"Rather than resting on their laurels, the UCLA Health System asked, 'How can we be better?' This excellent book reveals how they choose their direction and develop their future through the transformation to an even greater institution because they are committed to care."

—JOYCELYN ELDERS, M.D.,
former U.S. Surgeon General

"Most leadership authors describe how to apply commonsense principles. Michelli is a notable exception. Now he artfully describes the compelling, *un*common leadership practices that transformed the UCLA Health System. The resulting lessons are plentiful and powerful for today's business leader."

—LEE J. COLAN, PH.D., author of
Sticking to It: The Art of Adherence

"A hospital, like any business, must be true to its core values in order to succeed. 'Trickle down values' start at the top with the best leadership so all the stakeholders understand and carry out the mission of the institution. That is the gift that David Feinberg has brought to UCLA. I am in awe of his management skills and deeply appreciate his huge heart."

—LYNDA RESNICK, owner of Pom Wonderful,
Fiji Water, Teleflora, and Wonderful Pistachios

"This story of the transformation of the UCLA medical care system to a focus on caring and compassion is for all of us: patients and families, caregivers, healthcare system leaders, and policy makers. The UCLA community shows how to make dramatic improvements in a complex system in just a few short years. With clear purpose, unwavering principles, and steadfast leadership, the people at UCLA have established a new bar, a compelling promise, for what healthcare can and should be."

—DAVID M. LAWRENCE, M.D., former CEO, Kaiser Permanente

"Joseph Michelli has written an absorbing and educational account of an astonishing transformation of a large institution led by Dr. David Feinberg. The strong, courageous, and focused leadership of David Feinberg and his outstanding team is evident on every page. His team is energized and dedicated to the vision of customer satisfaction and never resting until the next patient is well taken care of. This metamorphosis is a tremendous lesson for all large enterprises, whether in the not-for-profit or in the for-profit sector."

—WILLIAM E. SIMON, JR., cochairman of William E. Simon & Sons

"In my more than 50 years of business experience, I have operated some very large public and private companies, highlighted by what was at that time the most well-known hotel gaming company in the world. We were open 24 hours a day, 365 days a year under extraordinarily difficult circumstances. When you take care of as many as 40,000 people on one property in a single day, it makes you very aware of the importance of customer satisfaction. The analogy to operating a hospital is obvious, because so many of the services are the same. This book diligently emphasizes some of the major differences. The vision statement deals with 'healing humankind' and does not allow return on investment a position to compromise those objectives."

—HENRY GLUCK, Chairman of the Board of Advisors for Ronald Reagan UCLA Medical Center and former CEO and Chairman of the Board of Caesars World

Prescription

for

Excellence

LEADERSHIP LESSONS FOR
CREATING A WORLD-CLASS
CUSTOMER EXPERIENCE FROM
UCLA HEALTH SYSTEM

JOSEPH A. MICHELLI

NEW YORK   CHICAGO   SAN FRANCISCO
LISBON   LONDON   MADRID   MEXICO CITY   MILAN
NEW DELHI   SAN JUAN   SEOUL   SINGAPORE
SYDNEY   TORONTO

1 2 3 4 5 6 7 8 9 0   DOC/DOC   1 6 5 4 3 2 1

ISBN: 978-0-07-177354-6
MHID: 0-07-177354-1

e-ISBN: 978-0-07-177390-4
e-MHID: 0-07-177390-8

Copublished with Second River Healthcare Press.
Design by Lee Fukui and Mauna Eichner

Any patient-specific information was obtained either directly from the patient, with the patient's permission, or through publically available information.

This book was prepared with the assistance of UCLA Health System.

Service Serves Us™ is a trademark of Joseph A. Michelli.

McGraw-Hill books are available at special quantity discounts to use as premiums and sales promotions, or for use in corporate training programs. To contact a representative please e-mail us at bulksales@mcgraw-hill.com.

This book is printed on acid-free paper.

Contents

Foreword

In the big picture of premier U.S. health system centers, UCLA is a veritable newcomer. However, despite its short 50-plus-year history, UCLA has had a significant impact on medical education, clinical care, and revolutionary medical research. Similarly, in the history of UCLA's tremendous leadership legacy, I am relatively new on the scene. Because this book shares insights concerning leadership practices that were in place prior to my arrival, my enthusiasm for it is not a result of its reflections on my own leadership. But it does celebrate a tradition that attracted me to UCLA.

Fundamentally, *Prescription for Excellence* focuses on the attributes that have made UCLA one of the top-tier health service providers worldwide, but it is also a template for outstanding leadership principles that apply across business settings. In essence, it is a book about people, collaboration, and a vision of service. Consistent with my long-held belief that that the lifeblood of great institutions can be found in the quality of their people, this book captures how UCLA has uniquely positioned itself to excel in the future as a result of the extraordinarily talented and committed individuals it has attracted and the community support it has garnered.

As you will see throughout the book, the leaders at UCLA appreciate that talented staff members are necessary but not sufficient for the overall success of a healthcare or business enterprise. Talent without collaboration produces limited results. Having had experience with other institutions across the United States, I have seen an impressive array of exceptionally talented individuals with variable degrees of team commitment. At UCLA, I've appreciated a spirit of collegiality that enables our talented people to bring innovation to life.

Consistent with a theme that is echoed throughout this book, the talent and collaboration of UCLA's staff members have been accentuated by a clear leadership vision for unyielding excellence and growth. The UCLA community has been led on a quest to constantly be better. Across the health system campus, there is a hunger to continue to "make the best better" and "create the future."

Joseph Michelli does an excellent job of not only showing the principled leadership of the UCLA Health System campus, but also sharing its humanity. From stories of hallway conversations between the hospital CEO and patients or staff members to prescriptive summaries that mobilize you to action, Joseph has painted a warm, compelling, and useful picture of UCLA's success drivers. Most important, *Prescription for Excellence* is presented at an important time for leaders in healthcare and business.

The book addresses the new tools, knowledge, and insights that will allow us to transform the health of populations and businesses worldwide in ways that would have been unimaginable even 10 years ago. From a healthcare perspective, we have unprecedented opportunities to make substantial and significant contributions to overall health. At the same time, we are faced with millions of individuals who die prematurely or who suffer diseases unnecessarily, and we also continue to look at wide and alarming disparities in healthcare. From a business perspective, we have the chance to take an evidence-based approach to best practices that will improve the work environment for our staff members and the overall experience of those whom we serve.

I am glad that you have this book in your hand, and I am delighted to have the opportunity to play a part in leading UCLA Health System at this important time in history. When I look at the opportunities as well as the needs that face healthcare and business today, I feel that there is a handful of institutions that can effectively pursue solutions to the most pressing of problems. I came to UCLA because I believe it is one of those institutions that can and will improve the lives of future generations. I hope the lessons found herein serve you in your pursuit of similarly important objectives.

—A. Eugene Washington, M.D., M.Sc.
vice chancellor, UCLA Health Sciences
dean, David Geffen School of Medicine at UCLA

Acknowledgments

This all started years ago when I toured the yet-to-be-opened Ronald Reagan UCLA Medical Center with Dr. David Feinberg. While I was overwhelmed by the beauty, grandeur, and futuristic technology of the complex, I was ostensibly visiting it in preparation for a presentation that I was to give to Dr. Feinberg's leadership team. That presentation was focused on making sure that the patient experience at UCLA was commensurate with the quality of the soon-to-be-opened new hospital.

While I had no idea that this book would emerge from that early work at UCLA, I suspect that Dr. Feinberg had already envisioned this outcome. I will forever be grateful to David for his ability to see and make this book possible. Moreover, I am in debt to him for his mentorship on developing a service-centric culture and his living example of what it takes to put your patient/customer first.

Lest you think that Dr. Feinberg was solely responsible for this book or for the amazing level of care provided throughout UCLA Health System, I must quickly acknowledge all the members of the senior leadership team and of the medical community who shared their time and wisdom. Of special note are Amir Dan Rubin, Dr. Gerald Levey, Dr. Tom Rosenthal, and Mark Speare. Each of these people made extraordinary contributions to *Prescription for Excellence*. They stand out for the significance of their contribution and their passion for service.

Pattie Cuen, director of marketing at UCLA Health System, and her team (particularly Jake Scherzer and Marina Lawson) were my gracious guides and coordinators at UCLA. Pattie helped with finding appropriate UCLA staff members and scheduling meetings with them, streamlining my meetings with leaders, securing releases, overseeing the editing of the manuscript, and generally keeping a seemingly implausible process running flawlessly. Pattie did all of this with positivity, graciousness, and humor. Without Pattie, this would have been a concept, not a book.

There are far too many UCLA contributors for me to recognize all of them by name in this section. However, in the back pages of the book, you will find what is intended to be a list of all those who participated in this project.

I am becoming increasingly embarrassed that my name is the only one that appears on the covers of the books on which I have worked. Don't get me wrong, I am proud to have my name on the cover; it is just that one person can't produce a project of this size. In this instance, I have benefited from three amazingly talented research assistants, Ryan Walsh, Kelly Merkel, and Jill Merkel. The administrative duties and interviews conducted by this trio serve as the foundation on which this book is assembled. Lloyd Rich, publishing attorney extraordinaire, keeps my writing career moving smoothly, and Terry Moore uses his photographic talents to smooth out my wrinkles. Thanks to both of you for allowing me to benefit from your sizable talents.

So now to the not-so-big secret, at least for anyone who has had the pleasure of working with her. Lynn Stenftenagel, my SVP of operations, has been *most* instrumental to this book's existence. In fact, this is the third book I have worked on with Lynn, and I am not sure how I wrote my first two without her. Suffice it to say that I can't envision ever again doing a book without her involvement. She is my friend, business partner, supporter, taskmaster, organizer, and project manager. When it comes to this book and my overall business success, one name stands out—Lynn.

The last couple of years have been a time of significant challenge and interpersonal growth. As a result of this turmoil and evolution, I have come to appreciate my family and friends at an even deeper level. Fiona, you have always brought a warmth, charm, and presence wherever you go. I am so grateful that you are and always will be "my girl." Dance, act, sing—the world needs your joy. Andrew, just yesterday you were a boy, and now you are a man. I am inspired by your rapid interpersonal growth and maturation. I cherish the adult-to-adult relationship we are developing. Andrew and Fiona, I am so proud of both of you, and I welcome the opportunities to share your victories and your sorrows. Nora, your strength, patience, forgiveness, faith, and laughter are gifts that I will never deserve. Thanks for sharing them unwaveringly and for keeping our family together through so much adversity. You have silently toiled and nurtured the children and me, always doing so without the appreciation, respect, and recognition that you deserved.

The support of friends and colleagues is central to my being able to do what I love. Special recognition goes to Dr. Dale Mann, Rob Graf, Paul Prouty, Tim Horne, Dr. Dwight Gaudet, Michael Pollard, Dr. Bill Dove, Doug Fleener, and Dr. Jeff Wooddell.

I am not one to mention my faith in the context of my professional life, but I must thank God for abounding love, uplifting hope, and truly amazing grace.

Wow, are you still reading these acknowledgments? Then I guess it is time that you were finally recognized. I understand the formula: no readers = no books. Your supportive readership is so important to me and has made this book possible. The only way I know to repay you is to try to meet your needs with each word. My gratitude lives in the benefits I hope you will derive from *Prescription for Excellence.*

To Marie C. Michelli, whose relentless support
has been profoundly felt, if not sufficiently acknowledged,
for more than half a century. Mom, I love you.

The UCLA Health System Experience: What Everyone Can Learn from Greatness in Healthcare

Greatness is so often a courteous synonym for great success.
—PHILIP GUEDALLA

Imagine having to run a successful business that requires the innovation of Apple, the commitment to safety of NASA, and the customer service of Ritz-Carlton. Furthermore, imagine that your mandate demands that you be a world-class educator, your work product holds life and death in the balance, and you are responsible for discoveries that shape the future of medicine. But wait; there's more! You have to achieve your complex mission in a highly political, cost-competitive industry. From imagination to reality, you are about to dive deeply into the challenges and leadership lessons of UCLA Health System!

While a book about a premier medical research and training center is obviously relevant for anyone who is in healthcare, its appropriateness for other industries might not be readily apparent. In fact, you may be asking: what does UCLA Health System, a leader in a complicated and often maligned sector of our economy, have to offer me if my business is banking, retail, hospitality, or something else? The short, albeit incomplete, answer is how to

- Catapult your business to preeminence at an unusually rapid pace.

- Transform the satisfaction and engagement of your customers through a service-centric approach.

- Achieve meteoric profitability during economic downturns—despite aggressive competition.

- Achieve decades of recognition as a quality and safety leader.

- Create revolutionary improvement in your employee engagement and empowerment.

- Redesign, elevate, and humanize your customer experience.

Despite having a background working as an organizational development specialist, when UCLA approached me to write this book I was initially skeptical about whether UCLA Health System would be the "right" source for business lessons. (Of course, my cynicism may have been amplified by my not having been accepted by UCLA's graduate school years ago, and instead having attended its crosstown rival USC.)

For me, an author of books about businesses that provide great customer and employee experiences, such as the Pike Place Fish Market in Seattle, Starbucks Coffee and Tea Company, and the Ritz-Carlton Hotel Company, UCLA Health System seemed an unlikely subject for a book. Suffice it to say that my experiences with the UCLA leadership convinced me that these lessons needed to be told. In fact, the profits from this book will be donated to Operation Mend (more on this program in Chapter 11) in support of UCLA Health System's overall mission.

Are you ready to learn from one of America's top healthcare systems, owned by 30 million citizens of California, with 4 hospitals; more than 75 clinics; in excess of 80,000 inpatient hospital contacts; 1,000,000 clinic visits annually; 1,500 physicians; 1,500 residents and fellows; 3,500 nurses, therapists, technologists, and support personnel; 1,000 volunteers; 120 physicians cited in the "Best Doctors in America" poll; and a world-renowned medical school that is among the top 10 in the nation in medical-research funding, the David Geffen School of Medicine at UCLA? If so, your lessons are about to begin. But let's first examine UCLA Health System's humble start and rapid ascent to the top tier of medical excellence.

GOING WEST IN THE ATOMIC AGE

Traditionally, centers of medical excellence were found in the northeastern and Great Lakes regions of the United States, with highly revered institutions such as Johns Hopkins in Baltimore, Maryland, and the Mayo Clinic in Rochester, Minnesota. As World War II came to a close, however, a group of physicians began pressuring the University of California to create a premier medical center in southern California. In response to these influential physicians, the University of California Board of Regents voted in 1945 to appropriate $7 million to fund a medical school at UCLA.

In 1947, Stafford L. Warren, a professor from the University of Rochester Medical School in New York, was appointed as the UCLA medical school's first dean. Picking a handful of exceptional faculty leaders from the University of Rochester and Johns Hopkins, UCLA School of Medicine began without a hospital or advanced research facilities. Scientists instead worked in temporary Quonset huts in distant locations around the campus. As construction of the new medical center began in 1951, the first UCLA School of Medicine class was being admitted. Fifteen faculty members provided courses to 28 students—26 men and 2 women—who attended classes in a reception lounge of an old religious conference building.

In 1950, just prior to the beginning of construction on the medical center building, a *Los Angeles Times* reporter called it "one of the greatest medical meccas in the world." Newspaper reports indicated that the medical center would "combine a complete undergraduate medical school, a fully equipped and staffed hospital and the most advanced research facilities possible." In the article, Dean Stafford Warren remarked that the medical campus would be "the first structure of its size and nature to be specifically designed for the Atomic Age with operating rooms and radiology department built where they serve both the flow of function and, incidentally, protection against disaster."

That protection from disaster served the UCLA medical complex well from its opening in 1955 until 1994, when the main medical building experienced interior structural damage as a result of the Northridge earthquake. Given concerns for patient safety in the context of earthquake risks, the California legislature amended existing legislation and required all hospitals to house their acute- and intensive-care units in earthquake-safe buildings by 2008. As a result of that legislation, the "medical mecca" of the 1950s gave way to the Ronald Reagan UCLA Medical Center (RRUCLA).

SCOPE OF THE MODERN ENTERPRISE

The Ronald Reagan UCLA Medical Center is named after the former U.S. president and California governor. Including state-of-the-art equipment purchases, the construction costs exceeded $1 billion. Funding sources included more than $300 million in private donations, including $150 million in the name of President Reagan; $432 million in federal earthquake relief funds; and $44 million in California state contributions. The 10-story building, with more than a million square feet, has 520 private patient rooms and employs 1,500 full-time physicians and more than 2,500 support staff. The building, which opened to patients in June 2008, is constructed to withstand an 8.0 magnitude earthquake and was one of the first buildings in California created to meet the state's elevated seismic standards.

The Mattel Children's Hospital UCLA occupies a 90-bed unit in the Ronald Reagan UCLA Medical Center. Similarly, the medical center houses the Stewart and Lynda Resnick Neuropsychiatric Hospital at UCLA, a 74-bed independently accredited and licensed hospital.

In addition to the hospitals housed in the Ronald Reagan UCLA Medical Center on UCLA's Westwood, California, campus, UCLA Health System also owns and operates the 271-bed acute-care Santa Monica–UCLA Medical Center and Orthopaedic Hospital in the neighboring community of Santa Monica. The Santa Monica hospital has had a presence in its community since 1926 and was acquired in 1995. Much like the Ronald Reagan UCLA campus, the Santa Monica–UCLA Medical Center has been modernized to the highest technology standards and serves as a parallel extension of the academic medical center in Westwood.

Adjacent to the Ronald Reagan UCLA Medical Center are three professional office buildings that make up the UCLA Medical Plaza. These buildings house more than 75 outpatient clinics providing care across a wide range of medical specialties. In addition to these clinics, UCLA Health System oversees the UCLA Medical Group, which is composed primarily of UCLA faculty physicians from the David Geffen School of Medicine at UCLA. The UCLA Medical Group provides traditional community-based outpatient health services to private-pay patients, as well as those covered by all forms of insurance, via regional clinics found in the Los Angeles area.

The hospitals and clinics exist not only for the clinical care of patients, but also to support the educational and research objectives of the David Geffen School of Medicine at UCLA. While providing world-class education for medical students, residents, and fellows, the medical school also participates in research designed to create breakthroughs in diagnosis, treatment, and medical-care delivery. The integration of medical school training, research, and clinical care is reflected in the institutes and centers that are a part of UCLA Health System. A list of these programs can be found in Appendix A.

IT'S COMPLICATED, IT'S BROAD IN SCOPE, BUT HOW IS IT EXCELLENT?

While you now have a sense of the wide scope of UCLA Health System, scope should not be confused with significance, and we all know that bigger often does not mean better. So, what has the leadership at UCLA done to warrant your time and attention? From UCLA Health System's inception, its leaders have achieved success in four areas that are critical to every business enterprise:

1. Growing while maintaining quality

2. Inspiring innovation while generating cohesion

3. Balancing technological advances with humanity

4. Achieving recognition and respect for extraordinary accomplishments

A GLIMPSE AT BREAKTHROUGHS

The chapters that follow will primarily address issues of growth, quality, innovation, and service excellence; very little time will be spent talking about the recognition and reputation that UCLA has achieved. Clearly a book could be written on UCLA's medical break-throughs alone, but for our purposes, a few highlights should suffice.

In the 1950s, UCLA surgeons performed the first open-heart surgeries on the West Coast of the United States, and researchers developed the initial techniques for fetal monitoring. In the 1960s, surgeons at UCLA brought the first mother-to-daughter kidney transplants to the western United States. In the 1970s, UCLA physicians and scientists developed a durable artificial hip, and surgeons performed the first shoulder replacement. During the 1980s, UCLA doctors innovated and delivered the first PET scan services and identified the nation's first case of AIDS. In the decade of the 1990s, Dr. Hillel Laks pioneered the first Alternative Heart Transplant Program in the United States and was the first U.S. cardiac surgeon to perform bypass surgery on a donor heart prior to transplantation. In the same time period, UCLA surgeons and transplant specialists were the first in the west to perform a remarkably successful combined small bowel/liver transplant.

Since 2000, doctors and researchers at UCLA Health System have continued to generate innumerable research breakthroughs, innovative accomplishments, and medical firsts. For instance, cardiothoracic surgeons developed a technique to harvest an artery from a patient's wrist for heart bypass surgery, and Dr. Ronald Busuttil performed the nation's first combined unrelated living liver and "domino" transplant in response to the national shortage of livers for transplant. This process essentially saves two patients through one liver donation. The donated liver comes from a nonrelated living donor and is transplanted into a patient with an otherwise genetically deficient liver. The genetically deficient liver is then transplanted into the second patient, who suffers from liver cancer. The genetically deficient liver, while less than perfect, dramatically extends the life expectancy of the patient with liver cancer.

Similarly, a team of more than 50 surgeons, nurses, and technicians led by Dr. Jorge Lazareff and Dr. Henry Kawamoto successfully separated two-year-old craniopagus twin girls from Guatemala in a 22-hour surgery. Fused at the tops of their heads, craniopagus twins are among the rarest of conjoined twins, accounting for just 2 percent of cases worldwide.

UCLA Health System's hospitals also became the world's first to introduce remote presence robots in its neurosurgery intensive-care unit. This allows doctors to "virtually" consult with patients, family members, and healthcare staff at a moment's notice, even if they are miles away from the hospital.

RECOGNITION ABOUNDS

From the standpoint of peer and organizational recognition, a select few of UCLA Health System's noteworthy achievements include:

- *U.S. News & World Report's* America's Best Hospital Honor Roll consistently ranks Ronald Reagan UCLA Medical Center as one of the top hospitals in the nation and, for more than 21 years, as the best hospital in the western United States. UCLA's nationally recognized programs based in Westwood and in Santa Monica have been ranked among the top 20 in 15 of the 16 medical specialties. At least 12 of those specialties have achieved ranks in the top 10.

- Integrated Healthcare Association consistently ranks UCLA Medical Group as one of California's top-performing physicians' organizations.

- UCLA Medical Group was one of only 6 organizations in California and one of only 28 in the United States to meet the strict standards required to receive a Certificate in Credentialing and Recredentialing through the National Committee for Quality Assurance (NCQA) Physician Organization Certification Program.

- UCLA Stroke Center received the American Heart Association's (AHA) Get with the Guidelines™ Gold Performance Achievement Award for commitment and success in implementing a higher standard of stroke care by ensuring that stroke patients receive treatment according to nationally accepted standards and recommendations. In fact, UCLA cardiologist Dr. Gregg Fonarow was recognized as generating one of the top research advances for establishing the Cardiovascular Hospitalization Atherosclerosis Management Program guidelines promoted by the AHA.

- The National Cancer Institute has designated the Lung Cancer Program at UCLA Health System's Jonsson Comprehensive Cancer Center a Specialized Program of Research Excellence (SPORE), making it one of only a handful of programs nationwide to receive national recognition and substantial research funding to improve the prevention, detection, and treatment of lung cancer.

- The National Cancer Institute designated UCLA Health System's Prostate Cancer Program as a Specialized Program of Research Excellence, distinguishing the program as one of only a few nationwide that was tapped to improve the prevention, detection, and treatment of prostate cancer.

- National Institutes of Health (NIH) has designated UCLA Health System's prostate cancer and kidney cancer programs as Centers of Excellence according to NIH guidelines.

- UCLA's Jonsson Comprehensive Cancer Center was officially designated by the National Cancer Institute as one of only 40 comprehensive cancer centers in the United States.

- UCLA's Heart Transplant Program was recognized as the nation's best by the U.S. Department of Health and Human Services.

- Ronald Reagan UCLA Medical Center was honored by OneLegacy, the transplant donor network serving southern California, for achieving a high organ conversion rate.

- The American Alliance of Healthcare Providers (AAHP) recognized Ronald Reagan UCLA Medical Center as one of America's Most Customer-Friendly Hospitals in the organization's Hospital of Choice Award.

- Ronald Reagan UCLA Medical Center and Santa Monica–UCLA Medical Center and Orthopaedic Hospital rank among the top three hospitals in Los Angeles County for the highest percentages of mothers discharged from the hospital while feeding their babies exclusively with breast milk.

- UCLA Health System has earned the American Society for Metabolic & Bariatric Surgery (ASMBS) Center of Excellence designation by demonstrating a track record of favorable outcomes in bariatric surgery.

- Ronald Reagan UCLA Medical Center earned Magnet Status for Nursing Excellence from the American Nurses Credentialing Center.

- The Leapfrog Group named Ronald Reagan UCLA Medical Center as a Leapfrog Top Hospital based on results from an annual Leapfrog Hospital Quality and Safety Survey.

- UCLA Medical Group is a qualified data registry under the Physician Quality Reporting Initiative (PQRI), a Medicare pay-for-reporting program. UCLA Medical Group was one of only 10 organizations in the nation affiliated with teaching or academic medical centers to earn this designation from the Centers for Medicare and Medicaid Services (CMS).

- *U.S. News & World Report* ranks Mattel Children's Hospital UCLA among the top pediatric hospitals in the United States.

- Resnick Neuropsychiatric Hospital UCLA consistently ranks number one in the west and number six in the country in *U.S. News & World Report.*

- Ophthalmology services at Jules Stein Eye Institute rank number five in the country in *U.S. News & World Report.*

WHERE IT MATTERS MOST

While breakthroughs and critical acclaim are vital to business success, for the leaders at UCLA Health System, the ultimate validation comes from the countless stories of appreciation offered by the medical professionals that the system trains, the staff members it employs, and the patients it serves. In essence, the greatest measure of success for the UCLA leadership is the degree to which compassionate care matches or exceeds the quality of the clinical outcomes.

Jennifer Rosenthal is one such example of a patient's heartfelt recognition of UCLA's excellence. Jennifer had lapsed into a coma and was taken to a nearby hospital. When doctors at the other hospital could not determine the cause of the liver failure she was experiencing, they airlifted Jennifer to UCLA to evaluate her for a liver transplant. Jennifer notes, "While my transplant was miraculous, it's often the little things that stand out most. For example, the ICU nurses at UCLA brought to the forefront that a dietary supplement I was taking was probably the cause of my liver failure. It wasn't enough for those nurses to provide outstanding acute crisis care for me; they found out why I had experienced such a rapid decline. In the process, they not only helped me get to the source of my liver failure but contributed to an awareness that will protect others. These nurses took their own time to investigate the supplement on the Internet. Then the doctors took it from there. I was healthy, but when I took the supplement for two weeks at half of the recommended dosage, I ended up in a coma with 48 hours to live.

"The skill, care, compassion, and personal investment of the nursing staff and doctors at UCLA not only saved my life through liver transplantation but prompted me to rethink and change my life as well. I began to realize that I could be a part of giving people a chance to emerge from the precipice of death and go on to live a purposeful and fulfilled life. To that end, I just graduated from nursing school, and I'm waiting to take my boards. I wanted to come back to UCLA, so I worked as a unit secretary, and hoped to soon be working as a nurse on the transplant unit. [Jennifer is now a licensed vocational nurse working in one of UCLA's outpatient clinics.] I want to give back to patients what UCLA gave to me. I remember some of the feelings I had, and I want to be the nurse who can say to a transplant patient, 'I've been there, and look where I am now; I've walked in your shoes.'" Receiving excellent care from talented staff members was not only lifesaving for Jennifer, but transformational and magnetic as well. It was transformational in that she completely changed her career path and magnetic in that it drew her to work at UCLA.

UCLA Health System has a magnetic pull for talent thanks to its compassionate staff. Consistent with his comments in the foreword, A. Eugene Washington, M.D., M.Sc., who became the vice chancellor of UCLA Health Sciences and the dean of the David Geffen School of Medicine at UCLA in 2010, puts it best when he says, "Great people are the lifeblood of great institutions. And we are inarguably one of the world's preeminent health-sciences campuses today precisely because of our exceptional people." An organization can have no more significant achievement than the respect and support of the communities it serves and the ability of its talented people to inspire and attract individuals such as Jennifer Rosenthal and Dr. Washington.

AN OUTSIDER'S VIEW

While this is a book about lessons that you can learn and apply from UCLA Health System, it is not solely a discussion of the extraordinary things that the system's leaders and staff members have accomplished. There is much to be learned from leadership missteps and faulty service delivery. For example, you will read about a rather significant set of problems involving patient confidentiality breaches and a period in which patient satisfaction fell below nationwide hospital standards. In every case where a leadership or service breakdown is outlined, lessons will be presented so that you might be able to avert a similar challenge and instead create a breakthrough in your business. Obviously, most of the book will be dedicated to benchmarking what UCLA Health System is doing well, so that you can adapt its ideas, systems, and leadership principles for your setting.

To ease your experience as a reader, I will be referring to UCLA Health System simply as UCLA. In addition, UCLA's primary customers are patients and will routinely be referred to as such. I'm sure you will be able to relate the patient experience examples to the experience of the customers you serve.

While UCLA Health System is a complex entity to study and medical jargon can be daunting, this book is designed for readers both inside and outside of healthcare. Accordingly, its structure and content are meant to be broadly accessible. The book is structured around five key action-oriented principles that, when executed effectively, result in catalytic impact for healthcare-specific and general business success.

These principles are

1. Commit to care.

2. Leave no room for error.

3. Make the best better.

4. Create the future.

5. Service Serves Us™.

By applying these leadership principles, UCLA quickly took a medical school without a dedicated classroom building or hospital and transformed it into a world-renowned center of healthcare excellence. Continued adherence to these principles has guided UCLA to financial strength, social significance, and sustainability, despite its having to operate in the context of swirling political debates, react to volatile government service reimbursement mechanisms, adhere to complex regulatory demands, and respond to aggressive direct competition from other healthcare providers for higher-paying customer groups. All the while, the leadership has been treating not only a large population of California residents, but some of the most ill patients in the United States and the world.

In the vortex of this challenge, change, and complexity, the CEO of UCLA Hospital System, Dr. David Feinberg, offers a singular, simple, and unifying perspective: "We are in the business of taking care of people. It doesn't matter if you are a doctor, a nurse, or a janitor or if you carry a leadership title, we all must champion and execute on the common goal of coming in every day to make sure we take care of our next patient."

Whether it's healthcare, finance, or a neighborhood hair salon, all business starts and ends with a focus on "coming in every day to make sure" you take care of those you serve. In essence, all business is personal. So let's begin your personal journey into the leadership principles of UCLA Health System.

1

COMMIT
TO
CARE

CHAPTER 2

Care Takes Vision, Clarity, and Consistency

The capacity to care gives life its deepest significance.
—Pablo Casals

Nicole Draper didn't have a lot of experience with hospitals, but that changed quickly with the birth of her twin boys. Nicole notes, "Nick and Nate were born with a rare heart condition called dilated cardiomyopathy. We were told that there was no surgery or hope for the condition other than heart transplants. At the time, our home state of Arizona didn't perform infant heart transplants, so our family was off to UCLA, where my very sick boys were initially treated in the Neonatal Intensive Care Unit. My husband and I were obviously impressed by the knowledge and intelligence of the treatment providers, but also with their empathy, which was demonstrated in the way they communicated sensitive information." Initially, Nicole and her husband were advised that Nick was eligible for a heart transplant, but that Nate had experienced brain hemorrhaging that would affect his eligibility. Nicole adds, "In all of our meetings, staff members just kept communicating in such a compassionate way and spent so much time with us." During the course of Nick and Nate's care, a *Los Angeles Times* photographer and reporter followed the twins' treatment and wrote a series of stories about what ultimately turned out to be extremely successful medical outcomes for each of the brothers. Nicole notes, "Through the entire odyssey, we were amazed by UCLA. The medical professionals are incredibly skilled, and they are also really good with people. We were very impressed with the whole experience."

While stories of seemingly miraculous outcomes have consistently been common at UCLA, the leadership did not always hear that patients were "impressed with the whole experience." In fact, when David Feinberg, MD, MBA, the CEO of UCLA Hospital System, was promoted to his current position, he inherited an organization that had rich existing strengths in medical training, cutting-edge research, and the delivery of extraordinary clinical outcomes. But he was also faced with a significant opportunity. UCLA's overall patient satisfaction scores were in the 30th to 40th percentile range and in need of considerable improvement.

Prior to becoming CEO for the entire hospital system, Dr. Feinberg, then medical director of the Resnick Neuropsychiatric Hospital (RNPH) at UCLA, had led a turnaround in patient satisfaction scores in a challenging setting with neurologic and psychiatric patients. As a result of that success, he was prepared to create a similar turnaround throughout the UCLA system. Dr. Feinberg admits, "To be honest, being chosen for this job was rather daunting. This is a place where miracles are performed every day; however, when I talked to patients, I heard some disconcerting things. I'd gone to business school, and they told me that you should know your customer. But how much were we talking to our customers at UCLA, and why were our satisfaction scores so low? Furthermore, why weren't more of our customers willing to refer us to their family or friends? As I asked these questions, I received some interesting responses, such as, 'We'll never be like other hospitals that get scores much higher than ours, say in the 60th or 70th percentile, because those hospitals don't treat cases at our level of complexity or they are not training facilities.' I just couldn't accept that."

Dr. Feinberg's lack of acceptance of "status quo" performance translated into a mission to enhance the patient experience and elevate the satisfaction level for every patient throughout the UCLA Health System. To that end, Dr. Feinberg inserted the "face of the patient" into every business discussion at UCLA by starting every meeting with a patient story. He also began asking leaders in the organization if they were talking with patients about their experience at UCLA. Mark Speare, senior associate director, Patient Affairs, Marketing and Human Resources, notes, "Shortly after Dr. Feinberg took over as CEO, he asked me if I 'rounded.' I self-assuredly replied, 'Yes,' thinking that he was referring to staff rounds. He pressed me further by asking, 'But do you see patients?' I realized at that point that my contact with patients was merely incidental and not the focus of what I needed to be doing as a leader. It was a significant 'aha' moment for me. Dr. Feinberg expressed confidence that connecting face-to-face with patients was something that I was very capable of and encouraged me to get out of my comfort zone to do so. In the weeks that followed, he supported me and would ask how visits with patients and their families were going. And yes, the first visits were a little awkward and angst producing. Initially, the staff members were perplexed, if not suspicious of my intentions, when I would visit the floors. Yet, at the very early stages, it became evident that listening to the patients was the only way anyone could truly learn how to serve them. It was clear that patients wanted us to listen. I was rarely turned away once I introduced myself. Now, some years later, visits with patients and their families come naturally. All of our directors and managers participate in patient rounds, and our staff members enjoy seeing us and getting feedback on how we are doing at making the patient experience better. We all look forward to rounds as the most connected and genuine part of our work, as we realize that there are real persons in our beds who have something valuable to share with us every day."

As Mark suggested, at UCLA, informal processes of listening have evolved into systems that increase the consistency of service delivery and ardently solicit the voice of the patient. Dr. Feinberg notes, "To turn our patient satisfaction numbers around, we knew we had to go back to the basics. We took our important mission statement, 'Delivering leading-edge patient care, research, and education,' and personalized it for staff members with a strong emphasis on care delivery. Specifically, our work to recraft our vision statement resulted in 'Healing humankind, one patient at a time, by improving health, alleviating suffering, and delivering acts of kindness.' We linked that vision statement to our underlying values of integrity, compassion, respect, teamwork, excellence, and discovery and built a framework to solicit the staff's commitment to caring. In fact, we created a 'Commitment to Care' statement that expressly states, 'I will always keep my commitment to care, as I have been entrusted by patients, colleagues, and society.' Once we had all these foundational pieces in place, we could fully launch the structures [the UCLA operating system] needed to transform patient satisfaction."

Tony Padilla, director of Patient Affairs and Volunteer Services, says, "I have compared notes with people in my role in other healthcare organizations in the 1980s and 1990s, as I go back that far. In those days, a patient service program was something that senior leaders would delegate to someone like me, and those leaders would receive periodic updates. It has become clear to many of us, in this industry and other industries, that service has to start at the top. Being able to have a CEO who states unequivocally that this 'caring' for patients is our number one mission has made a huge difference for us at UCLA."

Tony adds, "Dr. Feinberg says that we deliver great clinical outcomes and that we are one of the finest healthcare facilities in the world, but we need to be known first and foremost for our compassion and our relationships with patients and their families. When your CEO consistently communicates and acts on that message, you are halfway to achieving the objective. Better yet, when he partners with a talented senior leadership team, you can inspire second-tier managers to prioritize service excellence and carry that enthusiasm right to the patient level. That really is our secret formula. It is a matter of leadership priorities, leaders who walk their talk, and who offer constant, singular-focused communication and a lot of discipline. That's how we transformed our satisfaction levels from the thirties to greater than 95 percent systemwide." Those systemwide improvements have led to UCLA's often being recognized as the number one–rated academic medical center in the country from a patient satisfaction standpoint.

UCLA's patient satisfaction surge occurred consistently and swiftly across hospital and outpatient units. In my career, I have never seen or heard of any other business transforming, in a matter of just a few years, its satisfaction levels from around the 35th percentile to the number one position among its peers. Dr. Feinberg claimed patient satisfaction and maximizing "care" in UCLA's healthcare system as his central leadership theme. The remainder of this chapter addresses the mechanics and specific steps taken to achieve a swift, consistent, industry-leading culture shift.

Whatever your business, pleasing the customer is an important aspect of emotional engagement and customer loyalty. The UCLA leaders offer key lessons in how to maximize customer satisfaction levels by establishing operational objectives that drive customer-centric outcomes.

CICARE AND "WORLD CLASS PRACTICES" ARE BORN

Effective leadership depends upon influence, not control. This type of influence is reflected in a leader's ability to paint such a compelling picture of the future that colleagues can embrace the vision and enlist others in its pursuit. Bindu Danee, unit director of Oncology/Hematology/Stem Cell Transplants, notes, "From my perspective, senior leadership sold managers on the importance of creating a patient-care revolution at UCLA. More important, they specifically outlined the behaviors needed to achieve our goals and gave us the structures to guide us along the journey." Those guidelines came in the areas of communication, courtesy, respect, and professionalism.

Specific communication behaviors were highlighted through a template called CICARE (pronounced "See–I–Care"). CICARE is an acronym for actions that include

Connect with the patient or family member using Mr./Ms. or their preferred name.

Introduce yourself and your role.

Communicate what you are going to do, how it will affect the patient, and other needed information.

Ask for and anticipate patient and/or family needs, questions, or concerns.

Respond to patient and/or family questions and requests with immediacy.

Exit, courteously explaining what will come next or when you will return.

CICARE reflects a broad set of communication behaviors that can be practiced by everyone in a healthcare setting, including food service workers, housekeeping, administration, volunteers, nurses, and doctors. This CICARE template was further augmented with guidelines referred to as "World Class Practices" addressing issues that go beyond the process of respectful communication. Specifically, "World Class Practices" includes the following types of guidelines:

Courtesy

- Always exercise courtesy whenever patients, family members, and visitors are present. This includes the cafeteria, patient and visitor waiting areas, hallways, elevators, treatment areas, and patient rooms.

- Make eye contact and smile with patients, visitors, and staff. Offer a greeting when passing, such as, "Good morning."
- Allow patients and visitors to go first when getting into or out of elevators or doorways and in the hallways.
- Offer to help visitors get to their destination, or provide directions.
- Speak in moderate tones; be aware of the level of your voice.

Professionalism

- Maintain appropriate conversations, being respectful of patient and employee confidentiality.
- In order to provide a safe environment of care, speak only English or the language of the patient or visitor you are helping. Arrange for interpretation services when needed.
- Personal cell phones or listening devices may be used only during break times and only in designated break areas.
- Show pride by maintaining a professional appearance while on duty. Adhere to organizational appearance standards.
- Demonstrate ongoing responsibility and commitment through good attendance and by being on time to work.
- Demonstrate pride in UCLA Health System by keeping areas clean and safe.

Respect

- Respect privacy and dignity.
- Knock on a patient's door before entering and ask permission to enter.
- Ask permission before examining a patient, and provide an explanation of the examination or procedure.

- Do not make disparaging remarks about other departments or staff members in front of patients or visitors.

- Respect individual and cultural differences.

At UCLA, these world-class practices have been codified into a document titled "World Class Practices: My Commitment to Care," which is discussed when a prospect seeks a job at UCLA and is signed by all employees prior to being hired. Requiring employees to sign such a document obviously does not ensure that each employee will live up to his commitments, but the signing process has several positive leadership benefits, including

1. A clear baseline for expectations of universal caring behaviors

2. A delineation of the priority that the leadership places on customer care

3. A behavioral commitment from the employee

4. The message that peers will be held accountable for service behavior in interactions with patients and other staff

While the first two leadership benefits are fairly obvious (setting expectations and highlighting the importance of those expectations), the very act of securing a behavioral commitment does affect employee behavior. While human beings do not always act in accordance with their commitments, social psychologists have established that people attempt to be internally consistent. That is to say, we try to behave in accordance with our prior statements and commitments. By securing a verbal or written commitment, leaders increase the likelihood that staff members will attempt to align their behavior with that commitment. Additionally, the "World Class Practices" document highlights the broad target of care. For example, caring behavior is not reserved exclusively for patients, but is also a way of interacting with other staff members. The document specifically states, "My commitment to fulfill these communication, courtesy, respect, and professionalism expectations recognizes that I would want to be treated in a similar fashion as a patient or coworker. My personal pledge to the UCLA Health System is to conduct myself in a manner that will model caring for my team and others." The language of the "World Class Practices" document appreciates that a fundamental component in achieving buy-in to any leadership initiative is a willingness to address the "What's in it for me?" question for those you lead. At UCLA, engaging a commitment to care leads to compassionate treatment of patients, to increased institutional strength, and to an environment in which each employee reaps the benefits of respect, courtesy, and teamwork.

In addition to having the commitment to care included in the orientation process, the UCLA leadership has taken the behaviors outlined in that document and placed them in the job descriptions of all employees. Those job descriptions are also accompanied by language that acknowledges that "employees will be responsible for fulfilling these expectations on a daily basis as they apply to each position and they will be measured in the performance evaluation process." Mark Speare, senior associate director, Patient Relations, Marketing and Human Resources, notes, "Although we make it clear that you need to meet our caring expectations, our ultimate goal is to develop talent in the direction of maximum caring, not punitively respond to performance gaps. We need to ensure that people don't willfully disregard these expectations, but we are more interested in encouraging people to grow in their service professionalism." It has been said that people change because of either inspiration or desperation. The UCLA leadership has chosen to inspire a service movement by encouraging personal accountability for service skills development.

YOUR DIAGNOSTIC CHECKUP

- How aligned is your senior leadership team when it comes to a vision of service excellence? What can you do to increase that alignment?

- Have you placed the "face of the customer" in all aspects of your business discussions? Do you start meetings with customer service stories? Have you elevated your corporate vision to address aspects of compassionate care of your customers?

- How have you identified the specific communication behaviors you would like to see in all interactions with customers?

- Have you outlined a broad set of service behaviors that represent expectations for interactions with colleagues and customers?

- Are customer service behaviors included in the job description of all employees?

OPERATIONALIZING CICARE

Outlining brand-consistent communication and service behaviors like those identified in the CICARE model is a substantial first step in communicating the expectations of the leaders. Soliciting a personal commitment from employees further personalizes those expectations and mobilizes staff members in the direction of desired actions. Unfortunately, for many businesses, the behaviors just mentioned reflect the totality of service-enhancing strategies. At UCLA, however, those steps are just the beginning of a very involved process that includes talent selection, training, managerial oversight, and coaching.

SELECTING CARING STAFF

Mark Speare, senior associate director, Patient Relations, Marketing and Human Resources, was instrumental in championing the importance of systematically selecting for service talent and defining "talent" in the context of an individual's ability to excel when presented with training. Mark notes, "Service talent can be compared with athletic ability. If two individuals are offered the same skill training and one of the individuals has far more natural athletic talent, the talented individual will advance much faster and farther as a result of the training. In our case at UCLA, we are looking for talented people who naturally go the extra mile in truly caring about those they serve and the quality of their everyday work." Like many other great businesses that depend on "service talent" (e.g., the Ritz-Carlton Hotel Company), UCLA solicited the services of the company Talent Plus to provide scientific tools to increase the probability that UCLA's leaders will select employees with a high aptitude for caring professionalism.

Rachel Lemkau, the client relationship manager at Talent Plus who supports the UCLA account, notes, "Talent Plus and UCLA Health System have partnered over the past several years to select and develop highly talented team members based on the thoughts, feelings, and behaviors of applicants. UCLA Health System instituted the Talent Plus Healthcare Professional (HCP) Interview to select and train nurses and administrators, and we have conducted research to validate this approach to selection specifically at UCLA. Starting with focus groups where we analyzed potential key characteristics for highly successful job performance and moving on to the formulation of structured interviews that assessed the level of intensity of these characteristics, we ultimately validated a quantitatively based set of tools that enables UCLA to assess characteristics that are critical to the priorities it has set for service professionalism."

Tools developed with Talent Plus are a part of a systematic process of selecting "service-oriented" individuals. For example,

once job applicants are screened for skills that match job requirements, an initial interview process begins. That interview includes
questions that address specific types of service behaviors, such as
"Are you familiar with our World Class Standards here at UCLA?";
"Can you give me an example of when you followed one of these
standards at your current or previous employer?"; and "What would
you say are the most important qualities of someone in the job you
are seeking?"

Once candidates clear those initial screening hurdles, they encounter the Talent Plus Behavioral Interviewing Tool. That tool
essentially begins with 20 online screening questions and esca-
lates to a 45-minute behavioral interview. These two data collection efforts result in an analytic report of the applicant's underlying
talents, including her work intensity, values-based orientation,
positivity, resourcefulness, and facility in relationships. The Talent
Plus report offers recommendations to management with regard to
moving forward with the selection process or passing over a given
individual. At that point, UCLA managers conduct their own interviews with viable job applicants. Robin Epstein Ludewig, director
of Staffing and Workforce Planning, says, "Our recruitment process
is really a talent-based journey. In fact, all of our senior leaders, including Dr. Feinberg, have had their talent profiles charted, and we
have done a lot of work around leadership development by helping
managers focus on the strengths of their staff members to assist their
staff members in building on those strengths. In many ways, a talent
focus is about not only selection but a transition to a more apprecia-
tive culture, appreciating the gifts of your people, acknowledging
those talents, and helping people take care of the development of
their strengths in the service of and collaboration with others."

While some business leaders might think the war for talent
wanes during periods of increased unemployment, trends in healthcare suggest otherwise. In fact, a survey of healthcare CFOs published by Healthmedia.com suggests that talent selection and
retention (particularly among professional providers) is the single

most pressing issue for business success over the foreseeable future (followed by cost management and patient-centric care delivery). This healthcare trend toward talent acquisition and retention has specific application to all industries. Retention of the best talent is universally essential to business success, independent of levels of unemployment or economic cycles. Excellent staff members want to be surrounded by other talented teammates. Talent begets talent! Vigilant selection practices fuel the pursuit of excellence and facilitate the growth of teams.

Like many things in business, the ability to attract talented service staff has a "chicken/egg" quality. Service-oriented staff members are drawn to service-oriented cultures. But where does a leader start in creating a culture that makes a business more desirable to the types of employees that will help strengthen the service mindset? Dr. Neil Martin, chair of the Department of Neurosurgery, notes, "By the leadership giving voice to the importance of service and focusing the staff on CICARE concepts, I have seen a fundamental change not only in the way staff members treat patients, but also in the way we treat one another. This used to be the kind of place where if you had an emergency admission, you might have to wait for the admissions person to end a personal conversation before talking to you, or possibly telling you that emergencies were someone else's job. It could feel as if you were slugging through a marsh up to your chest to get things done. We lacked professional appearance, and there were no uniforms to signify areas of specialty. The nurses wore whatever they wanted, and that lack of focus on service detail made this a place where even patients would say to me, 'Thank God for the medical care I received because I was saved, but I don't really ever want to come back to UCLA.'"

Going from a place where some patients "endured" care and some staff members struggled to receive supportive service from peers to a place with world-class levels of patient satisfaction was no easy task. Despite the challenging journey, UCLA's satisfaction scores reflect a changing sentiment about the quality of care. This is articulated by Alicia Weintraub, who gave birth in a fire station and was then transported to the emergency room at UCLA: "I had had a prior child at a nearby hospital with an outstanding reputation for care, so when I was being transported, I asked if I was being taken back to that hospital, but the medical transport driver said, 'No, we're taking you to UCLA. We promise it will be okay.' It was the best thing that ever happened. I am so glad I was there. It was such a nice facility. Everyone spent so much time with us. You could tell that it chose great people who take a lot of pride in their work. When my daughter Lauren needed to go to the neonatal intensive-care unit at UCLA for a small matter, the people there were so great as well. Everyone was respectful and made it a point to introduce themselves and find out what my goals were in terms of feeding and to not intrude but offer support. At UCLA, they were great at listening to my needs."

In addition to refining the process for selecting service professionals, the centerpiece for the cultural shift at UCLA was its structured program of service and a tenacious effort to achieve buy-in to the CICARE program throughout the middle-level manager and front-line ranks.

Involving Staff in the Creation of CICARE

All too often, service initiatives are just that—initiatives. Frequently they are preprogrammed service systems created by an outside vendor. By contrast, CICARE is an organic program designed in a partnership between the UCLA leadership and staff members at all levels of the organization. In fact, training videos, which offer an orientation to CICARE concepts, are customized for applications in various areas of the healthcare system and involve staff members from those areas. For example, while the acronym CICARE reflects the same service expectations whether a staff member works in food service or nursing, the way those behaviors are applied may vary with the setting. Departmental training videos reflect those differences in application. They also model optimal examples that are relevant to the recipient of the training. In addition to the video presentation of the CICARE templates, staff members are given personalized training in the UCLA way of caring through a "buddy" or "preceptor" and by having their supervisor set expectations, connect service to mission, and establish performance expectations.

Barbara Anderson, RN, unit director of Neuroscience/Trauma ICU, notes, "I think the CICARE behaviors were already in us as healthcare professionals; they just weren't embraced as consistently as they are now. By appealing to our humanity and the reasons we came into nursing, CICARE gave us a way to talk to one another about what we all wanted. For me as a unit director, I want our patients and staff members to know that we care about them deeply and we think about their needs before they have to ask to have those needs fulfilled. CICARE is a way of inviting all leaders and staff members to consistently join together to realize a mutually desired outcome." Barbara's concept that the CICARE approach to service excellence draws out "behaviors that were already in" healthcare professionals speaks to the art of corporate education. Education, which comes from the Latin *educere*, literally meaning to "draw out," is at its best when people intrinsically embrace concepts, as opposed to having them imposed by top-down authority.

Amir Dan Rubin, one of the instrumental contributors to the CICARE approach and former COO, shares, "Our desire was to have staff members own this CICARE concept because it was an underpinning for consistent service that matched what professionals aspire to do. Rather than making it an aspiration, we wanted it to become a service standard that assured respectful care. To do that, everyone from the top of the organization to the newest employee had to be held accountable, through observation and coaching."

Once he has been trained on CICARE behaviors, a new staff member is essentially certified by managers to ensure that he can manifest the CICARE steps in real interactions. Once it is determined that new staff members can behave in a way that is consistent with the CICARE guidelines, managers and leaders are responsible for auditing each employee's CICARE practice patterns on a regular basis and immediately coaching employees to excellence. The expectation for managers is that they will perform CICARE audits of a new hire in the first week that the new hire is on the job. The manager is then to perform regular audits on her employees every month thereafter. In addition to offering immediate feedback from those audits to the employee, managers are expected to set aside additional check-in meetings with every employee throughout the year. Each meeting is to focus on trends in CICARE audits and other performance data, including information solicited from patients, as well as address questions from the employee and assist him in his ability to serve.

We all know that just because senior leaders want managers to conduct regular audits of certain employee behaviors or engage in a certain level of employee contact doesn't mean that managers will follow through on those expectations. At UCLA, managers are required to document and report the frequency of audits. Frequency data concerning manager audits are posted on a Web site for all managers to see, along with patient satisfaction scores for each unit. Amir Dan Rubin notes, "In a gentle way, we appreciate that peers hold one another accountable when data are provided in a transparent way. Most important, we see that managers who conduct the most audits tend to have the highest patient satisfaction scores. That, in and of itself, can inspire a manager to redouble her efforts to get more involved in the day-to-day coaching processes that change the service level in her area."

As an example of this auditing and coaching, Posie Carpenter, RN, MSN, MPH, chief administrative officer of Santa Monica–UCLA Medical Center and Orthopaedic Hospital, shares, "On Fridays, when I first walk around a unit, I'll say, 'Happy Patient Experience Friday.' As the hospital administrator at Santa Monica, I spend time on the same unit for about a month and then rotate.

I tell staff members that I am going to be interacting with our patients, and that I would appreciate it if they would grab me because I want to accompany them into the room. The staff is great about finding me and telling me that they would like to give some medications now, or that they are going in to clean the room. Another manager or I will observe the staff member going through all of the desired CICARE behaviors. At the conclusion of the interaction with the patient, we will offer private coaching and give feedback about where the staff member offered excellent execution of CICARE and where he might consider other things."

When the chief administrator or CEO of a business is out of her office and actively engaged in service discussions with staff members, a clear message is sent about the importance of service. Many leaders might feel uncomfortable with this level of involvement and fear that their presence will make their staff uncomfortable, but Posie notes, "This entire Patient Experience Friday adventure has really been positive for us. For example, the other day I sat and listened to a unit secretary, and she did most of the CICARE behaviors well, but there was one additional part that I thought she could enhance. As soon as I finished coaching her, she answered the telephone and incorporated that additional piece into her conversation and did it smoothly each time the phone rang that day. We both felt good about that."

While Posie's coaching on telephone service had immediate results, she acknowledges that coaching isn't always that well received. "I sat on another nursing unit and listened to a secretary who was working really hard. She was taking off orders and was very intent on what she was doing, but if a staff member asked her for something, she gave a one-word answer. The telephone would ring and she'd say, 'Hello.' The call light would go off, and she'd give a terse response that implied, 'What do you want?' I listened to this and tried to give her some coaching. In response to my feedback, she looked at me like, 'Who the heck are you?' I got absolutely nowhere. I went back to her manager and asked why this person was working at UCLA. The manager explained that the employee had been at UCLA for a long time and that the manager was trying to get the employee on board with CICARE, but it wasn't clear that the staff member was going to make it in a more patient-centric environment. A short time later, that employee visited my office and said, 'You know that day you were upstairs and you were observing me? Well, I want to apologize. I can do better than that, and I've changed the way I serve people and take feedback.' That situation made me reflect on how long we can let employees languish in their service abilities when we aren't coaching from the top of our organization."

All too often, "service strategies" are reduced to senior leaders giving middle managers the task of enhancing service levels without the senior leaders participating in the same service improvement process. At UCLA, service coaching around CICARE is a standard part of conversations at the senior leadership, management, and peer-to-peer levels. Moreover, these conversations have expanded to engage another important stakeholder in the service process—the patient.

YOUR DIAGNOSTIC CHECKUP

- Are you selecting for service talent? Have you leveraged scientific approaches to talent selection to increase the probability that you are choosing staff members with natural service abilities?

- Has leadership development included a focus on enhancing the talent of existing staff members, as opposed to remediating employee deficits?

- Are your staff certified and regularly audited on your desired service behaviors?

- How are managers held accountable for monitoring frontline service behaviors?

> Is service coaching taking place at all levels of your organization? When was the last time you coached or were coached about service?

CICARE CARDS

Ultimately, the test of any service-oriented business is the perception of the individual who is receiving the care. At UCLA, the voice of the customer (VOC) is regularly assessed in both traditional and atypical ways. Even when typical methods of collecting customer feedback are used, the execution at UCLA is often both wise and unusually impassioned. From the standpoint of wise execution, CICARE comment cards are well positioned in high-traffic locations, and the scope of the questions presented on the comment cards follows directly from the CICARE behaviors tailored for each department. For example, if you are at a cash register at the exit from the central dining area, you would encounter a well-positioned display of CICARE comment cards that ask about your most recent transaction. The example of the content of those cards that is shown here reflects an adaptation of CICARE behaviors for the dining setting.

Dining staff members are trained and coached concerning their specific service responsibilities in the context of CICARE, and customers are given an opportunity to evaluate staff members on the specific behaviors highlighted in the employee's training and coaching. All business leaders should determine whether they have developed an overarching service umbrella like CICARE, modified behavioral expectations to meet the service requirements of each of their work areas, and aligned customer and manager evaluations of performance with those specifically defined expectations.

Comment cards are one way to get real-time data concerning customers' perceptions of service, but many of us have seen customer comment collection boxes that are seldom used and even less frequently checked by administrators. At UCLA, many staff members

---

UCLA Health System

We at Dining Commons want you to have the Best Dining Experience. Please check the box "yes" or "no" next to each statement below to let us know how we are doing.

Thank you!

CICARE

Did our team member:

Yes ☐ No ☐ Address you as Sir or Madam, or by your name?

Yes ☐ No ☐ Handle him/herself cordially and attentively in processing your order?

Yes ☐ No ☐ Did the quality of our food meet your expectations?

Yes ☐ No ☐ Did our staff respond to your request with promptness and efficiency?

Yes ☐ No ☐ Did our cashier give you your receipt?

Yes ☐ No ☐ Did he/she end by wishing you an enjoyable Dining Experience?

Date: _____ Phone: _____

Completed by: _____

Department: _____

Comments:

---

not only have embraced excellence in delivering CICARE, but also have demonstrated a commitment to soliciting feedback from patients and their families at a rare and fervent pace. One example of this ardent desire to capture the voice of the customer comes from Security Officer Virgil Jones. "When the CICARE program was implemented, it fit me. In a nutshell, it's all about caring for patients, visitors, staff, and faculty. You have patients coming here from all over the world to get the best healthcare, and I get to help them. Administration said they wanted feedback from all our visitors, so I turned in more than 2,000 CICARE comment cards. To be honest with you, if I had had people fill out a card every time they received help, I would have about 4,000 right now. While I lead the security department for most cards turned in, I am also assisting fellow officers in delivering quality CICARE and making sure we are asking for and collecting input from those we serve." When your security officers are collecting thousands of customer feedback cards, you have clearly communicated the importance of collecting data that capture customer perception.

WALKING THE TALK OF COLLECTING CUSTOMER INPUT

While most leaders understand intuitively that their actions speak louder than their words when it comes to giving priority to behaviors like soliciting customer opinions, CEO Dr. David Feinberg demonstrates the power of "walking your talk." Following Dr. Feinberg through a day at UCLA is like taking an intensive course on "how to talk to your customers." Whether it is staff members, patients, or family, he has an insatiable appetite for seeking input. Dr. Feinberg notes, "I try to be out of my office as much as possible because I am 100 percent about relationships, and relationships are a lot about listening." In addition to walking onto units following CICARE behaviors (knocking on doors, asking permission to enter, introducing himself to patients, and so on) and asking patients about themselves and about their care at UCLA, Dr. Feinberg actively creates ways to hear from hospital staff members about their work experience. Every week, Dr. Feinberg invites random staff members to share a meal with him and give him their opinions on their work environment and anything that will improve UCLA's care of employees, patients, and families. Dr. Feinberg notes that even the process of listening has necessitated additional listening and refinement: "In the beginning, I thought inviting people to lunch was a good idea. Then at one of the lunches, I found out that an individual had worked the overnight shift, changed out of uniform, and caught a couple of hours of sleep prior to joining me for lunch. This person didn't have enough time to go home and come back for our lunch, and didn't want to miss the opportunity to accept a lunch invitation from the CEO. From that day forward, I knew that I had to have meals with staff members at rotating hours that fit into their schedules, not into mine. Even to listen, you have to make yourself available to the logistic needs of others."

Dr. Feinberg's approach to sharing meals with staff members is part of his broader effort to meet all 7,000 members of the UCLA team. He shares, "I am on a quest 10 people at a time, and while I can't remember the names of all our staff members the way I used to be able to do when I oversaw 400 people at the Resnick Neuropsychiatric Hospital (RNPH) at UCLA, I am fully committed to spending time with each person." Every leader can gain inspiration and direction from Dr. Feinberg's ambitious goal of spending time with all 7,000 staff members. If you are going to champion service one customer at a time, you have to serve your staff—one employee at a time or one meal at a time.

All senior leaders are out of their offices making "management rounds" with patients. In addition, they have crafted processes to ensure that every level of leadership is doing the same. One example of these processes is PCAT rounds. PCAT stands for "Peer CICARE Assessment Tool," and the rounding process for this tool involves all managers throughout the system. The PCAT tool is used by managers to ask patients if their experience is consistent with delivery of CICARE and World Class Practices. Furthermore, the assessment addresses whether the care is meeting or exceeding other core needs.

Heidi Crooks, RN, chief nursing officer at UCLA and senior associate director, Operations & Patient Care Services, shares, "I think PCAT rounds are ingenious and invaluable. All managers come together and are assigned areas of the hospital to visit, and they ask standardized questions of patients. The managers then come back together and discuss the information they acquired. It breaks managers out of the mold of simply fixing problems and puts them in a place where they are listening to customers throughout the hospital."

Having participated in PCAT rounds, I will attempt to offer an example of this rather unique managerial "hands-on" approach for collecting input about the patient experience. Let's assume that you are a food service manager, and you are attending mandatory PCAT rounds. You and your fellow managers meet in an auditorium to hear some preliminary remarks that focus you on getting out of your comfort zones to authentically seek input from patients and families. You are then grouped with a small team of other managers and sent to a unit of the hospital. You pair up with a partner, and the two of you check with the unit director to determine which patients are well enough to receive a management visit. You and your partner approach each room, sanitize your hands, knock on the door, ask permission to enter, introduce yourselves, establish rapport, and begin an informal dialogue with the patient and his family members. While you are provided with possible areas of inquiry, the focus of PCAT rounds is to engage in an authentic discussion of the patient and family experience at UCLA. You inquire, actively listen, forge an interpersonal connection, and explore issues that are important to the patient's overall care. Conversations might include effective pain management, responsiveness of nursing staff, approachability of physicians, and specific areas of concern like parking fees.

You and your partner then address issues that require immediate attention. For example, one administrator I observed went downstairs to buy a patient her preferred newspaper, and another spoke to a nursing supervisor regarding a pain management issue. You then thank the patient, leave the room, resanitize your hands, and repeat the process until it's time to reconvene and be debriefed with other managers in the auditorium. There managers share what they heard from patients and their families and offer suggestions for quality improvement based on their engaged listening. During my involvement, these types of suggestions included improving signage in a particular area of the hospital and clarifying an ambiguous policy. As PCAT rounds come to an end, stories of positive service are shared.

The PCAT process offers many essential leadership lessons, including the importance of mobilizing managers to leave the refuge of their offices and listen to the perceptions of customers, increasing managerial team behavior, and helping managers listen to patients in other departments. In the process, managers are mobilized to take specific actions that address customer concerns and remedy process breakdowns.

In addition to patient rounds conducted with management peers, each department has CICARE rounds (CAT rounds) to evaluate the employees' adherence to departmental CICARE standards. This on-unit patient rounding process pairs a leader with a direct report to solicit feedback from patients they serve. This process, which includes observations of the healthcare provider as well as feedback from patients, not only ensures that managers continue to conduct rounds for patient satisfaction, but also includes the providers of the service. This inclusion has the benefit of allowing front-line staff to hear the direct feedback of patients.

In addition to all of the management rounds being conducted with patients at UCLA, student volunteers conduct independent patient-care audits. Undergraduate students interview patients to ensure that medical school residents are performing their duties in accordance with CICARE guidelines. Timothy Wen, a student volunteer, shares, "We go to a patient's room, knock, introduce ourselves, tell him that we are there to do a survey from the school of medicine, and ask if he has five minutes. We make it clear that the survey is optional and confidential, and that it will help residents in their professional development. Once we have the patient's consent, we ask if he knows his resident's name. If he does not, we ask if he can identify the resident from a group of pictures we provide. We ask him the degree to which his resident follows each behavior of CICARE."

When asked how residents typically perform, Timothy notes, "Residents are doing very well with the quality and consistency of communication. Patients report that residents typically speak very courteously. Patients are extremely happy with the care they receive. If there are any problems, feedback from our audits is used to help the resident improve her communication and care behavior." Timothy suggests that patients welcome the opportunity to talk about their care experience and that the audits are a win/win/win. "The patients benefit, the resident benefits, and as an interviewer, I get a lot out of this opportunity. I want to be a doctor, and this process has helped me appreciate that healthcare is more than just terrific skill and knowledge. A lot of quality healthcare has to do with simple communication skills that can be overlooked if you don't take a disciplined approach to communication."

The impact of disciplined communication skills and the satisfaction of customers is echoed by Posie Carpenter, RN, MSN, MPH, chief administrative officer, Santa Monica–UCLA Medical Center and Orthopaedic Hospital, "At times during our journey to elevate patient satisfaction at Santa Monica, I've become frustrated when satisfaction scores start to plateau. On one occasion, I talked to David Feinberg about our satisfaction scores flattening out. He suggested that it was a matter of redoubling efforts on the CICARE program. So I went back through CICARE and asked myself what were the main things that we could be doing to pick up the momentum. We focused on using our daily huddles (conversations with staff) to reemphasize CICARE behavior. We did more CICARE rounds and had managers build time into their daily schedules exclusively for the 'management rounding' process. We closely tracked our managers' follow-through with these rounds. Most important, we took the information we gained from patients and revamped our processes, redesigned units, and created options like our emergency 'fast track.' Because of those changes, we have literally seen areas of our hospital go from the 10th percentile of patient satisfaction to the 99th."

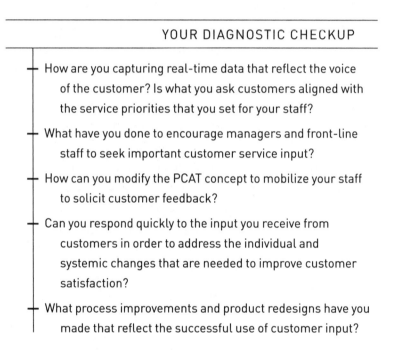

YOUR DIAGNOSTIC CHECKUP

— How are you capturing real-time data that reflect the voice of the customer? Is what you ask customers aligned with the service priorities that you set for your staff?

— What have you done to encourage managers and front-line staff to seek important customer service input?

— How can you modify the PCAT concept to mobilize your staff to solicit customer feedback?

— Can you respond quickly to the input you receive from customers in order to address the individual and systemic changes that are needed to improve customer satisfaction?

— What process improvements and product redesigns have you made that reflect the successful use of customer input?

EXECUTION BEYOND ROBOTICS

When I first heard about UCLA's CICARE program, I harked back to the 1980s, when I worked as an organizational development specialist for a hospital system. More than 25 years ago, the concept of "scripted" care enjoyed popularity, and CICARE initially seemed to be reminiscent of those arcane scripted communication concepts. However, UCLA's execution of CICARE is a fundamentally different approach from those failed efforts at scripting that were tried decades ago. UCLA adds important ingredients to the mix, such as talent selection, staff involvement in the development of training materials, daily discussions of CICARE behaviors (daily huddles), peer management rounds, leader/staff care rounds, leadership accountability for making rounds, and activation of quality improvements based on information gained during rounds. Furthermore, UCLA has connected making patient rounds to desired satisfaction outcomes that affect overall business viability.

On the downside, CICARE (like any communication template) can become a robotic process. It can drive operational consistency, but it can do so at the expense of passion, warmth, and humanity. Chapter 3 explores ways in which UCLA's leadership makes sure that CICARE does not become robotic or impersonal, but instead serves as the launch pad for extraordinary patient experiences. To that end, Chapter 3 offers a rich and often poignant look into the subtle and heroic efforts of UCLA staff members as they deliver transformational, compassionate, and memorable care.

Prescriptive Summary

▶ Appreciate that successful service cultures need champions from the top of the organization.

▶ Evaluate your vision statement to determine whether service needs to have a more prominent and relevant presence.

▶ Define the key service behaviors that you want to see in your culture.

▶ Establish a communication template.

▶ Leverage the science of selection to increase service talent.

▶ Get managers actively involved in developing talent.

▶ Come out of your office more. Listen more.

▶ Develop mechanisms to get your managers out of their offices more to observe staff service behaviors and seek customer feedback.

▶ Measure service performance against preestablished objectives and expectations.

▶ Share a meal with a widening circle of staff members.

▶ Empower staff members to fix customers' problems immediately and to look for opportunities to affect processes that regularly dissatisfy customers.

CHAPTER 3

Never Enough Care

*How far you go in life depends on your being tender
with the young, compassionate with the aged,
sympathetic with the striving and tolerant of
the weak and strong. Because someday in your life
you will have been all of these.*

—GEORGE WASHINGTON CARVER

Candie Goldbronn has been a patient at a number of UCLA clinics, and, like most people who seek treatment at UCLA, she has noticed consistent service, but also an intangible level of care. "I've had Lasik eye surgery done at UCLA and been treated in the emergency room for a back muscle strain. Every time, I'm greeted with a smile. Volunteers, nurses, doctors, and other staff members introduce themselves, ask to examine me, listen to me, answer my questions, and let me know what is going on with my care. I've never been to another healthcare system that didn't feel just like a hospital. UCLA is more like being cared for at a nice hotel or a fine restaurant. I've never received that type of healthcare anywhere else."

The CICARE program outline in Chapter 2 was designed to provide service consistency. However, it is part of a larger leadership strategy that elevates "service" to the "relationship-based" or "customer experience" level. Consistency drives predictable patterns of care and ultimately generates customer satisfaction—a consumer's assessment of your business's competence and reliability. UCLA's leaders seek to achieve not just satisfaction, but also patient engagement—an emotional sense of connection between the patient and UCLA.

When a business achieves engagement, consumers are likely to refer their family and friends to that business and remain loyal in the face of increasing competition. At UCLA, this focus on patient engagement also sets a stretch goal of reaching beyond being a "good" service provider in an industry that is fraught with service challenges. The leadership wants to inspire and drive memorable patient experiences that not only stand out in healthcare but also leave people like Candie Goldbronn comparing the service they receive at UCLA to the service they receive at legendary providers like luxury hotels.

Throughout this chapter, we will look at leadership practices at UCLA and how those practices help the staff create deeper relationship-based and emotional connections with patients. We will also glean insights from the relationship wisdom of UCLA staff members.

SINCE ALL BUSINESS IS PERSONAL, FOCUS ON RELATIONSHIPS

It can be argued that certain business transactions, such as fueling your car or buying a product online, are impersonal. By contrast, businesses like childcare and healthcare are high-touch industries. In healthcare, personal connections obviously matter, and the ability of staff members to create authentic caring relationships leads to success. However, even in businesses where service seems secondary to product, strong customer connections drive brand differentiation and other positive business outcomes. Starbucks and Ritz-Carlton sell commodities (coffee and housing, respectively), but their leadership teams also help staff members give priority to relationship building in a way that has lifted those brands to a "beloved" status with customers. To measure that customer "love,"

Ritz-Carlton utilizes the Gallup Corporation's CE11 (customer engagement tool), which asks customers to endorse responses like the degree to which the brand is perfect for someone like them, or whether the customer is a proud supporter of the brand. These items drill down much deeper than questions like "Are you satisfied with our service?" Instead, they measure whether customers are passionate about your company.

In order to build referrals effectively and inspire customers to essentially become part of your sales team, you have to connect with those customers at a level similar to that described by Rachel Vollmer. Rachel, whose son Aiden experienced a life-changing surgery at UCLA, communicates her emotional connection to the healthcare system in a way that reflects the essence of what tools like the CE11 are trying to measure. "Hospitals are not exactly the most fun place to be, and it's going to sound odd, but I actually look forward to going to UCLA when we have postoperative appointments. I look forward to seeing those people, and I don't want to think of a world without UCLA."

While most leaders want to have their people create relationships with customers, so that those customers "can't imagine a world" without their company, many of those leaders often fail to engage their staff members in conversations about the types of relationships that produce high levels of customer engagement. In essence, leaders might identify CICARE-type behaviors, but fail to follow through on accountability, let alone deepen conversations about customer "experiences" or consumer "relationships."

UCLA's leadership has not left an understanding of healthy service relationships to chance. In fact, the leaders facilitate rich conversations with and between staff members about the essential ingredients necessary to generate healthy and healing bonds. For example, the nursing department at UCLA has adopted and modified a model of relationship-based care championed by Creative Health Care Management. That model asserts that relationship-based care is a commitment from bedside to boardroom and builds on evolving theory and research that began in the late 1970s when Jean Watson, a distinguished professor of nursing and founder of the Center for Human Caring, first began to look at "care" from both the giver's and the receiver's perspective.

Based on the work of individuals like Jean Watson and Mary Koloroutis, vice president of Creative Health Care Management, and the commitment of their own nursing leadership, UCLA is exposing staff members to training and conversations about the importance of self-care, support of colleagues, and service to patients. These discussions, personal-renewal programs, and skills development tools help nurses create a healing environment, serve together effectively in teams, and practice service leadership. By offering a formal relationship-care delivery model, UCLA nursing provides a context for ways to deliver care to oneself, the team, and the patient. Leadership also helps make important service distinctions about varied ways for patients to achieve a sense of well-being.

This chapter is structured around a model of service that UCLA leaders have modified to help staff members understand the diverse ways they can serve and build relationships with one another and with patients. The model, the "five caring processes," was originally crafted by Dr. Kristen Swanson, affiliate professor of parent and child nursing at the University of Washington, and reflects the following core tenets:

- *Maintaining belief* (believing in a patient or holding him in esteem and maintaining hope on his behalf)

- *Knowing* (avoiding assumptions, thoroughly assessing a patient, getting to know her, and centering care on her)

- *Being with* (offering time and conveying a sense of availability)

- *Doing for* (comforting, protecting, and anticipating)

- *Enabling* (informing/explaining, advocating, validating, and generating alternatives)

By helping staff members understand the various ways in which they can develop caring relationships, the leaders encourage teams to grow beyond a preferred way of caring and toward proactive relationships that are fitted to the needs of each patient. While an authoritative staff member might prefer to demonstrate caring by taking charge and "doing for" a patient, that patient might best be served if the staff member "enables" him. Throughout much of this chapter, staff examples will be offered in the context of these well-differentiated caring processes.

As you approach this content, you may wish to consider what, if any, efforts you have made to create a "model of care" that encourages relationship-based as opposed to transactional service. You may also wish to think whether you have encouraged your staff members to target care toward the well-being of the individual staff member, her teammates, and your customers. Additionally, the chapter will provide insights into ways of expanding your staff's toolkit of caring behaviors. By providing staff members with a wider set of service tools, leaders offer tangible strategies that enable all employees to forge relevant, deep, and loyalty-building relationships with one another and with consumers.

YOUR DIAGNOSTIC CHECKUP

- Have you made distinctions between "service" and "experience"?
- What are the elements necessary for your staff to create relationships that will fuel referrals and more customers?
- What percentage of your customers would say that they are proud to purchase from you, "can't imagine a world without your company," or view your service level as extraordinary for your industry? What changes would be necessary to increase this percentage?
- Which models or approaches have you used to discuss constructive, relationship-based sales and service?

SERVING BY MAINTAINING BELIEF

Most leaders think of service as a set of transactional behaviors (observable actions on behalf of a customer), but the UCLA leadership helps staff members appreciate that the foundation of service involves fostering an environment of dignity and hope. This caring process of "maintaining belief" emphasizes the affirmation of individual worth and the importance of encouraging hope and positivity. Paul Watkins, associate director of operations for UCLA Hospital System, notes, "I oversee a lot of people who don't have direct clinical-care responsibilities. They may be in environmental services or engineering. No matter what their direct contact with patients, it is essential that staff members know that they play an important role in creating an environment of caring that benefits their coworkers, the patients, and even themselves. When staff members interact with a patient in an area like transport or food service, the way they connect with the patient has therapeutic value. In a hospital environment, privacy and dignity can be hard to come by, and a food service worker can contribute to or detract from a patient's sense of well-being. It is my responsibility to help staff members understand how to serve so that they create an environment that dignifies the patient's experience. You'd be surprised how often I receive letters from patients that talk about the respectfulness or cheerfulness of staff members in areas like transport."

CEO Dr. David Feinberg notes, "Some of what is built into CICARE, like knocking on a door before you enter a room, introducing yourself, or asking permission before you touch or intrude on a patient, is based on a fundamental understanding that service must come from a place that honors dignity. Even well-intentioned people get busy and forget those common courtesies; that's why formats like CICARE are important. CICARE can't just be an end unto itself. You have to elevate service through a conscious effort to demonstrate how much value you hold in others. That's why we as leaders need to model genuine caring that affirms the integrity of those we serve and encourages them to do the same with one another and with their patients."

In the spirit of honoring the dignity and worth of coworkers, the nursing leadership has implemented a "commitment to my coworkers" card developed by Creative Health Care Management. The pocket card, which is disseminated to staff members throughout the organization, includes a number of commitments that affirm the value of coworkers, as seen in the sample below:

As your coworker and with our shared organizational goal of excellent patient care, I commit to the following:

- I will accept responsibility for establishing and maintaining healthy interpersonal relationships with you and every other member of this team.

- I will accept you as you are today, forgiving past problems, and ask you to do the same with me.

- I will remember that neither of us is perfect and that human errors are opportunities, not for shame or guilt, but for forgiveness and growth.

- I will not engage in the "3Bs" (Bickering, Back-biting, and Blaming). I will practice the "3Cs" (Caring, Committing, and Collaborating) in my relationship with you and ask you to do the same with me.

Dr. Cathy Rodgers Ward, RN, DNSc, director of nursing at UCLA, notes, "Once you recruit the best talent, leadership and peers have to support those talented individuals so that they can deliver the highest care to our patients. Peers should make commitments to one another to ensure an environment of respect, and we as leaders need to do all we can to care about the overall well-being of our staff."

This focus on human dignity, hope, and positivity has application in all aspects of care, whether that care is focused on the patient, on the team, or in the direction of personal well-being. To that end, leaders like Dr. Ward have invested in helping nurses care for themselves. "It's hard for most people to fathom the challenges that nurses face every day. Take pediatric ICU nurses, for example. They regularly endure the sadness of children dying mixed with the joy of patients who recover. We've long recognized that nurses need self-renewal and self-care support. The nursing literature emphasizes the importance of services to help avert burnout. As leaders, we have to constantly innovate self-care services for our caregivers. At UCLA, we started by doing unit self-renewal retreats annually. However, it became clear that for some staff members, a four- or eight-hour annual retreat was just not enough time to revitalize their passion and purpose for nursing. So we set up a three-day program at a mountain location. This type of retreat has significant impact in helping nurses maintain belief in themselves and in our profession. It sets aside time for renewal and self-care, and provides opportunities to explore the calling that led to their career choice." Given the pace, paperwork, crises, and technology of medicine, care professionals are at risk of losing their focus on caring relationships and are vulnerable to becoming task-oriented instead. To avert these unwanted outcomes, the leadership creates opportunities and guidance for reaffirmation and a rekindled sense of hope.

Dr. Ward notes, "When nurses reidentify what drives them to serve others, they are better able to connect, care, and collaborate with their patients. We talk about consistently connecting with patients as part of relationship-based care. We emphasize the idea of 'every nurse, every time.' Essentially, we are in the business of believing in and serving people, even when they may have lost their own sense of dignity or worth. We need to deliver human dignity with a spirit of hopefulness 100 percent of the time. 'Every nurse, every time' is an important mantra for us to achieve our goals associated with excellence in patient experience." Dr. Ward's comments speak to the important role that leaders play in inspiring staff members to care for themselves, their coworkers, and their customers. Furthermore, she demonstrates that lofty expectations can reasonably be placed on staff members (100 percent execution of relationship-based service components like "maintaining belief") when those same leaders invest in caring for staff in a similar way.

Cindy Jaeger, inpatient rehabilitation manager at UCLA, understands how consistently maintaining belief in patients is an important aspect of being a relationship provider. "We often treat patients who either have given up hope or have a poor prognosis. As therapists, we continue to encourage those patients to do just a little bit more, and over time these patients achieve recovery goals that they never thought possible."

The concept of delivering service by "maintaining hope" does not imply encouraging unrealistic expectations or engaging in overly optimistic behavior. Sara Devaney, child life specialist, CCLS, MS, notes, "I work with our grief, bereavement, and palliative program, which is called Children's Comfort Care. In some cases, maintaining a positive belief isn't about recovery, but instead involves a belief in the individual or family's ability to address end-of-life issues with comfort. In many cases, I'm responsible for helping families maintain a different kind of optimism—positivity to find peace and meaning in the process. If we know a patient is dying, my colleagues and I work with the entire family. We facilitate each family member's grief and loss experience. We offer family members the opportunity to express themselves constructively, or at times we get clothing and blankets so that parents can hold a child after he or she has passed away. We help the parents say good-bye with dignity. For me, the most important services I have to offer are comfort, dignity, and hope."

Relationship-based care often starts with a belief in the worth and dignity of others. It can also be manifested through a spirit of hope and positivity, even if outcomes are not optimal. Being respectful and hopeful are readily available service options, even when other behaviors are not. The leaders help staff members see opportunities for building meaningful connections with customers simply through maintaining a positive regard for those individuals. The subtext of every service relationship is, "I am here for you because you matter. How can I help?" It is the job of leaders to discuss this powerful foundation of relationship-based care.

KNOWING AS A FORM OF SERVICE

To create emotionally connected relationships, service providers must understand the wants, needs, and desires of their customers. Lee Iacocca, former CEO of Chrysler Corporation, once said, "I only wish I could find an institute that teaches people how to listen. Business people need to listen. . . . Too many people fail to realize that real communication goes in both directions." Of course, listening to serve others occurs on at least two levels: listening to fulfill stated needs and listening to create emotional connections. Listening to fulfill stated needs means that you offer transactional services: I ask for a pillow, and you provide the pillow. That is a fulfillment transaction. To build deeper relationships, customer experience providers listen for opportunities to serve unstated needs. These service professionals are acutely attentive to people and get to know them in more subtle ways. This same process of attentive "knowing" is at play in leadership, with effective leaders exerting effort to subtly attend to those they serve. A rough estimate of employee engagement can often be made by simply asking managers what they know about their employees. How many children does that direct report have? What motivates that employee? What are the aspirations of your sales director? Managers who attentively and continually seek to understand the values and drivers of their people often have the most engaged staff members, who, in turn, actively seek to "know" their customers.

Elizabeth George, unit director at the Nethercutt Emergency Center at Santa Monica–UCLA Medical Center and Orthopaedic Hospital, demonstrates the power of listening to the stated and unstated needs of her staff members and customers. "We had dissatisfied staff and the turnover rates to prove it. As I assumed leadership, we increased our listening, both formally and informally. At the beginning of this journey, we received data on customer satisfaction, and we were horrified to learn that patient satisfaction scores were at the 15th percentile. But the more we as leaders listened openly, the more opportunities we had to serve. Employees became engaged; our level of relationship-based care improved; we innovated service breakthroughs that responded to what our staff members and patients told us they needed. We improved records technology, enhanced staff productivity, drove revenues, justified increased staffing levels, and developed a 'fast track' guarantee. This means that for most conditions that conform with fast track criteria, patients will be in and out of our ER in 90 minutes or less. Because we listened and listened, our patient satisfaction scores climbed from the 15th percentile to the 35th, to the 55th, to the 80th, and now we rank at the 99th percentile. To me, listening is service unto itself, and it is also the foundation for action that can transform any business."

Dr. Bonny Sham, R.N., PsyD, unit director, Neonatal ICU, notes that healthcare is taking revolutionary strides to find ways to listen and "know" the needs of patients in areas that it did not years ago. "We have nurses who are training in a special relationship-based program called NIDCAP, which stands for Newborn Individualized Developmental Care and Assessment Program. This program helps those nurses become resources for our team in caring for preterm newborns in a highly personalized way. Rather than subjecting vulnerable babies to a nurse's style or process of care, the NIDCAP approach helps nurses accommodate to the often subtle needs that are being communicated by these preemies. The speed of activity and the level of stimulation are guided by careful ongoing assessment of the newborns. Those nurses look for body language cues from a baby to distinguish how to approach a process as basic as the speed of diapering. This is a novel concept to some, but it makes perfect sense—customize care to the developmental needs of your patient and become expert in your ability to read the cues being given by patients at high risk. Astute assessment is the foundation of personalized care."

Hilary Gan, MA, CCLS II, UCLA child life specialist, keys in on the idea that listening requires finely tuned sensitivity and a willingness to grow and adapt. "I am constantly learning how to listen. I served a girl who came to UCLA and remained in the hospital for about two years. She was primarily in our intensive-care unit. When I met her, she had been intubated for a long time, but she was awake, alert, and engaging. She eventually was extubated and had some expressive language difficulties, although she seemed to understand most things. For a long time, staff members debated about whether she should go home or continue to stay at UCLA. The concern was whether she would survive outside of the hospital environment. Ultimately, it was determined that her best interest would be served by returning home. I spent a lot of time getting to know how she felt about going home to her mom, dad, and sister. I felt that I had listened to her effectively, and we readied for the transition. She was going to be taken home by ambulance, and her parents would be waiting at home for her. I escorted her to the ambulance on the day she left the hospital. I remember explaining all about the ambulance ride and what she could expect. I introduced her to the ambulance staff, and she smiled and nodded. I gave her a hug and told her that she was going to see mommy and daddy. She nodded again. I stepped out of the ambulance, and her arm popped up. She had this terror on her face. That's when it hit me. I hadn't listened well enough to understand that for her, UCLA had been home for such a long time, and I had been preparing her for a concept of home that made sense to me but of which she was fearful. I realized that I could have thought this through more from her perspective. My heart just sank." Hilary's passion for learning ways to "know" and "listen" beyond a patient's stated words reflects mature service professionalism. Despite the fact that the patient ultimately made a successful and healthy transition to her home, Hilary is always looking for ways to improve her ability to "listen" and "know" even the unstated needs of her patients.

UCLA leaders formally develop active, consistent, and evolving listening processes. For example, management rounds and CICARE comment cards are formalized listening processes. Virgie Mosley, manager of the UCLA Patient Liaison Program, suggests that listening is often the linchpin not only of service excellence, but also of effective service recovery. "Most of my job is simply listening and getting to know a patient's wants and needs. Hospitals have regulations, procedures, and so on, but when you're sick, you don't care about those things. You care that someone understands what you are going through. My job is to get to know people and help them understand what is possible in our hospital environment. Often service breakdowns occur when, in the course of clinical care, patients feel that a staff member was rushed or didn't take the time to understand their point of view. After listening attentively, I often only need to say, 'I'm sorry.' I'm careful not to say that the problem won't happen again, because I can't control all the variables in the system, but I can show that I understand the discomfort that the situation created, apologize, and take steps to make the patient more comfortable. Through listening and seeking to know the patient's experience, acceptable resolutions often emerge. If I go in with a predetermined fix to a problem, that fix often fails to lead to a patient's satisfaction." Virgie appreciates that stepping into the patient's experience by listening is a partial solution in itself. The act of taking the time to honor the customer's experience (without unrealistic promises or defensiveness) places the customer and the service provider in a collaborative relationship, as opposed to an adversarial one. Georgetown professor of linguistics Deborah Tannen remarks, "To say that a person feels listened to means a lot more than just their ideas get heard. It's a sign of respect. It makes people feel valued." Once people feel valued, viable acts of problem resolution can be explored. Virgie's comments, much like the wisdom that Hilary Gan obtained from preparing her young patient for a trip "home," suggest that effective "knowing" or listening starts with a willingness to let go of preconceived ideas or bias, while exploring and assessing the needs of the customer.

Whether it is disgruntled customers, premature babies, or disengaged staff members, leaders help their staff members understand that listening is an essential and underutilized service behavior. Those same leaders typically facilitate their staff's understanding of the importance of listening through the leader's own listening behaviors. Every day you have the opportunity to strengthen your relationships with staff members and customers by listening to them and helping them see the power that comes from "knowing" their customer.

BEING WITH AS A FORM OF SERVICE

Although listening to customers and actively assessing their needs are often overlooked forms of caring, most staff members quickly come to understand that those actions are essential to customer service. However, passive activities such as simply spending time with a customer or giving a customer a sense of your accessibility are less obvious forms of relationship-based care. Clara Huerta, a sign language interpreter at UCLA, notes, "Some of my greatest moments occur when I am doing little more than being present with patients and their families. It is in those inactive moments that patients draw a great deal of strength and comfort. This is particularly true in the roller coaster of emotions that patients and their families can experience. I was paged during a lunch hour and ran to the ICU to interpret for a family where the young wife was dying from a heart attack and ensuing heart failure. The doctors were concerned that she wouldn't make it through the night and wanted to place her on the list for a donor heart. After I had interpreted for the deaf patient and her deaf husband, the family was crying and tired. Those events took us until late in the evening, and the family decided to get dinner at a restaurant in the nearby community and asked if I would join them." Clara reports that despite an initial reluctance, she felt that it was important for her to "be with" the family, and "although we did not communicate much, I knew they felt supported. We returned to the hospital after dinner, and the patient's husband literally said a good-bye that he feared would be his last. As I headed to my car, physically and emotionally exhausted, my pager went off again. Just that quickly, a donor heart had been located. I ran through the parking lot screaming and racing to the family to let them know that the patient would be getting a heart that night. She is alive and well today, raising her children. While interpreting the complexities of these rapidly changing medical circumstances was important to this patient and her family, I think just being with them during that time may have mattered more."

UCLA nurse Elaine Rosso Severa, RN, suggests that the ability to be present with patients in a time of need is what distinguishes professional caregivers from those who simply transact medicine. "We treat bowel patients who can be with us for months or even a year. I have come to realize that for many of these patients, we are their family. We are their social system; we're more than just the nurse that does the needed treatment. I am convinced that anyone can hang an IV and anybody can do patient dressings, but a real caregiver offers her full presence for as long as a patient or family needs it. I often attend the funerals of patients because I have connected with the family and they deserve my presence at their time of grief." Barbara Abrams, RN, suggests, "Most service comes down to your presence during an important life event and how much that means to the person served. Patients remember your being there. It's really not about me. It's about connecting with them. If there is a reason for me to cry about something, I cry with the family. If there is a reason to be happy, I am happy with them. I just allow myself to be present and involved."

Like many other businesses, medicine can become so technically focused that staff members lose sight of the importance of their "presence" as a form of care. Given the pace of business today, leaders must help their staff understand that customers want ready access to human beings. Customers crave human service from people who are not too harried to give the customer their time and attention. Great leaders help employees appreciate that service occurs when staff members are fully present with customers, often doing little more than "being with" them.

YOUR DIAGNOSTIC CHECKUP

- Have you delineated various ways of offering service, including "maintaining belief," "knowing," and "being with" the customer?
- How do you demonstrate these service behaviors with those you lead and serve?
- Are positivity, hopefulness, and creating a sense of availability key aspects of your leadership style? If you increased these service qualities, how would it affect your customers' experience and relationships between your staff members and your customers?

DOING FOR AS A FORM OF SERVICE

All this focus on treating individuals with hope, integrity, open listening, and a physical and emotional presence does not mean that discussions about excellent and active service behavior aren't taking place at UCLA. CEO Dr. David Feinberg notes, "I am in relationships with patients and their families all day long. I can't help but share stories of how our staff members constantly go the extra mile for patients. The great thing about these stories is that they not only put faces to the service provider/patient relationship, but also inspire us all to creatively take action above and beyond CICARE to do the big and small things that transform experiences at UCLA from good to extraordinary."

Dennis Gonzales, RN, pediatric oncology clinical nurse, notes, "I love hearing stories of excellent care because they motivate me to action. Shortly after I heard some 'extra mile' nursing stories, I noticed that a young patient who adamantly refused hospital food had run out of the frozen meals he had brought from home. The poor kid was waiting for his supply to be replenished, so I asked other nurses to cover me while I ran out and got him some healthy frozen chicken dinners and beverages." When asked where he got the money to buy those items, Dennis casually noted, "It was my money, but that wasn't important. The point was that I was inspired to be of greater service because my peers are doing small and big things every day that are transforming unpleasant circumstances into memorable and special moments."

Lynette DeFrancia, occupational therapist, builds on Dennis's point about the importance of taking action to create moments of specialness in an environment that can be quite painful and hostile. "There are many times in this job where we have reached the limits of medicine and have to turn to what is limitless—caring action. I had a 17-year-old patient who had been healthy most of her life until she was diagnosed with viral cardiomyopathy and was awaiting a donor heart. During this waiting period, she suffered an infarct to her spinal cord and was rendered paraplegic, with no use of her legs. We attempted to maximize her function in her wheelchair, but it was hard to motivate her at that point." Lynette notes that she was with the patient in a hospital classroom when the patient's teacher announced that the patient would be graduating from high school on a given date. Lynette asked the patient if she would like to have a graduation party at the hospital.

According to Lynette, "The patient was motivated by the idea of a graduation party. She thought the party would be something to work toward, and she did really well the day the idea surfaced. Unfortunately, the next day our patient had a significant stroke, so we were back to square one. She was unstable, so it took a couple of weeks before she started trying to sit up again and get back into her wheelchair. Her stroke was severe enough that she was no longer an optimal candidate for a transplant. However, none of us gave up on her graduation party. We poured out the effort to celebrate that graduation, and the patient's brother even traveled in from out of state. Staff members came in on their day off to attend the party, give the patient presents, and wish her well. Doctors joined us in the same way. The patient wanted to feel like a regular teenager again, and during that party, she truly did. I think the party was her happiest time in the hospital. She sat in her wheelchair for a long time, even though that was challenging for her." Lynette goes on to note that the patient died a short time after the party. "When I went to console the mother, the first thing her mother said was, 'Thank you for giving her the party. It meant the world to her and to us.'"

By sharing stories of service excellence like the party created by Lynette DeFrancia and her team, people like Dennis Gonzales are inspired to greater levels of service excellence. Leaders spotlight staff members who are "doing for others" in a noteworthy way and use those examples as teachable lessons for service greatness. Put simply, from a leadership perspective, a front-line worker perspective, and a human-to-human perspective, service *is* synonymous with giving to and "doing for" others. Great leaders readily offer examples of situations where large and small "doing for" actions occur.

ENABLING AS A FORM OF SERVICE

When is an act of service not service? When that act renders a person less capable than he would have been had you not helped him. Leaders at UCLA readily talk about acts of service that enable and empower those who are being served. Lana Wohlschlegel, clinical social worker, Mattel Children's Hospital UCLA, sees "enabling" as a duty for service professionals. "Part of my job is empowering families to reach out for help in their communities because many of these people have never been in such a challenging position and don't know how to access community resources. It's important that I guide them through this process and not take over for them." Dan Alivia, RN, clinical case manager, offers an example of how he guides and advocates for those he serves. "Our patients encounter many hurdles beyond the diseases they face. For them the challenges are new, but for me they are familiar. In many cases I have to intervene, but I'm also looking to give the patient and her family the tools to take action." Dan continues, "I had a patient from a nearby state who stayed at UCLA for about a month. She had renal cancer, incontinence, severe pain, and then brain metastases. The patient experienced some confusion because of her metastatic disease, but she wanted to be involved in her care nonetheless. It was, in part, my job to advocate for that involvement."

According to Dan, the patient's out-of-state insurance company was closely regulating her care, and that produced challenges for her family. Dan notes, "With information provided concerning her options, the patient and her family decided that she wanted to be placed in hospice in her community. While the patient was saddened by her prognosis, she reported being glad that we were there to educate her and involve her in this important decision." Dan indicates that the patient's insurance company supported the plan to discharge her to hospice, but it would not pay for an ambulance to transport her back to her community, and the patient was too ill to travel by private vehicle. At this point, Dan and his team reengaged a process of empowerment. "The ambulance cost was estimated at around $3,000, so we deployed all our service options. We had our doctors talking to the doctors at the insurance company. The social worker and I continued to talk to the insurance representatives, but mostly we were enabling the family to work with the hospice program and the insurance company. All of that pressure and the mobilization of the family resulted in a split of ambulance costs among the hospice program, the insurance company, and the family. Consistent with her wishes, the patient died near her home with the nearby support of family and friends. It is rewarding to empower people so that they can get their needs met, even in the most adverse circumstances."

Cullen Torsney, RN, Neurological Disorders Unit at UCLA, puts it somewhat differently, noting, "To be successful in healthcare means putting yourself in the shoes of every patient. When you understand the frightening nature of a hospital stay, or how foreign an experience a series of outpatient procedures can be, you realize that your role is to help people master their fears and uncertainties. I live in this world, and I need to help patients make it through the foreign and frightening terrain."

Employee ownership behavior is reflected in an ability and willingness to empathize with customers and show those customers how to use company resources to help them help themselves. Relationship-based care is often about empowerment. Empowerment starts with leaders giving staff members the tools and the trust they need to provide extraordinary service. Those tools include structured service behaviors like CICARE to drive consistency and diverse constructs like the five caring processes to build relationships based on empathy and support. When well-selected employees are given resources, trained, and empowered effectively, extraordinary service relationships develop, and customers are empowered to build skills that meet their needs.

UNRELENTING PURSUIT OF SERVICE EXCELLENCE

At the beginning of this chapter, I shared a service example from Candie Goldbronn, a patient who noted that her many experiences at UCLA led her to conclude that UCLA's service levels are higher than what she expects from healthcare. That patient perception is the result of relentless efforts from leaders like Lynn Sullivan, community health program manager, The BirthPlace at UCLA Santa Monica, to benchmark service levels outside of her industry.

Lynn notes, "Wherever I go, I look for extraordinary service. I then discuss the ideas I collect with my colleagues, and wherever possible, we implement them. I pick up many ideas from resort hotels, including the way they present food and beverage service or little perks like a bento box snack. Our dietary department had been one of our biggest complaint areas, so when Rey Hernandez joined us as assistant director, nutrition, we went to work on bringing more organic food to our menu and having patients call down and order what they wanted, much as if they were selecting a hotel's room service option. Our dietary ambassadors or hostesses now come up to the floor and serve the patients what they ordered. Historically, we would deliver prepoured coffee or tea, but now it's poured at bedside. We used to have a celebration tea in the afternoon that we put in our family dining room, but it was underutilized by patients, so now we pour the hot coffee or tea and provide patients with a beautiful snack. Having seen a resort hotel provide bento boxes (with a ciabatta sandwich, cheese, and some fruit) at poolside, I talked to Rey, and he made it happen. We are planning to offer a bento box for our moms after they deliver their baby. So if they give birth at 3 a.m. and they're hungry, they have a special presentation of these ready-made snack boxes, including a congratulations card." Lynn adds that not all of the service ideas she emulates involve product development or a flair for presentation. "I was at a nice hotel and noticed that everyone acknowledged me verbally. It wasn't always 'good morning' or 'good afternoon'; often it was something that a person observed about me and commented on. It felt very personal. So that became my objective—to have every staff member talk to families, congratulate them, and say something personal. We need to engage that human connection at every opportunity, much like service in a luxury setting."

Similarly, Laurie Johnson, director of ambulatory operations, UCLA Faculty Practice Group, remarks, "In our outpatient clinics at UCLA, our staff members are offering customer service that can be compared to that of world-class service providers in other industries. Much of the job done by the clinic staff involves scheduling and interfacing with patients who are coming for appointments. We needed to benchmark industries outside of healthcare to offer the best service possible, so we looked at allied industries where those same functions were also critical." Ana Esquival, director of operations, Community Physician Network, shares, "From this benchmarking, a set of world-class customer interaction skills were brought together into formal training for our office staff." Angie Price, director, clinical operations, Orthopaedic Surgery, reports, "Our benchmark training allows us to drive a consistent patient service experience across all outpatient clinics throughout the UCLA system, so that the Faculty Practice Group can have service consistency that is congruent with brand standards." Lillian Martinez, director of operations, UCLA Department of Medicine, adds, "This training also ties in with the service standards that we measure all clinics against, whether those standards involve customer satisfaction, scheduling protocols, reminder calls, or timely phone answering. To be world class, we need to impose the same rigorous training and accountability standards that you would find among office staff at premier service businesses outside of healthcare."

Leaders set expectations and establish the standards by which all performance can be measured. At UCLA, ideas, expectations, and standards are established not only in relation to other healthcare industry leaders, but also based on best service practices in industries playing at the highest levels of service excellence. To which industries might you look for ideas and measurement comparisons that will stretch the level of customer experience offered at your business?

RECOGNITION BEGETS RECOGNITION
AT ALL LEVELS

Clearly UCLA's leadership is executing a patient experience and relationship-based care strategy, helping staff members engage in self-care and teamwork, engaging discussions of caring processes, and benchmarking service excellence outside of healthcare. All the while, UCLA leaders are celebrating those who demonstrate excellence in patient care. Reward and recognition approaches at UCLA that spotlight service excellence include unit employee of the month, the "STAR" program (which stands for Service and Teamwork Achieve Results), and Hospital Hero acknowledgments. One employee of the month, a nurse on the Neurological Disorders Unit, noted that, by recognizing individual excellence, the company reinforces the high value that it places on service. Mei Lani Renger, RN, senior nurse in the Neuroscience/Trauma ICU, was acknowledged as a Hospital Hero for being "a model of inspiration and compassion." When asked about the honor, Mei Lani instantly shared her recognition with her peers: "It's great that the leaders celebrate people they think are offering service excellence, but in truth we serve in teams, and my teammates deserve recognition. A classic example of the care that we collectively provide was the case of a Greek family. The patient was a woman who had been riddled with cerebrospinal disease and lived with her elderly mother. The daughter, our patient, fell while walking upstairs and was transported to our Emergency Department. The mother of the patient spoke very little English, and an amazing UCLA surgeon of Greek descent, Dr. Areti Tillou, looked in on the family, communicated with the mother in Greek, and built rapport. In the meantime, the daughter lost consciousness; her bleeding got worse. She lapsed into a coma, had a breathing tube placed, and was admitted to our unit. I got to care for the patient shortly after her arrival, and as another nurse was giving me a report about the patient, that nurse began to cry. I asked the nurse, 'Why are you crying?' She said, 'This is such a touching case.' When I looked in on the patient, I experienced what that nurse must have felt; it was a picture of love in action. There was this frail, very elderly mother hovering over her comatose daughter. That mother kept a constant vigil, essentially living in her daughter's room. On our breaks, nurses went out and bought food for the elderly woman. Dr. Tillou, who was not formally involved in the case, took the mother to her own home every two days so that she could shower. Dr. Tillou even helped the patient's mother receive the medication she needed, and my colleagues and I made sure she took the medicine as prescribed. Ultimately, the patient died, and for closure I went to her funeral. The mother went back home with another daughter, and our team did what teams here do every day at UCLA—we focused on the next patient and served him as well as, if not better than, we did this family."

When asked what inspires her to serve at this high level every day, Mei Lani gave a wide range of answers that included her upbringing by a caring mother, her patients' zest for life, the professionalism of her peers, and the servant leadership she observes from the top down at UCLA. Mei Lani notes, "I consider senior leadership right up to CEO Dr. Feinberg to be members of my service team. I had a patient who was hit by a car and was suffering with multiple lung contusions. Sadly, he could not get off his breathing tube. He even lost his will to push toward that goal. So a number of our nurses got together to strategize what we could do to inspire him. He was breathing on his own only 20 minutes a day, and we wanted to offer him a graph that could inspire his progress. We knew that he loved biking, so his EEG technician said that he was going to call a biking company and see if it would donate some posters. On our lunch break, we called two bike businesses, and our charge nurse went and got supplies, posters, magazines, and calendars. We put posters together, and with the patient's permission, we plastered his room with images of biking and a graph chart for his tracheotomy tube care. I asked Dr. Feinberg to come up and look at the posters, and of course he did. Dr. Feinberg spent a considerable amount of time listening to and inspiring the patient. When Dr. Feinberg found out that the patient was a Chicago Cubs fan, he used his connections and secured Chicago Cubs posters, pencils, and other Cubs materials for the patient. All those efforts from the top down inspire me and, more important, they make for incredible service experiences for our patients."

When front-line staff members view senior leaders as "members of their service team," organizations elevate one another, acknowledge one another's contribution, and build compelling experiences. By contrast, when leaders talk about service but fail to live it, relationship-based care becomes nothing more than a platitude that is manifested inconsistently for staff and customers.

YOUR DIAGNOSTIC CHECKUP

- What mechanisms have you developed for consistently offering inspirational stories of service excellence and recognizing your service stars?
- How have you communicated the service distinction between "doing for" and "enabling" customers? Where is each form of service most appropriate in your business?
- What organizations outside of your industry do you benchmark to broaden your standards for extraordinary service?
- Would front-line staff members describe senior leaders as members of their service team? If not, what changes need to be made to effect that perception?

THE PROOF OF RELATIONSHIP-BASED CARE AND CUSTOMER-CENTRIC EXPERIENCES

In the end, the test of service excellence comes down to whether customers feel the outpouring of care. The proof at UCLA can, in part, be found in the transformation of customer satisfaction scores from mediocre to world-class and achieving a highly regarded reputation for satisfaction among academic healthcare centers. Additionally, there are important soft measures of customer engagement that are worthy of tracking as well. I have long held that brands are nothing more than what customers say about them when representatives of the brand are not around. Increasingly, UCLA Health System is enjoying highly favorable unedited reviews, such as the following, on customer feedback sites like YELP:

Tom C. writes:

"After months of being treated by <a competitor>, circumstances have allowed me to transfer my care to UCLA Medical Center, both in Westwood and in Santa Monica. I think <blogger> Victoria put it best when she said, 'We've been floating out in the middle of the ocean on a raft cobbled together out of driftwood and old tires. Suddenly, we've been rescued by the QEII.'

"The difference is beyond night and day. Within the first 24 hours of being a UCLA patient, we accomplished what would have taken weeks at <the competitor>.

"I can live with this. I mean that literally. I think I can LIVE with this."

Linda M. notes:

"I had my first baby <at UCLA> and I can't say enough about the nursing staff and the doctors. From the moment I walked in the door to the moment I left, all of the nurses and doctors made me feel as if I was the most important person there. They treated me with respect and kindness. The first nurse I had even came to my room after I had given birth to say congratulations because she was not on duty at the time. Even

my husband who hates hospitals was thoroughly impressed. I
would trust this hospital and its staff with my (and my family's)
life and would never think of going anywhere else."

From a business perspective, most leaders would love to develop a culture where customers contrast its offerings to the competition's service by suggesting a difference between the *QE II*
and a raft cobbled out of driftwood. It would also be heartening
to think that people who dislike typical experiences in your area of
business will find your service refreshing, worthy of referral, and
such that they would "never think of going anywhere else."

Consistently applying service templates like CICARE, listening for the voice of the customer through management rounds and
other processes, selecting for service talent, encouraging self-care
as well as teamwork, offering distinctions on varied caring processes, acknowledging staff members who excel at service, and having relationship-based care start at the top have fueled UCLA's
service revolution. What might the disciplined application of these
strategies do for your business? Moreover, what benefits might
your business derive from the application of these strategies?

In the chapters that follow, we will look at issues of operational
excellence that are necessary if excellent clinical outcomes are to
occur in the first place. We will examine the building blocks that
are essential for "world-class service"—foremost among which is
the development of an uncompromising culture of safety.

Prescriptive Summary

▸ Talk about customer experiences and relationship-based care.

▸ Identify various ways to serve customers, such as maintaining belief, knowing, being with, doing for, and enabling.

▸ Evaluate the degree to which you and other leaders are extending these service approaches to your staff.

▸ Have regular conversations about various ways of caring for peers and customers.

▸ Look for ways to encourage self-care and renewal.

▸ Identify and benchmark providers of service excellence from outside your industry.

▸ Recognize and systematize recognition of the service achievements of your staff.

▸ Seek to have the company's leaders be viewed as members of the front-line staff's "service team."

LEAVE NO ROOM FOR ERROR

CHAPTER 4

Setting the Foundation: Safety Is a Matter of Culture

*The way to be safe is never
to be secure.*
—Benjamin Franklin

A service revolution like the one that was achieved at UCLA can occur only on a platform of operational excellence. UCLA grounds its service success in a commitment to the safety of its staff members, patients, and families. Although it is not always a conscious consideration, every business leader shares the common challenge of providing for the safety and security of the business's stakeholders. Often leaders underestimate the significance of safety, so the chapters that follow offer an opportunity to ensure that safety is always a relevant and monitored aspect of daily business decisions.

Clearly, the focus on safety in healthcare, the auto industry, food service, and aviation exceeds that in most other industries. Given healthcare's rather unique interest in public safety, some readers might disconnect from this involved level of conversation about safety management. In the event that you believe that your attention to safety does not need to be on a par with that in healthcare, I would encourage you to read these chapters from the perspective of leadership lessons that you can apply to change facilitation or human performance management.

Fundamentally, safety must come before everything else for companies to even have a chance to serve customers or sustain success. In 1943, Abraham Maslow theorized that human beings are motivated to fulfill an escalating hierarchy of needs, with safety concerns being among the more primitive and basic aspects of human existence. Although Maslow focused on what drives human behavior, his theory also offers insights into fundamental aspects of successful business leadership.

While business leaders talk a lot about the importance of staff empowerment, the customer experience, consumer loyalty, employee innovation, or even social networking, Maslow's theory suggests that none of these higher-level objectives can be achieved unless employees and customers understand that their safety is unequivocally protected. This was the case for Jennifer Fine, whose 18-month-old daughter Ella was cared for in an intensive-care unit at UCLA. Jennifer notes, "The overall care of my daughter was outstanding at UCLA; however, their concern for her safety was paramount. Given that my daughter was in an isolation bubble, the hospital staff restricted contact with everyone, including my husband, who had recently donated part of his liver to Ella. While I felt that this restriction was unnecessary at the time, I now realize that UCLA safeguarded our daughter by overruling our wishes for my husband to be able to visit with us in the ICU."

We have all been exposed to conventional wisdom and common-sense slogans like "safety first"; however, real business practices give credence to humorist Will Rogers's observation that "common sense ain't so common." In fact, during difficult economic times, it is *not* unusual to see business owners cut back on safety expenditures that may be invisible to consumers. This practice prompted Warren Brown, president of the Society of Safety Engineers, to note, "If companies believe they will save money by reducing or ignoring safety for their workers, customers, and communities . . . they are mistaken. . . . Not only does [a company's] bottom line benefit positively [from a safety commitment], but their company's reputation stays intact, employees stay safe and healthy; thus, reducing health care, workers comp, training, and turnover cost—not to mention keeping customers, the communities they do business in, vendors, and employees happy. Safety is good business." As proof of Mr. Brown's point, one need only look at the adverse impact Toyota Motor Company experienced in 2010, when its reputation for quality and operational excellence was severely tarnished by a series of safety lapses.

Consistent with Mr. Brown's observations about the importance of a "strong safety culture" and "investing and implementing effective safety processes," UCLA leaders understand that safety is, in fact, "good business." Mark Speare, senior associate director, Patient Affairs, Marketing and Human Resources at UCLA, shares, "As I walk down the halls of these hospitals and clinics, I'm constantly reminded that we are in the business of trust. Patients are looking to us to ensure that their safety and well-being are our highest priority. As we work to assume that responsibility, our business successes naturally follow." To honor that trust, UCLA administrators have focused on key leadership behaviors that champion a message to everyone in the organization that they must "leave no room for error."

SAFETY CULTURE—PROACTIVE, NOT REACTIVE

When I go into a business, I am looking at culture on three levels: (1) what the leadership claims the culture to be, (2) how things really get done at the employee level, and (3) what the end users (patients/ customers) experience. When it comes to the creation of a safety culture, Stanford University researchers Sara Singer and Anita Tucker put it well: "A culture of safety is a shared value and belief among employees, managers, and leaders regarding the primary importance of ensuring that the organization's equipment and processes cause no physical harm to employees or customers."

Singer and Tucker's definition of a "safety culture" homes in on an essential aspect of any functional workplace, namely, "a shared value and belief among employees, managers, and leaders." While safety must be a key component of the leadership's vision, a company's culture reflects the degree to which that vision is shared at all levels of an organization.

Dr. Tom Rosenthal, chief medical officer at UCLA and an expert on medical safety issues, addresses the work involved in creating a safety culture. "If all you do is send out a memo saying, 'Be more careful,' it accomplishes absolutely nothing. That's why at UCLA we have a group of people from medical and administrative leadership who are actively and consistently involved in stewarding our safety mission. These individuals share expertise from the external world and from within the practice of medicine. This team understands hospital environments and that we can, at any time, be working on 500 safety-related concerns, but we *must* track and flawlessly succeed on a select few critical safety targets." In essence, Dr. Rosenthal suggests that leaders must create an overarching theme and key objectives to ensure a safety culture.

From Dr. Rosenthal's perspective, keeping safety targets focused and simple allows for a consistent message throughout the organization. Without hesitation, Dr. Rosenthal offered UCLA's key patient safety goals: "Don't kill me; don't give me a horrible infection; don't operate on the wrong body part; don't give me a medication that harms me. In essence, think through the most important protections a patient would want to have and prioritize your safety objectives from that starting place." With this level of patient-centric empathy, communication of priorities is an easier task.

Although the safety objectives that Dr. Rosenthal shared may seem obvious, for safety awareness to become part of the fabric of a culture, that awareness must connect with the existing values and mission of the business. Otherwise, safety is seen as a freestanding set of initiatives or an optional, intermittently important component of the business. Dr. Rosenthal indicates, "When it comes to folding in safety messages, you will have better success building on your core identity. People don't come to work intending to harm others when it comes to healthcare. That is a deep-seated part of our culture—*primum non nocere* [Latin for "first do no harm"]. In fact, it is a deeply felt core value of people here at UCLA that they will do no harm, and our safety culture is built on that foundation."

Given that shared baseline, Dr. Nasim Afsar-manesh, director of quality, Internal Medicine and Neurosurgery, translates the concept of a safety culture into the conscious, day-to-day actions of everyone in a workplace. "When I think about a safety culture, I think about the cumulative actions of the workforce when it comes to the things that each of us do to get from one day to the next. So if it's the valet at the front door, the nurse on the floor, or a physician, it's all about being on the lookout to make sure that things are being done safely. If I'm a valet and I see a patient who isn't stable on his feet getting out of his car, I own responsibility for jumping up and not only assisting the patient in exiting his vehicle, but also making sure that he receives safe transport to wherever he is heading in the hospital. A safety culture is understanding your core values and seeing the big picture or the leadership vision through your day-to-day actions." In the words of author and consultant Dr. Terry Paulson, "The difference between a vision and an hallucination is how many people see it." When it comes to safety at UCLA, the vision is widely shared and acted upon.

YOUR DIAGNOSTIC CHECKUP

- What are the five business-critical safety objectives for your business?
- Are those objectives aligned with the core values and mission of your company?
- Are those objectives known and understood at all levels of your organization?
- What percentage of people at the front line, in middle management, and in the senior leadership could list those five areas if asked?

How would you describe safety in your business? Is it a series of strategies or a component of your culture? Are people seeing the "big picture" of safety, and is that picture guiding them in their daily actions?

VISION PLUS COMMUNICATION CONSISTENCY

From a leadership perspective, the clarification of priorities around a safety vision is just the first step in a process of constant communication and organizational execution. Amir Dan Rubin, former COO, notes, "UCLA experienced dramatic changes in various aspects of the culture when it applied a disciplined process to drive change. That is evident in the transformation experienced in patient satisfaction scores. As a result, UCLA learned the steps necessary to drive organizational excellence and then replicated those steps in all important aspects of our mission. UCLA calls those steps the 'operating system,' and the elements of that system are as important to the development of a safety culture as they are to a service culture." By referring to these processes as an operating system, Amir emphasizes that long-term success in creating a safe business depends upon establishing processes that "ubiquitously run in the background like a computer's operating system."

The leaders at UCLA generally believe that the operating system should be anchored to organizational values, mission, and purpose. They suggest that an operating system must be buttressed by the consistent communication and involvement of all leaders and managers. Much as in the creation of a service revolution, senior leaders at UCLA emphasize that alignment has to be reflected in selection, training, and development priorities and in the creation of performance and improvement management tools. Once safety priorities are set, they must be translated into actionable goals and performance objectives. In turn, measurement tools and usable analytics need to be provided. In UCLA's case, the leaders have made those analytics available as computer dashboard items and linked performance on those objectives with regular performance reviews and budgetary planning processes.

In essence, to have a culture that embraces safety, leaders must

1. Identify safety as a priority.

2. Connect it to values.

3. Select, orient, and train for that which is valued.

4. Set critical targets.

5. Develop meaningful measurements.

6. Offer usable and timely data to guide quality improvement.

7. Monitor, reward, celebrate, and constantly problem-solve ways to move performance in the direction of the targets.

In contrast to this disciplined operational approach to a safety culture, Dr. Rosenthal notes, "All too often, in many businesses, safety can become a matter of problem solving in reaction to unsafe events. The event that happened this morning becomes the most important event, and people respond with individual corrective actions or by assembling a safety improvement team. That team gets excited about working on the problem, but after a few months with no similar events, a more pressing issue captures the safety attention." While there will always be some level of safety reactivity, the key to a safety culture is developing an operating system that allows you to keep making progress on important priorities so that there is less need for crisis reaction.

YOUR DIAGNOSTIC CHECKUP

- What are you doing to consistently hold safety as a corporate priority?
- How are you addressing safety awareness in your selection, orientation, and training processes?

- Have you set safety targets that are associated with your core objectives?
- What usable measurement and analytic tools have you deployed to track your progress toward your objectives?
- How would you describe the bulk of your safety focus? (Is it reactive, made up largely of quality improvement committees addressing past breakdowns, or is it proactive, tracking and managing progress toward desired outcomes?)

MANAGING THE DYNAMIC "NONEVENT"

Dr. Rosenthal's comments about being proactive when you can and reactive when you must reflect one of the greatest challenges in building safety cultures—namely, the ability to maintain passion and focus on dynamic nonevents. By dynamic nonevents, I am talking about the ability to have people maintain an effort to achieve goals that involve eliminating occurrences of unwanted events. In the UCLA safety operating plan, for example, the target for patient falls is set at zero, suggesting a goal to achieve the absence of falls (a dynamic nonevent).

When it comes to dynamic nonevents like *no* deaths caused by hospital staff members or doctors, *no* surgeries on the wrong patient, *no* harmful medication errors, and *no* hospital-based infections, the broad objectives require a focus on many specific safety-related behaviors (for example, a 100 percent hand-washing target as a component of achieving zero infections) and systems with multiple levels of fail-safe redundancy.

In essence, it is easier to gain leverage on change when your target is the commission of specific behaviors, such as hand washing, than when it is the absence of a multifactorial phenomenon like infections. By extension, the more important it is to achieve the "nonevent," the more duplicative systems need to be in play. So, if you run a bank and it is critically important to decrease employee theft, you may wish to create safeguards like supervisor cash counts and video monitoring. If the behavior you wish to eliminate is less high priority, you might rely on a single monitoring system.

The challenge of creating a safety culture that is committed to achieving dynamic nonevents is easily demonstrated with UCLA's goal of zero medication errors. That goal is both relevant and important, given data that suggest that a half million medication errors occur in the United States each year. Also, the goal is well aligned with healthcare workers' passion to "do no harm" and UCLA's vision to "improve health and alleviate suffering." Thanks to the efforts of individuals like Diane Zalba, PharmD, director of Pharmaceutical Services, the central element of operational excellence in UCLA's effort to achieve zero medication errors is a state-of-the-art bar-code system that adds additional safeguards to an otherwise error-prone process.

Much as bar coding has been used in many other industries, such as shipping, to increase delivery accuracy, the process has recently been deployed to achieve the goal of total medication accuracy. The system works as follows:

- A physician writes a medication order, which is sent to the pharmacy.

- The medication order appears on the patient's electronic medication record.

- The nurse verifies the electronic order against the physician's order and obtains the medicine.

- The nurse then logs on to the computer in the patient's room and accesses the electronic medication record.

- The nurse scans the patient's armband (which contains unique patient identifiers) and then scans the bar code attached to each medicine before the medicine is administered.

Ellen Pollack, RN, director, Clinical Systems at UCLA, shares her experience with the bar-code system. "Let's say that I gathered 30 mg of a drug, and I am supposed to be giving 20 mg. The system will provide an alert to make sure the nurse is aware that there is a discrepancy between what was ordered and what was scanned. Or, say I am really busy. I get your medications, and I think I am going into your room, but I accidentally go into another room. The system is going to stop me when I scan the ID band and provide a warning that I have the wrong patient. Those errors do happen, and the bar coding definitely is a huge safety piece."

Ellen suggests that the positive benefits of bar coding have led to safety innovations in other related areas. "We have begun a project to implement bar-coded lab specimen collection. The phlebotomists actually have been using this system for a while, but nurses who draw blood are now also using it." In this process, Ellen reports, "If you are drawing blood, the bar-code system ensures that the blood was drawn from the right patient and that it matches the physician's order. A lot of hospitals don't have these safeguards. We feel so strongly about ensuring that these safety initiatives are used consistently that we have a computer and a bar-code scanner at every bedside."

From a safety perspective, bar codes serve as cross-checks to reduce the likelihood of an event occurring. Essentially, humans check the paperwork, the medication, and the patient's identity, and computer systems offer double checks to prevent human error. The conversion to the bar-code system was costly and time-consuming at UCLA. For example, the FDA requires drugs sold to hospitals to have bar codes, but there is no standardization requirement for the codes; thus, a great deal of time was spent just finding a scanning system that could accurately identify all the diverse bar-coding formats.

On an even more practical level, Ellen Pollack notes that the new computerized system adds a step to the already hectic life of a nurse. "As nurses, we are really busy. We give a lot of medications,

SETTING THE FOUNDATION | **85**

and now we have to stop, get the medication, scan the ID band, scan every medication, and finally give the medication. However, despite the fact that it makes more work and takes more time, the bar-code system has been well received. I think that as nurses, we have embraced the system because it helps us standardize our practices through a critical safety process. It is helpful to have established what the best practice is and then set that as our procedure for how to give medications. Over the years, units have delivered medications in different ways, and now we are going back to a standardized process to give medications safely at UCLA." Evidence for the emergence of a safety culture can be found when front-line staff members warmly embrace safety initiatives that create more work for them because they believe those initiatives have great value for those they serve.

ACCOUNTABILITY/BLAME/EMPOWERMENT

While hospitals in California are required to report injurious events such as falls, Chief Medical Officer Dr. Tom Rosenthal notes, "Not all data are created equal when it comes to tracking safety. We are not looking to just produce compliance reports. We need actionable and timely information." To that end, UCLA invested in a highly advanced electronic data collection system to expedite the capture of information on safety breakdowns. The system eliminates the cumbersome forms that dissuaded staff members from reporting and instead offers easy access to every staff member at any computer terminal in the system. By using computer-guided screens and drop-down menus, a housekeeping staff member, physician, or nurse can select from 14 categories of safety incidents, such as medication errors, falls, medical treatment problems, or complications. The menus have subscreens to further define the nature of the problem and space to write a brief narrative of that problem. Once the electronic report is completed, it is submitted via e-mail to the hospital supervisor overseeing the unit, the supervisor of the person doing the reporting, and the UCLA quality director's office. In addition to the response by the area supervisor, there is additional follow-up by the hospital's quality director. By easing reporting and by making information quickly usable, the system decreases barriers to collecting safety data and assists in leveraging the data collected. Given that across the UCLA system, 500 to 600 such reports are submitted each month, it is clear that data are being collected to measure and make progress toward performance targets.

Lest you get the idea that ensuring safety requires nothing more than developing sophisticated technological solutions to compensate for or track human errors, one must realize that technology has its own share of imperfections—thus the duplicative nature of human and technological solutions. Although technology serves as a tool in developing safe workplaces, safety cultures typically depend upon the actions of people. Given that reality, how do you get people to feel comfortable talking about unsafe behaviors so that those behaviors can be improved? It is easier to have these discussions when people believe that they will not face consequences if they make an error—in essence, when they are in a completely "blame-free" environment. But healthcare, by its nature, cannot be a truly blame-free setting.

UCLA CMO Dr. Tom Rosenthal highlights the complexities of reporting, accountability, and blame. "Yearly we have 80,000 hospital stays, a million ambulatory visits, and more than 10,000 employees working for us. How can three or five of us sit in the senior ranks and expect to know when any safety problem is occurring unless people tell us? It is also part of the medical culture that if you confess your errors, you should be forgiven, as long as those errors don't meet the seldom-reached test of gross negligence." To achieve openness, Dr. Rosenthal makes a critical differentiation between forgivable and unforgivable safety transgressions. To make this distinction, he recounts safety literature that contrasts the moral error and the technical error.

From Dr. Rosenthal's perspective, "A moral error would be a physician who gets paged five times to go visit Ms. Jones but is too busy watching the Super Bowl and doesn't get to her until after she dies. That is a moral error that I believe can't be forgiven, no matter whether it meets a legal standard of negligence or not. Compare that to a technical error, where I get paged and I go up to the bedside and make a difficult call as to medication and finally order epinephrine, and it turns out that this was the wrong judgment. That is a technical error." When it comes to adverse events, business leaders create an environment for self-reporting safety breakdowns if they clarify that people who make, report, accept responsibility for, and learn from technical errors can be forgiven, but that those who fail to take those steps or who make moral errors are more likely to face adverse employment action or termination.

YOUR DIAGNOSTIC CHECKUP

- How easy is it to report a safety breakdown in your organization?
- Is the information you collect on safety problems translated into immediate action, or does it simply address compliance reporting standards?
- Do you have multiple levels of administrative follow-up for all safety event reports?
- Is your workplace a "blame-free environment," where people who report safety lapses are assured amnesty from consequences? If not, do employees understand the types of lapses that are forgivable, as opposed to those that will be met with consequences? Do they also understand the steps they must take to achieve forgiveness (for example, self-reporting, reporting others, owning responsibility for the breakdown, and having a responsibility to learn from the breakdown and not make the same mistake again)?

OVERCOMING HIERARCHIES OF SILENCE

Not only are people often silent about safety transgressions after they occur (for fear of consequences), but many individuals are silent about their concerns before an event happens. This silence may be heightened in healthcare, since hospitals have a history of well-established power hierarchies, making it difficult for nurses (let alone unit staff) to challenge physicians or surgeons on any medical-care issue, including safety. In one attempt to address this authoritative or hierarchical culture, UCLA leadership has studied the issue and has trained 1,200 people in the operating room on crew resource management techniques utilized in the airline industry. These aviation strategies empower and authorize any member of the airline crew (baggage handlers, ground personnel, flight attendants, and so on) to have equal authority with a pilot to halt a plane's takeoff out of a concern for safety.

Dr. Rosenthal notes, "Despite ongoing training, old patterns don't change quickly. Changing people's willingness to speak up, particularly in a medical culture, is a work in progress. You are never done with that one. You do things like having the surgeon explicitly say, 'I expect everyone to speak up and stop the process at any time safety is a concern.' The hope is that those words formally give permission to people in the room who would have been silenced by the surgeon's authority. We go over and over how everyone in healthcare is a fail-safe for one another and that everyone is responsible for speaking up and for listening when it comes to creating a safe environment."

Dr. Rosenthal's comments highlight the importance of offering training and empowerment to challenge existing "hierarchies of silence," while realizing that this training must be never-ending to address an undercurrent that pulls behavior in the direction of the informal, and powerful, "way things have always been done."

Dr. Nasim Afsar-manesh shares that, while the status quo may pull in the direction of hierarchies of silence, her research suggests that doctors prefer hearing from others when it comes to safety reminders. According to Dr. Afsar-manesh, "We gave medical residents a list of 10 ways in which they could be reminded about hand hygiene; for example, they might have a sign above the patient's bed or a sticker somewhere in the room. Among those 10 interventions was having the nurses remind them about hand hygiene. Of the 10 options we provided, 'being reminded by a nurse' was the most desired intervention by the residents. I think this result speaks to the fact that those in the new generation of physicians are increasingly seeing themselves as part of a healthcare team. People are realizing that this job has gotten far too complex for any one person to be able to do it alone, and that you truly need a multidisciplinary group that includes the janitor, the nurse, the respiratory therapist, residents, and the attending physician, all working together to make the patient-care process happen." Dr. Afsar-manesh adds, "Ten to twenty years ago, there were fewer medications, fewer interventions, and fewer diagnostic and therapeutic options for patients. The options have grown exponentially over the years, and it is impossible to ensure patient safety if it is left purely to the physicians. It is going to take the physician, the nurse, the patient, and all the other staff members that are involved in patient care to make sure that safe outcomes occur. It's exciting to move toward that." As businesses become increasingly complex, more voices need to be involved in safety conversations, and safe outcomes must expand from individual to team responsibilities.

WHEN METRICS ARE LACKING

Some targets, such as patient falls or wrongful surgeries, seem fairly easy to track; however, much of what contributes to an environment of safety in healthcare or in any business occurs in subtle, often difficult-to-measure behaviors. A classic example of this challenge at UCLA was the measurement of hand-washing behavior. If asked how often they sanitized their hands upon entering and exiting a patient's room, most healthcare professionals would provide a number that approximates 100 percent, demonstrating an awareness of the importance of good hand hygiene. The UCLA leaders, however, were unwilling to take those types of answers from staff and doctors on faith and instead decided to find a method to measure hand-hygiene behavior more objectively. While technological approaches to assess this issue, such as electronic measurement of sanitation liquid dispensed, have been tried in healthcare, no technological tracking method has proved useful. Undaunted, UCLA leadership went back to the basics of measurement—human observation.

Mary Erbeznik, RN, MN, NE-BC, project director, Relationship Based Care, talks about the evolution of this tracking program. "I was part of the group that developed the Measure to Achieve Patient Safety (MAPS) program. We were doing our own internal audits of hand washing, and our staff members reported 100 percent compliance. Then we had our staff members ask patients what they observed, and patients reported far less than perfection. Since we are located on the UCLA campus, we have access to a lot of young people who are interested in healthcare careers, and we developed a volunteer program where we recruited undergraduate students."

The volunteer MAPS program began in 2004 and involves approximately 20 students per year plus two student leaders. The students participate in weekly and monthly meetings with program leaders, are trained in observational measurement, and receive continuing education from the UCLA patient safety staff. The students' observations are systematically reported to clinicians, medical school department heads, and hospital leadership. The students are tracking hygienic behaviors consistent with the Centers for Disease Control (CDC) guidelines. Based on the data obtained from the students and efforts to improve behavior based on those data, hand-washing consistency increased from 50 percent to 93 percent.

In addition to monitoring hand-hygiene behavior, the same student observers were given the task of monitoring whether nurses were using proper protocols to identify patients before they provided the patients' medication (given that there were no bar-code technologies at the time) or before the patients were handed off to be taken to a procedure. Using those data, the leadership was able to improve compliance with patient identification protocols at medication administration from 50 percent to 95 percent and consistency in patient identification at the time of nurse-to-transporter handoffs to greater than 90 percent. In essence, UCLA effectively uses direct observation data to enhance other efforts to achieve important safety objectives. In the case of patient identification and medication errors, the student observations are yet another safeguard, in addition to bar coding, that increases the consistency of human action. When it comes to hand washing, student observations offer increased objectivity and awareness concerning a behavior that is unreliably self-reported, routinely forgotten, and critical to safety.

REWARDING POSITIVE BEHAVIOR

The UCLA MAPS program indicates the leadership's appreciation of offering staff members helpful feedback from direct observation. UCLA's leadership often takes those direct observation data one step further to afford staff members positive recognition as well. One such example can be found in the WIN program, which stands for "Wipe out Infections Now." The program was created to encourage hospital staff to be consistent in their isolation technique to stop the spread of antibiotic-resistant bacteria, which pose significant infection problems in hospitals—a concern shared by hospital administrators, care providers, regulatory agencies, and patients alike.

According to Geri Braddock, RN, nurse epidemiologist, "We found that there was just hit-and-miss compliance with putting on isolation gowns and gloves, and doing the things you are supposed to do consistently every time. People are busy, and they think that they will just run in and do something quickly, or that given their credentials, they don't need to comply with protocol. This notoriously leads to the spread of diseases in hospitals, and it is a serious issue."

As a result of their findings, Geri reports that she and fellow team members Dr. Zach Rubin, hospital epidemiologist, and Jocelyn Gulliver, RN, surveillance nurse, approached behavior change in part from an unexpected perspective. "We monitored isolation technique very closely, and we would hand out a business card to some of those we observed. That card has printed in large type "YOU GOT CAUGHT," and then in really small letters, it says "DOING THE RIGHT THING." We used the card to publicly recognize those who were doing isolation correctly, so that others could appreciate proper techniques. We also put the names of those individuals into a monthly drawing for an incentive prize. Additionally, these card recipients were recognized in front of all of the hospital managers." Geri notes, "You know, in part, when a program like this is having a positive impact because conversations about isolation technique increase. It's gotten to the point that a lot of staff members say, 'I did the right thing yesterday; you just didn't see me.' I tell them to just keep it up and we'll keep noticing. It is our way of trying to get adults to do the right thing all the time because their patients need it." Safety is very much about getting staff members to do the right thing every time, not just most of the time or when a specific behavior is highlighted by the leadership. To achieve that goal, leaders must often focus on positive behaviors and do something unusual to capture the attention of employees.

In the spirit of the "unusual" and playful attention-getting strategies, Geri Braddock adds, "I teach infection control issues by presenting the information through memorable characters. The staff, patients, and their visitors respond very well to these personalities and seem to remember the lessons better. For example, a Miss Piggy–type character educated on issues regarding 'swine' flu and the importance of getting two flu vaccinations." Even with issues as important as pandemics, the communication must be varied, engaging, and memorable, if for no other reason than to cut through the clutter of competing messages.

YOUR DIAGNOSTIC CHECKUP

- Do "hierarchies of silence" exist in your organization? If so, what have you done to utilize best practices from other industries that have tried to change these authoritative cultures? Are your efforts to empower all staff members to "stop" processes being effective? Are your efforts ongoing? Is safety shifting to teams, not just individuals?
- What safety-related behaviors are difficult to track or measure?
- Have you attempted novel strategies like UCLA's MAPS program to increase the objectivity of important behavioral data? Are those collection efforts and intervention attempts showing positive results?
- In addition to tracking behavioral shortcomings, have you devised systems for catching people doing the right things when it comes to safety? Are you varying those messages and positioning them in memorable and engaging ways?

ENTRENCHED CULTURE AND COMMUNICATION

I've previously written that there is a fine line between "cult" and "culture." When it comes to safety, leaders must constantly seek to build a cultlike following for identified mission-centric safety priorities. To do this, leaders need to identify priorities and share them clearly and consistently throughout the organization. Simultaneously, leaders must develop actionable measurement systems, provide timely results of measurement, establish multiple levels of safeguards (often incorporating human/technology interfaces), encourage a culture of reporting, and manage human inconsistencies with observation, education, and reward. When all these factors come together, organizations not only achieve their most pressing safety priorities, but also see increased safety awareness in seemingly unrelated ways.

While he is very comfortable with UCLA's progress in service delivery, CEO Dr. David Feinberg is always looking for ways to further grow the safety culture. He points to a meeting in a hospital hallway as evidence that there is work ahead. Dr. Feinberg reports, "An employee stopped me and said, 'I'm with occupational therapy, and it's good that I bumped into you because I've been concerned about a safety issue for a while. It involves the need for patients to step up to get into the showers and not having a well-placed vertical safety bar.'" Dr. Feinberg thanked the staff member for his input and had the problem fixed hospitalwide within a matter of weeks. But the incident demonstrated an important opportunity. Dr. Feinberg notes, "We are on the right track when our people feel comfortable approaching senior leaders with their observations concerning safety, but we are not there yet. We need to get to a point where people feel empowered to get those types of issues fixed immediately and not hold their concerns until they have a chance opportunity to speak to the CEO."

Courtney Real, RN, reports that UCLA's administration has been very clear that every staff member is responsible for addressing any safety concerns that he encounters, and the nurses on her unit have taken ownership of this responsibility, not only in areas of patient care, but in protecting one another from harm and creating a safe environment for vulnerable patients. Courtney notes, "As much as it may seem that hospitals are quiet, safe places, sometimes they are not. That is why we have policies about a visitor getting a badge before going into a unit. Even then, the hospital environment can be emotionally intense, and visitors' behavior must be managed. We are all responsible for making sure that we monitor our environment so that quality care can take place." Courtney re-counts, "I have had patients' family members who present on our ICU unit intoxicated and angry. We have to be alert to warning signs before situations escalate. We've had staff members threatened by a family member because she was asked to stop consuming alcohol in a patient-care area. We work with people whose injuries were the result of gang hits, and we have to work with our internal security staff and the outside police to ensure the safety of the patient, the staff, and all of our visitors."

Courtney says that she and her colleagues accepted responsibility for creating guidelines that would make her unit safer, more orderly, and therapeutic for all who visited. According to Courtney, "When we moved over to this amazingly modern and technologically advanced ICU from our old hospital, the advantages were obvious; however, the open, roomy nature of the unit had unintended disadvantages when it came to potentially disruptive visitor behavior, particularly as it related to intrusions and people being in places where they should not be. So as a nursing group on our unit, we surveyed the staff members and families about access to the unit, the appropriateness of 24-hour visitation, and other issues that affect overall order and safety. We then analyzed our results in the context of the existing scientific literature about policies and procedures that create constructive, orderly, and compassionately caring environments. As a result, we now have a set of guidelines published for visitors and staff alike. These guidelines have had such a positive impact in settling our environment, and we enjoyed subtle differences like fewer visitors using cell phones in places that interfere with care or inadvertently gawking at the care of someone else's loved one. By taking action, I believe we have made our environment safer and saner. We have gone from chaos, which is where we were a year ago, to a harmonious and positive involvement between families and staff. I think when we as staff members see problematic things happening, we now try to educate visitors by saying something like, 'Have you see our visitation guidelines?'

and bring the conversation back to the fact that we need to create a safe, respectful, and therapeutic environment. It is important to partner with families for the safety of all and the smooth functioning of our ICU. In the process of creating guidelines, we also have had families and staff members providing great feedback on our efforts. It's proven to be a win-win."

The efforts of Courtney and her nursing colleagues preview Chapter 5 as it relates to the importance of "evidence-based" safety innovations. It also begins an expansion of the concept of safety beyond simply the physical well-being of patients. The upcoming chapter addresses sweeping challenges that safety-oriented organizations commonly face.

In the end, CEO Dr. David Feinberg has a vision for a culture in which people not only think safety but act immediately to ensure flawlessly safe outcomes—in essence, to provide the safest care possible.

What is your vision? What ideas have you begun to consider as a result of UCLA? Is your company's safety reality approximating your vision? Ultimately, the wisdom of Dr. Terry Paulson proves true—organizations that fail to act in accordance with a leadership safety vision reduce that vision to nothing more than a leadership "hallucination."

Prescriptive Summary

▸ Identify five key safety priorities for your business.

▸ Ensure that those objectives are consistent with your core values and mission.

▸ Consistently communicate the importance of those priorities.

▸ Seek to develop a "safety culture."

▸ Select, orient, and train for safety.

▸ Set safety targets.

▸ Develop relevant and timely measurements of targets.

▸ Share safety data efficiently.

▸ Use data for quality improvement.

▸ Celebrate safety improvements and problem-solve shortcomings.

▸ Create multiple safeguards for mission-centric safety goals.

▸ Where possible, integrate human and technology interfaces for safety.

▸ Consider using direct observation techniques.

▸ Make safety reporting as easy and blameless as possible.

▸ Catch people "getting it right" when they demonstrate safety behavior.

CHAPTER 5

Safety—Science, Selection, and Challenge

*For safety is not a gadget
but a state of mind.*
        —Eleanor Everet

ere's a one-item quiz for everyone in your organization: "Who is responsible for safety?" Of course, the right answer is "me." Unfortunately, quite often the answers you'll hear will involve a person whose title has the word *safety* in it. At UCLA, Erik Eggins is an individual who fits that description, given that his name badge reads "Director of Safety." Erik notes that a healthy safety culture is reflected by the commitment to safety demonstrated by each individual in the organization every day. "I appreciate that at UCLA we actually talk about safety in the context of culture, and as such we have encouraged all staff to take an ownership position in championing projects. Such safety initiatives serve the well-being of our patients and staff members. Rather than having a top-down approach to safety or feeling that people view me as the 'safety advocate,' a passion for our shared security is broadly held throughout our organization." The reality of a safe work environment involves safety initiatives that emerge from the engagement of front-line workers.

One example of this level of proactive involvement occurred a number of years ago when Robin Rosemark, RN, MN, clinical nurse specialist, jumped in to improve performance on a routine patient transfer process. Robin notes, "An escort came to pick up a patient for an ERCP, an invasive procedure. I had read the physician's notes and knew about the likely occurrence of the procedure, but there was no written order for it. I was working with a new nurse, and I asked her, 'Do you feel it is safe to send the patient with the escort for the procedure?' She responded, 'Yes, why not?' to which I answered, 'Well, there isn't a physician order in the chart.'" That one incident sparked Robin to take the matter to Dr. Tom Rosenthal, chief medical officer, to see if a safe process could be defined.

According to Robin, "Working with Dr. Rosenthal, we embarked on a hospitalwide change to promote safer practice in patient identification. Often, scheduling of tests and procedures was done physician-to-physician. But a critical element was missing at times, and that was the actual tangible order in the chart—the missing thread of communication that ties all the loose ends together. We appreciated that the conditions for error existed because of a lack of consistency and uniformity in documentation and handoff."

To rectify the situation, Robin investigated best practices on patient identification protocols and the need for two confirmed identifications of a patient. Additionally, she looked at the breadth of situations across UCLA Health System in which these types of handoffs could occur. Robin notes, "I surveyed the patient identification process in the main operating room, main radiology, CT, MRI, interventional radiology, cardiac catheterization suite, bronchoscopy, and endoscopy procedure units. I found that there was variation in the process for getting the patient to these areas and the identification of the patient once he was there."

Dr. Rosenthal and Robin involved other key parties, and the changes necessary to implement a two-identifier system throughout UCLA Health System were highlighted. These changes in the process resulted in the following steps: the patient ID number is checked, a chart order is written, a direct interaction between the escort and the nurse occurs, and the order in the chart is validated. Additionally, a policy and clinical practice alert was written describing the process for two identifiers for all off-unit testing. This process then became the consistent, standardized practice within the medical center.

The observations of a single employee started this successful safety improvement program at UCLA. However, observations alone were not enough. The employee had to feel comfortable sharing her safety concerns with senior leaders. The leader she turned to had to be receptive and entertain the viability of the issue. Upon concluding that the concern had merit, the leader then had to empower the employee to research best practices within her industry and audit the diversity of practices across the business. Furthermore, the leader had to partner with the employee to champion safety recommendations through various committees to ensure systemwide implementation. In essence, when individuals take responsibility for identifying safety concerns—or any other business initiative, for that matter—leaders must responsibly listen, support, and empower those employees to move observations into tangible systemic changes.

RALLYING DE FACTO LEADERSHIP AND EXPERIENCE

Just as safety initiatives are not strictly the domain of people with safety titles, safety leadership is also not the domain only of people with leadership titles. For example, Robin Rosemark became a de facto safety leader when she championed the two-identifier policy. In the process, Robin created relationships throughout the healthcare system and gained great experience in effecting changes in hospital safety policy. Rather than letting Robin's experience and natural safety leadership skill go further untapped, organizational leaders enrolled Robin in other safety-related projects. Robin notes,

"The associate director of nursing had heard about my work on the two-identifier program. She stopped me in the hall and asked me to get involved in putting together a policy for non-ICU EKG monitoring. At issue was the consistency of the practice, the safety of the patients, and the uniform procedures to be followed by all involved. Once again, I got the 'owners' of the process together—the doctors, nurses, educators, unit directors, monitor techs, and so on—and we crafted a policy that was written by all participants in the process and then disseminated to everyone in the hospital."

All too often, leaders and managers fail to leverage the experience, knowledge, and influence of de facto leaders within their workforce. In describing effective communication and leadership skills, researcher Robert Cialdini explains the "principle of social proof," where people follow others who are most similar to them. Rather than trying to be all things to all people, great leaders identify the de facto leadership of people like Robin Rosemark and encourage them to leverage their natural leadership talents to constructively influence their peers and advance progress at the grassroots level.

YOUR DIAGNOSTIC CHECKUP

- Are front-line employees coming to your leaders with safety improvement ideas?
- Do the leaders in your organization readily empower employees to research best practices and audit the diversity of practices across your business?
- Is the leadership responsibly listening, supporting, and encouraging employees to move safety observations and best practice findings in the direction of tangible systemic changes?
- How effectively do you capitalize on de facto leadership and deploy the Cialdini principle of "social proof"?

BENCHMARK, RECORD, REPORT

Unlike businesses that operate outside of academic settings, UCLA's method for achieving safety solutions often uses an "evidence-based" approach, both relying on existing published best practices and willingly contributing to an evolving body of knowledge. In their book entitled *Hard Facts, Dangerous Half-Truths and Total Nonsense*, Jeffrey Pfeffer and Robert Sutton note, "Business decisions, as many of our colleagues in business and your own experience can attest, are frequently based on hope or fear, what others seem to be doing, what senior leaders have done and believe has worked in the past, and their dearly held ideologies—in short, on lots of things other than the facts. Although evidence-based practice may be coming to the field of medicine and, with more difficulty and delay, the world of education, it has had little impact on management or on how most companies operate. If doctors practiced medicine the way many companies practice management, there would be far more sick and dead patients, and many more doctors would be in jail."

At UCLA, the evidence-based approach to safety practice management is alive and well. For example, Deborah Suda, RN, MN, director of the Perinatal Unit, and Nicole Casalenuovo, RN, assistant director of the Perinatal Unit, report that they noticed a c-section surgical site infection problem and took a scientific and methodological approach to its resolution. According to Deborah, "Our infection rate was so high that we suspected it had to be coming from a multitude of factors across our environment. We thought it might be resulting from inconsistencies in proper attire in the operating room, the number of times the surgery suite door opens, nightly cleaning procedures, and/or the time a patient's surgical site was open in the context of our mission to teach first-year residents."

Rather than rushing in with multiple solutions and not being able to know which attempted solutions were helpful, Nicole notes, "We brought in our infection control department to help us study our situation. They assisted us in collecting data, conducting chart reviews, and getting on the right track. They helped us make observations across the process. We also did an anonymous survey of staff members, asking people to tell us about their own practice standards in areas such as scrubbing. We then forged recommendations and shared all the data with our surgeons."

Although the tightened aseptic practices that emerged from the audit and recommendation process led to significant progress from the baseline infection levels, Deborah reports, "We got infection rates down to maybe 6 to 7 percent, but we wanted them to be zero. So we started researching other factors that could still be affecting infection. As a result of that evidence-based research, we looked at changing our topical antiseptic from one that needs time to dry on the skin. If an emergency c-section happens and the baby's heart rate is down, we don't have time to wait for the antiseptic to dry on the abdomen. So we switched to a different product that is an instant kill upon contact antiseptic. After we changed to this product, the infection rates dropped to 1.2 percent." Whereas many businesses might keep their findings and breakthroughs private to gain an advantage over the competition (e.g., "our infection rates are lower than theirs"), Nicole reports, "We submitted our process and findings and had them accepted for publication, so that our peers can benefit from what we learned along our journey at UCLA."

On occasion, efforts to benchmark best safety practices or uncover research findings prove completely unsuccessful. In such situations, it is not unusual for UCLA leaders to assess the need for research and help set standards of practice. Deborah Suda notes, "Patient falls had never been a reported concern in obstetrics; however, when we moved to our new hospital, we started having falls. In obstetrics, a fall does not necessarily mean lying flat on the ground; it can also include losing one's balance or needing assistance to get back to stability."

UCLA had already adopted a gold standard of precautionary care practice that had a postdelivery patient contact the nurse for assistance the first time she needed to use the bathroom. However, Nicole Casalenuovo notes, "Despite that standard, we went from essentially zero falls in the preceding three or four years to seven in a short span of time upon changing hospitals. We couldn't figure out what was going on, so we initiated a process improvement program to develop guidelines to help nurses look at why women were falling." When the process improvement team looked for tools to measure the frequency and causes of falls, they determined that no tools had been created for obstetric populations. Instead, most of the existing risk assessments were developed for geriatric patient populations or those in neurological or medical/surgical environments. Using a network of her peers, Deborah Suda solicited e-mail responses concerning the existence of an obstetrics fall assessment tool. All the respondents indicated that they were unaware of such a tool, and most suggested that they would love to have access to one if it was ever developed. According to Deborah, "That prompted us to embark on creating an evidence-based obstetrics risk assessment measurement. We certainly had our work cut out for us because all the existing tools suggested that every obstetric patient had a zero risk for falling. Of course, those tools were listing risk factors such as dementia, loss of consciousness, post-brain tumor surgery, and other issues that simply did not apply to the obstetric patient population."

As UCLA leaders began working on the obstetrics fall risk assessment tool, they examined environmental and physiological changes encountered by women in their care. They paid attention to differences such as whether a woman came to the unit in labor or if she had been on the unit for weeks for bed rest because of preterm labor. They examined blood loss volumes and other clinical and biological differences between patients. Ultimately, these UCLA unit leaders developed a patient fall tool that assessed risk from admission to discharge. As Deborah notes, "The tool is an early warning system that alerts nurses to pay attention to a particular patient because of the factors we identified as contributing to falling. We are completing the testing phase on the tool now and are readying it for launch. Once we get the data to show the value of the tool, we would like to publish the results and share the tool with all interested colleagues so that they can detect problems early and avert falls as we have done."

Although academic institutions, by their nature, lend themselves to scientific approaches to safety knowledge acquisition, much can be gleaned from UCLA that can be used in the development of safety processes for nonacademic environments. Most notably, safety innovation is far more difficult than safety emulation. It is easier to modify breakthroughs made in other settings than it is to create breakthroughs from scratch. Furthermore, while many proprietary business products require information protection, safety innovations and practices commonly need not be proprietary and can be widely shared beyond the walls of your building.

YOUR DIAGNOSTIC CHECKUP

— How much of your approach to safety improvement could be described as being based on hope or fear, following what others seem to be doing, being connected to what senior leaders have done and believe has worked in the past, or being the result of dearly held ideologies?

— What processes do you have in place to encourage safety progress management through evidence-based approaches?

— Where have you taken a systematic and incremental approach to safety excellence, as opposed to trying to change multiple factors simultaneously?

— What safety process breakthroughs have you shared with others?

THINKING OUTSIDE THE BOX

The notion of taking safety outside the walls of your building fits nicely with the idea that safety is a widely shared social responsibility. As such, to achieve safety goals, company and departmental boundaries often have to be eroded. For example, much of the work on obstetric patient falls involves the assessment of patient risk factors in that particular unit, but other departments voluntarily look for ways that they can contribute to improvements in this safety area as well. Director of Safety Erik Eggins notes, "The joint commission annually publishes approximately 12 national patient safety goals, and expects each hospital to be proactive in assessing its performance in those target areas. Although the National Patient Safety Goal does not mention environmental factors as being complicit in situations such as falls, our committee does make sure to examine every fall that takes place here at UCLA to ensure that no environmental issue was involved. Although a patient's fall could be attributed to the medication that she was taking, we still evaluate the incident to be assured that the bed rail was working properly, that the floor wasn't slippery, or that some other environmental factor was not at play. There's no requirement for this evaluation, but we do it anyway."

Erik's perspective offers insights into a commitment not just to look for the expedient answer when it comes to safety, but to rule out all reasonable contributing factors. Safety is less about quick fixes and more about lasting process analyses that lead to long-term quality safety improvements. Erik's comments also speak to the fact that regulatory safety requirements should not be viewed as the upper threshold of your safety aspirations, but more as minimum standards of performance. Erik expands on this point by noting, "Even though at any given time we have hundreds of safety projects in progress, we've increased inspections in areas that we have identified as high risk. Our focus on inspecting high-risk targets is far in excess of regulatory demands." Erik points out, for example, that the joint commission requires that Environmental Safety inspect patient care areas twice a year and all other areas once a year. Patient care areas are those locations where patients receive care—the units, the clinics, and so forth. UCLA feels that patient care areas are too narrowly defined in the regulatory criteria, so its staff offers more frequent inspections in locations that are not strictly offering patient care. For example, multiple safety inspections of the grounds, cafeteria, chapel, lobby, and waiting rooms—anywhere patients are served, not just where they are receiving medical care—are conducted on a regular basis. In areas considered a higher safety risk, Erik reports that his team does inspections not on a twice-a-year basis but monthly: "The operating room is one such example. It is inspected monthly, even though we are required to do that inspection only twice a year. The kitchen and laboratories are also inspected monthly." Many corporate leaders become angered by safety mandates; however, safety cultures embrace them and use them as a springboard to set their own higher-level standards.

SAFETY IN THE ENVIRONMENT

I remember that on my first day of college, a political science professor told me, "Everything is political"; then I went to a psychology class, only to have that professor say, "Everything involves psychology." By the end of the day, I was left wondering, "What is everything? Psychological or political?" At the risk of sounding like those professors, safety truly is an aspect of almost every business decision that a leader makes—right down to details in the construction and maintenance of the physical environment.

Because the main hospital bed tower of UCLA's Westwood campus sustained damage in the 1994 Northridge earthquake and the impetus for the construction of the new Ronald Reagan UCLA Medical Center was legislation to ensure safety in the face of a similar (if not greater) natural disaster, the entire construction of UCLA's new campus has a strong safety design emphasis. Specifically, architects crafted the structure to sustain zero structural failures and ensure that no elements of the exterior cladding would fall off the building as a result of an earthquake greater than 8.0 on the Richter scale. Also, the hospital can remain fully operational, without the need for outside resources, for the most essential 72 hours following a major earthquake. In addition to construction for earthquake soundness, the building is also designed to withstand winds of 70 mph and intense rain conditions.

Because of unusually sized and shaped steel beams weighing 20 to 25 tons, the hospital's earthquake safety exceeds anything experienced in Los Angeles in the last 100 years. The sheer mass of the structural components is impressive, with every beam measuring 20 feet long by 4 feet deep with 4-inch-thick ridges. These beams are encased by steel columns that weigh more than 900 pounds per foot. Each large-scale weld made in construction of the building required about 20 hours to complete. That weld time is twice what it takes for a standard weld.

The 18,000 Ambralight travertine marble outer stone panels that sheathe the building are designed to move up to 3 feet, to add greater safety outside and inside the building should the ground begin to shake. While it is difficult for nonengineers to fully appreciate the significance of these safety design features, they reflect the exacting nature of UCLA's safety design commitment, which must also seamlessly flow through the physical design of all areas of the hospital. For example, the 20,000-square-foot David I. Saperstein Emergency Department, which serves nearly 40,000 patients each year, was crafted with painstaking attention to speedy and efficient care of critically ill or injured patients. With frequent involvement of treatment providers and administrators, mock drills for emergency patients were conducted prior to opening. Safety and efficiency were designed into the smallest details, including the placement of each treatment tool.

The UCLA Emergency Department is one of only seven Level 1 adult and pediatric trauma centers in Los Angeles County.

Janet Rimicci, director, Emergency and Trauma Services, explains, "Level 1 centers provide the highest level of surgical care for trauma patients. To achieve the designation, we must have specialists and equipment available 24 hours a day and admit a certain volume of severely injured patients. We must also have a designated number of surgeons and anesthesiologists on duty at all times and offer coverage by specialists, provide education, conduct outreach, and deliver preventive and research programs." In accordance with its status as a Level 1 facility for children and adults, UCLA must pay particular attention to safety systems, such as its helipads and the process by which patients are expeditiously and safely transferred from an emergency helicopter down an exclusively reserved elevator into an emergency-medical-care suite.

While most of us in business do not need to design our physical plant to address environmental hazards such as massive earthquakes or emergency service delivery issues such as designs of helipads and emergency treatment interfaces, the obvious takeaway from UCLA is that safety is not a module or an add-on. Safety is an intrinsic consideration that must be designed into a physical environment to ensure the successful achievement of a business's mission.

YOUR DIAGNOSTIC CHECKUP

- Are you seeing cross-departmental cooperation to meet your safety objectives?
- When safety lapses occur, how likely are you to look for contributing factors beyond the most expediently obvious ones?
- What role do regulatory requirements play in your safety aspirations? Are they the gold standard to which you aspire, or are they the minimum performance standard?
- How do you factor environmental safety design into your long-term service and mission objectives?

EDUCATING AND LISTENING TO THE CUSTOMER

Often business leaders think about safety as something that they do *for* customers. Increasingly in healthcare, and particularly at UCLA, it is something that is done *with* them. Whenever possible, the UCLA leaders and staff members empower patients to provide an additional level of safety against human error. For example, UCLA expressly advises patients, once they are admitted, that they will be given an identification band with their name and a medical record number on it. For their safety, patients are further advised not to remove that band until they are discharged from the hospital. Patients are also instructed that

UCLA nurses follow a careful procedure to ensure that the medications they give to the patient are the correct ones. If the medications you receive do not look familiar, alert your doctor or nurse. Chances are, despite its appearance, the medication is correct. But it is always advisable to be an informed patient. Don't forget to check your prescription labels when you take your medication at home.

We take your concerns seriously regarding the way you are feeling. If you or a family member thinks there has been a change in your condition, please tell a member of the health-care team (care partner, nurse, physician, et al.) immediately. You can feel confident that any concern you express will be addressed.

Good communication among patients, visitors and nursing staff is key to preventing falls. Visitors can help prevent falls by staying alert to the needs and capabilities of the person they are visiting and notifying a nurse with any concerns. Patients should use the call light to request assistance getting out of bed, and they should wear non-skid footwear when mobile.

UCLA policy mandates that every care provider, including doctors, nurses and other staff, wash their hands before and after performing any "hands on" procedures with patients. Overwhelming evidence shows that washing hands is the single most important precaution that anyone (including your doctor or nurse) can take to effectively prevent the spread of infection. If you notice any members of your healthcare team have forgotten to wash their hands, remind them—it is for everyone's benefit.

Make sure that you know who is in charge of your care. This is particularly important when many people are involved in your treatment, or when you have many health problems.

Make sure your healthcare professionals know who you are. All physicians, nurses or other staff members should check your identification bracelet before examination and treatment.

Speak up if you have questions or concerns.

You have the right to know about your care and to ask questions of any member of your care team.

If you have a test taken, don't assume that no news is good news. Always ask your doctor for the results.

When surgery is involved, be informed.

Make sure that you, your doctor and your surgeon all agree on what exactly needs to be done.

Get an advocate.

Ask a family member or trusted friend to serve as your advocate to protect your best interests, especially when you may be distracted by the stress of illness.

Cynics might view this advice as nothing more than required postings to mitigate liability in the event of a patient injury. In essence, they could be viewed as a "We warned you in advance, and you share responsibility for what happens to you" type of diffusion of legal responsibility. In truth, these forms of patient education play an important role in overall patient safety, and they reflect UCLA's culture of partnering with patients and their families.

Erik Eggins reports, "Because we invite patients to offer suggestions regarding safety, patients at UCLA are safer than in other hospitals. One such suggestion involved wheelchairs for patients to enter the hospital. In the past, the patient or the patient's family had to go to a central area to request that a wheelchair be provided at the hospital entrance. As a result of patient suggestions about this safety issue, wheelchairs have now been made available in our parking lots." Whether it's wheelchair availability, the occasional instance where a patient challenges a care provider to wash his hands, or a patient who averts a medication error by communicating that she doesn't recognize the medication that she has been handed, one important additional safeguard in all safety initiatives is the involvement of your patient or customer.

TRAINING AND DRILLS PAY

While many of us have been exposed to the adage "practice makes perfect," many business leaders fail to appreciate the importance of rehearsing responses to possible, albeit not likely, safety challenges. At UCLA, where safety drills and training are a commonplace component of healthcare delivery, disciplined practice may not always "make perfect," but it certainly makes for competent reactions.

Tamara Jean Gavilan, RN, Acute Care Pediatrics and Pediatrics Hematology/Oncology units, and chair of the Acute Pediatric Unit Practice Council, notes, "I know a lot of nurses in the industry, and we all talk. Unlike some of my colleagues outside of UCLA, I have always felt safe working here, and I think it relates to our overall level of preparedness. I am thinking about one of the worst weekends I've had as a nurse, when we actually had a chemical spill in the unit, and I was in charge. While I've seen small spills associated with chemotherapy across my 21-year career in nursing, this was the largest chemical spill that I'd personally encountered, and I have to say that our team's response went as smoothly as it could have gone. Basically, it was a matter of taking it step by step through our training and policy. We deployed our internal hazmat team, and we evacuated the patients. When the emergency struck, I had everything I needed right at my fingertips. Safety has always been important at UCLA, and when it was put to the test, that commitment to safety paid off."

It is difficult to justify safety training and drills in the context of busy production schedules. When people have so much to do to simply get through the demands of their day, why would you want to add a drill or training for a highly unlikely event? The answer can be found in the words of Tamara Jean Gavilan—so that everything your people need can be "right at [their] fingertips" if and when the unexpected happens!

YOUR DIAGNOSTIC CHECKUP

- What steps have you taken to involve the customer in contributing to safety?
- Specifically, what have customers shared that has contributed to their safety? Have you communicated those examples to your staff members so that they appreciate the value of partnering with customers?
- What drills are you currently conducting in your workplace? What additional training might you consider?
- How confident are you that your people will have "everything they need right at their fingertips" when the unexpected happens?

IT'S MORE THAN PHYSICAL

Up to this point, my focus on safety has been associated primarily with physical well-being, but the umbrella of safety clearly extends to many other factors beyond physical harm. For example, healthcare providers have the task of safeguarding the privacy of medical information and ensuring the emotional well-being of people who are often vulnerable. While healthcare providers have always been sensitive to the importance of protecting personal medical data, 1996 legislation paved the way for national standards to protect specific health information. By 2002, a set of formal guidelines was finalized, and mandates were initiated by 2003. These regulations are often referred to as the HIPAA (Health Insurance Portability and Accountability Act) Privacy Rule. In broad terms, federal guidelines identify the types of health information that need to be protected, while also appreciating the importance of sharing healthcare data among providers who are involved in the integrated care of a patient.

Like all other similar facilities, UCLA must comply with the HIPPA Privacy Rule; however, UCLA has faced a rather unique set of challenges. These circumstances emerge from the celebrity clientele that UCLA often serves (based on its location and reputation) and have produced much-publicized breaches of patient information.

Most leadership decisions concerning safety come down to helping people pay attention to and act in accordance with behaviors that avert dangerous outcomes. However, the leadership at UCLA has had to address the safety of medical records from the perspective that a small proportion of its staff members have willingly chosen to compromise the privacy of "high-profile" patients. For example, a celebrity suspected that her medical records were being leaked by UCLA staff. So in 2007, when her doctor at UCLA advised her that she had a recurrence of cancer, she intentionally withheld that information from her family and friends; within four days, the information was released by a tabloid. When she advised UCLA administrators of the breach, it was determined that an administrative assistant, Lawanda Jackson, had repeatedly accessed the celebrity's information.

Lawanda Jackson quit her job at UCLA as she was facing termination. She was later indicted by a federal grand jury and pleaded guilty to violating federal medical privacy laws for commercial purposes. According to prosecutors, starting in 2006, the *National Enquirer* paid Lawanda more than $4,600 for the celebrity's information. While Lawanda Jackson, a 32-year employee, made the choice to abandon ethical and legal behavior, her actions prompted a thorough investigation at UCLA. According to Marti Arvin, chief compliance officer, "UCLA did an investigation of Lawanda Jackson's accesses over a designated limited period of time, and it became clear that she was a problem employee. After following the appropriate processes, the decision was made to terminate her employment. Then when the records of a second celebrity were breached, the Department of Public Health asked UCLA to do an even more in-depth investigation going back to the date when HIPAA actually became enforceable in April 2003. At that time, more potentially improper accesses by Lawanda Jackson were uncovered. As a result of those findings, several additional evaluations of processes occurred—one that was internal, and one that was conducted by the Department of Public Health. The outcome of those investigations resulted in a new monitoring system that was established for a particular list of patients referred to as 'persons of interest.'"

As a result of these process audits, UCLA's leaders began aggressively addressing a wide-ranging set of strategies to avert records violations. The multilevel response to these records breaches includes, but is not limited to,

1. Deploying the science of selection to assist in screening of new hires

2. Technology solutions to preclude and monitor unauthorized access to records

3. Intensive education on medical privacy issues (see Appendix B)

4. A written contract with staff members regarding the impact of records violations

One step in the process involved UCLA leaders deploying the services of Talent Plus, the Lincoln, Nebraska–based company mentioned in Chapter 2, as a resource for choosing staff members with service talent. Talent Plus has been involved in research and corporate development since the 1960s. The company specializes in helping employers use scientific methodology to assess and select staff members in order to achieve a diverse set of business objectives. Kimberly Rath, president and managing director of Talent Plus, notes, "From the outset of our relationship with UCLA's leaders, they shared the importance of finding ways to augment their existing selection processes to look for people with the highest levels of personal values. While we have provided them with the tools and guidance to make strong selections for service and values-based staff, the leaders at UCLA have demonstrated a steadfast discipline not to move forward with candidates with a less-than-optimal values orientation. This discipline reflects a commitment to select people who not only possess the desired technical abilities but also have the character to perform with integrity."

Although UCLA's staff overall is committed to the protection of patient records, there will invariably be individuals who fail to live up to the moral obligations of the job. Talent Plus is a resource that is tapped by the leadership to substantially decrease the probability that current applicants with questionable personality traits will be allowed to slip through the hiring process. In addition to deploying the science of selection with Talent Plus, the UCLA leadership has added technological safeguards to the records process.

Long-standing leadership wisdom suggests that "what you track gets done." However, when it comes to privacy breaches, UCLA operates on the basis that "what gets tracked is less likely to occur." Specifically, in the UCLA information system, there are now two levels of security—password protection to access certain types of information, and tracking data on who has accessed the records of "persons of interest." Marti Arvin, chief compliance officer, notes, "A person of interest could be a celebrity, a local politician, or any employee who doesn't want her record accessed. On a routine basis, we do an assessment of access for the prior 24 hours. We rotate the monitoring so that staff members don't know which day the audit will occur. When we have a person of interest who draws a lot of media attention, we monitor that person's records on a daily basis until we reach a comfort level and resolution that there has not been an improper access or until the attention diminishes."

Doug Gunderson, executive director, Operative Services, and director, Performance Excellence at UCLA, believes that no system can be put in place that will absolutely prevent breaches of patient records, but that monitoring systems can catch people quickly if they make the wrong decision. "Our systems are definitely improving with time. Several years ago, when we had a breach of a celebrity's records, we detected it the next day, and we terminated about six people immediately. So already those processes were starting, and they are even more in place today. There have been significant changes."

In addition to closely monitoring for intrusions into the medical records of persons of interest, UCLA uses a number of other strategies to protect confidential information, including false names and password-protected systems. From the standpoint of pseudonyms, Marti Arvin indicates, "Persons of interest can be given confidential names, so if the president of the United States came in, he might be listed as Joe Smith, thus making it more difficult for people to look him up." Password protections assure that if an unauthorized person happens upon a staff member's user name and makes multiple attempts to guess the correct password, he is locked out of the system. Similarly, if an employee attempts to access an area of a record, such as financial information, without authority, she is advised to speak to a supervisor to clear her "need to know" before she is given approval to access that record type.

Lea Ann Cook, RN, MSN, director, Patient and Guest Services/International Relations, gives a more detailed view of the technological barriers that have been created. "Every employee has a certain level of access that is appropriate to his function. A clerical person may have access only to clerical and not clinical information. A clinical person would have a broader scope of access. Some people will have no access. Your job defines your level of access. First and foremost, when I log in with my ID number, I can go only where I am supposed to go. Let's use a clerk as an example. Suppose someone comes into the hospital and she is flagged for privacy monitoring, and let's say that she is here for neurology services. If a clerk in the gastroenterology department logged on to that chart, within 24 hours of the encounter, the audit would pop up, and the auditor would call the manager of gastroenterology and ask if there is any reason that the clerk should be accessing this record. It is that quick, and if there is no legitimate business purpose for the access, that employee is going to be called in for an interview to ask why this happened."

Since medical records are dynamic, with constantly evolving shifts in who is required to have access, a great deal of time has been spent in educational efforts to ensure that staff members understand their legal, moral, and ethical responsibilities as they relate to confidentiality. Dr. Mark Morocco, a successful screenwriter who later graduated from medical school, subsequently becoming a consultant to the long-running television series *ER* and currently specializing in emergency medicine at UCLA, makes keen observations about the challenges of providing care to a small subset of patients at UCLA. "There is a market for the stories about these patients because of who we are and the population we serve. The publishing entities in the paparazzi world and the tabloid world are very, very aggressive."

From Dr. Morocco's perspective, the best that can be done to counteract these powerful forces is to focus on education. "We do the best we can to layer different areas of protection with a strong emphasis on teaching and developing culture. If you have people who are mostly moral, take their job seriously, care about the patients, and follow the Golden Rule, you can combat the strong forces that are out to get the story. I tell my residents that a lot of the work that we do is very simple. Much of it comes down to treating others the way you would want to be treated. If you were a celebrity with a problem, you wouldn't want it to go past your doctors. You have to keep teaching that message, and you hope that you can load that equation with as many ethical people as possible. You still are never going to protect yourself against the information terrorists. Maybe someday our electronic walls will be thick enough that we will be able to prevent 99 percent of the breaches, but I don't think it is going to get to the point where it is perfect."

Despite the shortcomings of human character and the strong pressures of "information terrorists," Tony Padilla, director, Patient Affairs, agrees that education is the key to the battle. "I believe all of the awareness and training concerning our privacy policies is paying off, particularly when staff members challenge the leaders on variations from policy. Recently, I asked a patient to give me her release of medical forms, and I told her that I would forward them to the manager in medical records. That manager e-mailed me back saying that I was deviating from the process—that I needed to send those patients to him directly to make certain that the process is handled completely. Wow. We have made huge strides in securing patient information."

Most employees at UCLA, and at any workplace, for that matter, do the right thing most of the time. But to effectively remove those who do not, employers must clearly outline the consequences for transgressions, and swift action must be taken to mete out those consequences. Lea Ann Cook makes a distinction between the rare instances in which people actively seek financial gain from looking at records and those who transgress because of curiosity. "I think we've seen two different categories. The cases that most people hear about are those where information is sold to the paparazzi. Those cases are the most horrific, but inside healthcare, we are also talking a lot about access breaches made based on a curiosity factor. People are fascinated with celebrity. I will tell you that I've had situations where I had to intervene and seek disciplinary action against staff members, and when I asked, 'What is it about not looking at celebrities' records that you don't understand?' the person said, 'I thought it was okay because I didn't tell anyone.'"

Marti Arvin shares, "We require all staff members to sign a confidentiality agreement (see Appendix C) that commits them to protect the privacy of patient information and to protect the login data that they use to access our systems. If they breach those obligations, there can be disciplinary consequences up to and including termination. We take that policy very seriously. For example, I have been here a year, and we've had approximately 12 terminations for privacy violations in that time period. Since our systems have been in place, I would estimate that more than 230 employees have been disciplined for inappropriate access of records, and around 40 have been terminated specifically because of celebrity incidents."

Not only are these individuals terminated, but according to Marti, "At UCLA, we do everything we can to cooperate with state and federal officials. I know that an extensive amount of work was done to help the U.S. attorney prepare for the criminal trial of a gentleman named Huping Zhou. His case didn't go to trial, but it resulted in a guilty plea. We take cooperation with law enforcement officers very seriously and help them gather the information that we can legally provide to them if they are going to prosecute someone who improperly accesses information at UCLA."

Lea Ann Cook frames the problem well when she suggests, "There are violations all the time by other organizations in town because I read about them in journals and publications. It's not good no matter where it happens. It's not better if it happens at our competitor. Patients put their trust in healthcare providers, and we have to earn it. People share a level of intimacy with us as healthcare workers that they don't share with anyone else, even their spouse or partner. As leaders, we have to do everything in our power to help staff members understand that they can't violate that trust. It's sacrosanct. We just can't do it."

Vernon J. Goodwin, security director, sums up privacy issues under the broad umbrella of respect for others: "We have some unique challenges with protecting privacy for celebrities, but we have an untiring commitment to ensuring that everyone who enters this building is safe and respected. If we constantly champion that cause, we will get closer to our goal of flawless execution and completely compassionate care." Even if you aren't treating "high-profile" celebrities, your workplace probably has its share of challenges that interfere with flawless execution on delivering compassion and respect to your customers.

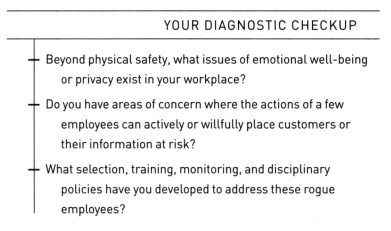

YOUR DIAGNOSTIC CHECKUP

- Beyond physical safety, what issues of emotional well-being or privacy exist in your workplace?
- Do you have areas of concern where the actions of a few employees can actively or willfully place customers or their information at risk?
- What selection, training, monitoring, and disciplinary policies have you developed to address these rogue employees?

THE TARGETS VARY, BUT THE OBJECTIVES REMAIN

Unless you are in aviation, healthcare, automotive manufacturing, or another such field, you may not face "life and death" safety decisions on a daily basis. However, all businesses have their share of risks to employees, visitors, and staff members. Those risks take the universal forms of natural disasters and random acts of violence, as well as routine behavioral management challenges (like hand washing in food service environments or procedural consistency in manufacturing settings). With the increasing complexity of work processes, great pressures to focus on productivity, and the inconsistencies or shortcomings of human nature, safety considerations can lose their priority. Hopefully, this look into UCLA's commitment to a safety culture will help you redouble your commitment and strategies to "leave no room for error."

The upcoming chapters build on this foundational commitment to safety and examine leadership lessons that emerge from UCLA's unyielding pursuit of "world-class" quality outcomes and clinical results. The next two chapters provide an opportunity for you to explore ways to elevate product and process quality throughout your organization.

Prescriptive Summary

▸ Ask each employee in your business to identify how he contributes to safety at work.

▸ Require employees to share their safety observations and acknowledge them for doing so.

▸ Empower employees to benchmark other safety practices in areas that are of concern to them.

▸ Actively seek out "de facto" leaders to influence safety policy and the behavior of their peers.

▸ Encourage an evidence-based approach to safety decision making.

▸ Share your evidence-based findings with others to elevate safety knowledge.

▸ Get customers involved as an extra safety layer in your business.

▸ Practice/drill and practice/drill more.

▸ Examine "well-being" issues (like privacy) that transcend physical safety.

▸ Deploy the science of selection to choose employees who have the desired talents and values.

▸ Incorporate technology to monitor security breaches.

▸ Consistently educate employees on safety expectations.

▶ Create a safety code of conduct, including conditions for termination.

▶ Investigate security breaches swiftly, act decisively, and ensure accountability.

▶ Don't be complacent. Safety is a forever thing—not a gadget, but a "state of mind."

MAKE THE BEST BETTER

CHAPTER 6

Delivering Exceptional Outcomes Here and Now

> *Quality is never an accident;*
> *it is always the result of high*
> *intention, sincere effort,*
> *intelligent direction,*
> *and skillful execution.*
> —WILLIAM FOSTER

U nless you are in a commoditized business in which offering the lowest price is the only essential component of your success, you have to consider how consumers perceive the value of your offerings. In most businesses, value can be calculated by combining the perceived quality of the products or services with the perceived quality of the consumer's experience and then subtracting the price charged for those goods or services.

Value = (Perceived Quality of Product + Perceived Quality of Service Experience) – Price

If consumers believe that the combined quality of the product and the experience exceeds the price, they impute positive value; if they do not, they feel fleeced.

In healthcare, this standard value calculation doesn't fully apply. Given that the "price" of healthcare is less obvious to consumers (particularly when payments are made through third-party payers such as private insurance or Medicare/Medicaid), a patient's perceived value can almost be reduced to, "Did I get the best outcome, and how was I cared for along the way?" Trends suggest that price transparency, cost/outcome statistics, and even patient satisfaction have become increasingly important components of calculating "value" in healthcare, and certainly these issues have been central in political conversations on healthcare reform. However, historically, from a patient's perspective, healthcare quality has had less to do with cost and more to do with outcomes and the process of care.

This chapter and the next offer insights into how UCLA's leadership consistently drives quality at both the product and the experiential levels. This chapter offers definitions of quality and an examination of the relationships among quality, patient outcomes, and ease of healthcare access. The next chapter will look at UCLA's quality in the areas of efficiency, equity, technology, and comfort. In the highly competitive world of business, a dedicated commitment to quality improvements at both the product and the service level is often the key to gaining competitive advantage; in healthcare, it can be the difference between favorable and unfavorable patient outcomes.

HEALTHCARE QUALITY DEFINED

It has often been said, "I don't know much about art, but I know what I like." A similar sentiment could be shared about healthcare quality. Consumers have difficulty evaluating the real success of complicated medical procedures. It is also challenging for patients to assess how a particular patient's outcome after receiving care from a given provider compares to the outcome of a similar patient with a similar condition who received care from a different provider. To better understand the unique intricacies involved in healthcare quality, let's examine attempts to define medical excellence. The federal Agency for Healthcare Research and Quality (AHRQ) simply defines exceptional healthcare as "doing the right thing, at the right time, for the right person, and having the best quality result."

To assess quality, agencies such as the AHRQ examine clinical outcome data and compare those data across providers to determine who is delivering the best results. Sometimes these side-by-side comparisons are referred to as *quality scorecards*. Of course, it is difficult to define which outcome measures are most relevant in grading healthcare performance and to ensure that the information is accurate, given that some of the data are self-reported. Moreover, clinical outcome data can tell only part of the story when it comes to healthcare quality. What if your provider offers above-average outcomes for the treatment of a common condition, but you must endure a great hardship to receive the care? Would you not be better served by going to a provider with comparable clinical outcomes and an easier process for service delivery? While this chapter and the chapter that follows will primarily focus on UCLA's fastidious commitment to exceptional clinical results, they will also touch on process improvements in service delivery. In business, it is critical to remember that a product is not enough; one must also consider how customers feel when they are being served that product.

According to the Institute of Medicine, quality occurs when products and services are

- *Safe.* Treatment helps patients and does not cause harm.

- *Effective.* Research shows that treatments have positive (good) results.

- *Patient-centered.* Healthcare providers (doctors, nurses, and others) treat all patients with respect. This means taking into account each patient's values regarding health and quality of life.

- *Timely.* Patients get the care they need at a time when it will do the most good.

- *Efficient.* Treatment does not waste doctors' or patients' money or time.

- *Equitable.* Everyone is entitled to high-quality healthcare. This includes men and women of all cultures, incomes, levels of education, and social status.

In essence, healthcare quality is reflected in timely, consistent, safe, and efficacious outcomes that are delivered efficiently and equitably. Chief Medical Officer Dr. Tom Rosenthal emphasizes the consistent delivery of high-quality care at UCLA and suggests that it is a matter of brand integrity. "Taking it from the patient's perspective, quality is inextricably linked to integrity. To have integrity with what we promise patients, we have to not only deliver outstanding outcomes but provide them every single time in every single encounter. That's integrity. Not 'I said I'd call you back, and I did,' but the integrity that comes from compassionate execution every time, efficiently delivering the highest performance fairly and with stability."

For the purpose of this chapter, I will examine two factors from the Institute of Medicine list that directly affect the integrity of the UCLA brand: effectiveness and timeliness. Every business either delivers or fails its brand promise to the degree that it executes on these two critical aspects.

YOUR DIAGNOSTIC CHECKUP

- How do you define quality and value in your business?

- What roles do the following play in your customer's determination of the quality of your experience and your products or services: efficiency, effectiveness, safety, customer-centricity, timeliness, and equity in access?

- Do you link your brand's integrity not only to overall quality performance measures, but also to your ability to deliver excellence every time with every customer?

┬ What metrics, certifications, or criteria should consumers
│ rely upon to determine quality in your industry? How do
│ you perform against those metrics? Do you educate the
│ consumer as to which criteria truly matter?

QUALITY AND EFFECTIVENESS

No matter what the business sector, advertising messages imply a business's quality by claiming that the company is "best," "world-class," "award-winning," and so on. Given the cluttered world of marketing claims, how does a consumer really know the effectiveness of a company's products or services? For example, if you go to the Web site of almost any healthcare provider, you will see awards, certifications, or recognitions that imply extraordinary effectiveness. However, what are worthwhile metrics and standards?

U.S. News & World Report has sought to create reliable criteria for comparing U.S. hospitals and each year ranks approximately 5,000 hospitals on the following criteria:

- Death rates

- Reputation among board-certified specialists (peer review—to whom would I send a member of my family?)

- Patient-care factors (for example, number of patients seen, items of technology for a given specialty area, and quality of staff members as measured by recognized certification agencies such as the Magnet nursing designation)

- Patient safety (as determined by performance against seven things that "should not happen" during a hospital stay (such as low-risk patients dying in a hospital)

Consistently, UCLA not only makes the honor roll of *U.S. News & World Report*'s best hospitals (consisting of approximately the top 20 hospitals in America), but routinely is "best in the west." In 2009, for example, UCLA ranked third, behind Johns Hopkins and the Mayo Clinic.

CEO Dr. David Feinberg emphasizes that the quest for quality has to be an internal one and must be gauged by an organization's success in achieving its maximum potential. According to Dr. Feinberg, "When it comes to being among the very top tier of U.S. hospitals, we don't see Johns Hopkins or Mayo as our competition. We are our competition! We have won every major healthcare award we could ever seek, and we have Nobel Prize winners on our staff. We do more solid organ transplants than any other facility in the country or the world. However, if you talk to our people here, none of that matters. What matters to us is the very next person that comes through the door. The rankings will take care of themselves. If we take care of patients, the finances will take care of themselves. Whether healthcare is reformed or not reformed, our friends and neighbors whom we have cared for in the community will make sure that UCLA survives." Despite the fact that UCLA's emergency rooms treat 80,000 people a year and about 800 people sleep in UCLA hospitals each night, Dr. Feinberg believes that the quality of "the next patient's outcome and experience is most important." It is through this focus on "the next patient" that UCLA's leaders have inspired a steadfast commitment to effectiveness—an effectiveness that can be measured in part by the breadth and scope of the populations that UCLA serves. How important is the next customer interaction to the quality and reputation of your business?

MORE THAN A NEIGHBORHOOD BUSINESS

While a corner convenience store may be able to rely on business from a nearby geographic area despite having marginal service or product (relying on location and a dearth of competition), great businesses produce outcomes that cause people to go beyond geographic convenience to seek them out. UCLA is an example of a center of excellence that draws people from a wide range of locations—from nearby catchment areas where local residents seek their best healthcare option all the way up to international patients.

CEO Dr. David Feinberg describes how operational excellence provides concentric rings of geographic attraction. "I look at our effectiveness as leading to three almost different types of businesses. The business that has the widest international appeal involves the treatment of complex coordinated diseases, such as transplant cases. To care for a transplant patient effectively, a healthcare system needs interventional skills (great surgeons, for example), but it also needs many other specialties in areas such as anesthesia, interventional radiology, and intensivist doctors who work in the ICUs. It also needs a lot of coordination because it takes many physicians, nurses, and specialized ICU staff members, as these patients may have to wait a few years before they receive an organ and are often very sick. So we have teams and nurse coordinators who follow the patients for life. Competitive quality advantages in this type of business emerge from both depth and breadth of subspecialties and a high volume of patients, which, in turn, supports the level of talent that you have to acquire."

In addition to these complex coordinated quality products, Dr. Feinberg identifies extraordinary talent and outcomes in specialized disease interventions. According to Dr. Feinberg, "We have experts who are among the world's best. For example, Kalyanam Shivkumar, M.D., Ph.D., who received his medical degree from the University of Madras, India, and his Ph.D. from UCLA, is the director of the UCLA Cardiac Arrhythmia Center at the David Geffen School of Medicine at UCLA. If you are a child or an adult with a cardiac arrhythmia, he and his team are the ones to see." In this quality product line, patients may travel a great distance for diagnostics, treatment interventions, and excellent nursing care, but those patients will return home to their country or neighboring state and need to have their care coordinated with a doctor in their community. In this business model, a hospital attracts patients from a great distance for specialized services, but these patients don't require the same level of onsite, long-term care coordination as those receiving a product like transplantation.

Dr. Feinberg acknowledges yet a third business model at UCLA that also relies on the delivery of excellent quality in what Dr. Feinberg calls "primary or secondary coordinated care, which is really how we function as a community hospital to people near us. Our geriatrics program, for example, has been ranked number 1 in *U.S. News & World Report*. Its level of expertise is no different from that of our international programs, but the issues that geriatrics deals with are more common and tend to serve people within the local geography. Using our geriatrics program as an example, this primary model of excellence and quality relates to specific local care and cutting-edge research on the management of an aging population with more chronic diseases and complex comorbidities." Despite differing levels of complexity, coordination, and areas of population served, outcomes, experience, and expertise all drive business into UCLA. Both wealthy and poor patients come to UCLA from local neighborhoods and distant countries, all searching for the same thing—"the best of the best" for themselves and for those they love.

The parents of nine-year-old Muhammed Alazmi, a UCLA patient, are examples of this search for excellence. Originally from Kuwait, the Alazmi family came to UCLA in 2008 when Muhammed was suffering from renal failure and required a transplant. Muhammed had previously had surgeries in hospitals in other parts of the world, including Germany, Kuwait, and England. One of those surgeries included a prior kidney transplant that had failed, where Muhammed's mother had provided the transplanted organ. After the failed transplant, Muhammed's family was referred to UCLA. When Muhammed first came to Los Angeles, he was on five medications that were proving unsuccessful in controlling his blood pressure. As UCLA specialists began to care for Muhammed, through sophisticated dialysis and improved kidney function management, his blood pressure was controlled with two medications. His family remained in the vicinity of UCLA, and Muhammed received the bulk of his care as an outpatient. Ultimately, a successful surgery at UCLA resulted in Muhammed's not needing any medications to regulate his blood pressure. Muhammed also enjoyed stabilization of associated conditions like neurofibromatosis.

One and one-half years after arriving at UCLA, Muhammed and his parents were finally getting ready to return to Kuwait to be with Muhammed's siblings and restore him to a much more normal life in a traditional classroom setting. Khalid Alazmi, Muhammed's father, shared, "It has been a long journey here in the United States, but it was worth every step because the doctors at UCLA were very meticulous about finding things to treat. They were very cautious along the way in taking care of Muhammed. If they suspected anything, even if it was minor, they addressed it completely. Muhammed's outcome is amazing, and the care we received here was exceptional, including the way they respected our customs. When Muhammed was hospitalized and his mother was staying with him, the staff would put a paper on Muhammed's door to make sure that people knocked before they entered so that my wife was ready to receive them. The respect shown to my wife and our customs was as reflective of UCLA's quality as the outcome that the doctors achieved for my son. Muhammed was hospitalized a few times while he was in Los Angeles, and it was impressive to me that the staff remembered Muhammed and what he liked every time." When asked about his experience at UCLA, Muhammed simply added, "I am happy, I am well, and I loved that I could laugh and that I am finally going home." The complexities, challenges, and rewards of dealing with the language and cultural needs of international patients will be significantly addressed in later chapters, but for the purposes of this discussion, the distance a customer is willing to travel for a service is often an indicator of the quality that a company provides.

Of course, drawing patients from outside local neighborhoods adds to the complexity of assuring an "overall quality experience" for the patient or her family. Unlike individuals who live near the hospital where they receive care, UCLA often has to assist families in securing lodging close to where treatment is provided. UCLA's Tiverton House was created to meet the needs of some of the patients and families receiving care at the Ronald Reagan UCLA Medical Center. Hotel rates in the general area are costly, and Tiverton House is a reasonably priced alternative for families. Peter Ji, general manager of UCLA Tiverton House, notes, "Thanks to donations and grants, a portion of those who stay at Tiverton House do so through a housing assistance program. We are always looking for ways to meet our objective of making it possible to be nearby when support and closeness are needed most."

Janina Krupa, programs coordinator/food service manager at UCLA Tiverton House, reports, "We play an important role for a hospital system that cares for so many people who travel from great distances. While patients are receiving terrific care, we must deliver a high-quality experience for families and for the patients when they aren't in the clinical treatment areas." Janina notes, "This job is amazingly rewarding, and I have so many stories of the important role we have been given. One such case is a couple from Australia. The husband was going through difficult times, and I did everything that I could for the wife, just as I would do for anybody else. Imagine not only that you're from out of town, but that this is your first time in America. They didn't know anything about where to go, what to do, or how to go about getting the things they needed. I took considerable time with them and tried to guide them, even to the point of helping them with shopping. I brought items from my home to help the wife, as she cooked a lot in our community kitchen. On and off, the couple stayed with us for more than a year. Fortunately, the husband's health improved considerably, and they returned to Perth. We became close during their stay, and I received many offers from them to have me visit them in Australia."

While UCLA could limit its focus on excellence to medical treatment areas, its leaders continue to look for ways to serve people throughout the United States and across the world. To that end, entire teams of people have to work together to create the infrastructure and attend to the vast array of details involved in serving people from distant locations.

When patients have traveled for care, staff members appreciate the significant responsibilities they carry to maintain outstanding clinical outcomes. David Niles White, a UCLA emergency trauma technician, notes, "I can't imagine that it gets any better than what we do. Especially with the new hospital, we now have a world-class facility. Some days I'm the first person in the ER who says, 'Hi. How can I help you?' or 'What's wrong today?' when a patient walks in the door, or limps in the door, or comes bleeding in the door. For some reason, I liken UCLA to the Luxor Hotel in Las Vegas, as that beam of light shoots up into the night sky from the top of the Luxor. I think people see UCLA like that. People will step out of their cars or their campers or whatever and say, 'Hi. I just drove three hours to get here.' And I might jokingly ask, 'Wasn't there another hospital near you?' and they'll say, 'I wanted to come to UCLA.' There's a reason that we're up there with the Mayo Clinic, Mass General, and the Cleveland Clinic. We do great work, and I am committed to keeping the light shining."

An example of a patient who will travel past nearby hospitals is Nancy Fowkes. "I moved to Los Angeles from New York, and my doctor in New York highly recommended a doctor at UCLA. There are many doctors in my husband's family, and they suggested that if I got a chance to choose which hospital I would go to, I should go to UCLA. The care at the hospital was so phenomenal that when we moved farther away, I knew I would be driving past other hospitals to have my second child at UCLA. I know a lot of people who go to the nearby hospitals, and I'm sure they are probably textbook good hospitals, but I've never heard from those other people that they received the extra mile of care."

The distinction between being "textbook" and providing the "extra mile" of care can make the difference between local commodity brands and beloved brands with a larger catchment area. Whether it is a function of providing outcomes that exceed the performance of competitors, receiving referrals from respected professionals, or developing product or service lines that draw customers well beyond local geography, performance matters when the goal is quality!

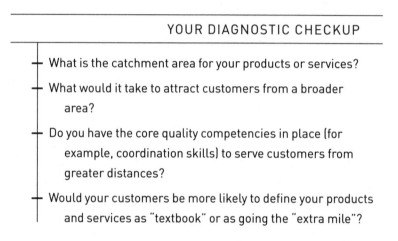

YOUR DIAGNOSTIC CHECKUP

- What is the catchment area for your products or services?
- What would it take to attract customers from a broader area?
- Do you have the core quality competencies in place (for example, coordination skills) to serve customers from greater distances?
- Would your customers be more likely to define your products and services as "textbook" or as going the "extra mile"?

QUALITY AND TIMELINESS

Let's assume that you have the "best of the best" products or services, and that customers come from great distances to acquire them. Can those customers get that product or service when they want or need it? As many can attest, U.S. healthcare is not known for the timeliness of its delivery, although some would argue that other healthcare models may perform even worse in terms of timely access. Whether you have waited for what seemed to be an interminable period to see a doctor, experienced delays in scheduling a procedure, longed to have your name finally called in an emergency waiting room, or anguished during the wait for an important lab result, healthcare often requires great patience. At UCLA and other cutting-edge healthcare centers, the leaders are constantly looking for ways to make sure that care is received based on an individual's prevailing need and is delivered in as timely and flexible a way as possible.

According to Dr. Michael Steinberg, UCLA chair of Radiation Oncology, the outpatient clinic had evolved into a place where timely patient scheduling didn't seem to be a priority. Dr. Steinberg notes, "It was almost as if there was some cap on how many patients you would put on a machine. So we decided to look at how we were doing business and expand our treatment times so that we would be more convenient for the patients' schedules. In the process, it turned out that we also scheduled patients more quickly, which was of great benefit to them." In the process of reanalyzing the timeliness of service delivery, Dr. Steinberg's department went from one that treated approximately 55 patients a day to one that now routinely treats more than 100 patients a day and peaks at about 125. Most noteworthy to Dr. Steinberg, "Ramping up to these numbers—to a place that we had never seen before—was very difficult for the staff at first, but patients were more satisfied with the quality of our care when we were seeing more of them. Quality can be delivered in a timely way if you are willing to make changes to meet the needs of your customers."

Dr. Michael W. Yeh, assistant professor of surgery and medicine and program director of Endocrine Surgery at UCLA, similarly addressed challenges involving the timely delivery of care when he took over leadership of his program. "One of the things that always bothered me about healthcare when I was a patient was that it seemed so difficult to access. The limiting factor in medicine isn't technology; it's healthcare professionals not helping patients to navigate in a foreign environment." Dr. Yeh even suggests that medical settings can become hostile for patients, who are often vulnerable and emotionally overwhelmed. In light of this vulnerability, Dr. Yeh notes that some healthcare providers have moved in the direction of care with additional amenities, where patients are offered concierge services. Unfortunately, not all of the providers who make care extremely comfortable are also delivering the highest level of clinical outcomes. Dr. Yeh adds, "It occurred to me that if you have the choice between having all the polish, but not necessarily the intellectual muscle, and going to another institution, say UCLA, that has all the intellectual muscle but could use a little more of the polish, the organization with substance would be in an enviable position." As a result of this observation, Dr. Yeh decided to add polish to patient access in the Endocrine Surgery program. "When I started here, I structured things so that we would be accessible—there would be no phone trees; there would be human beings. I answered my own phone for the first year; you always got a person when you called."

Dr. Yeh distinguishes between a surgeon and a technician by the degree to which the surgeon advocates on behalf of the patient. According to Dr. Yeh, "To advocate for patients, you have to take the time to get to know them and put systems in place to help them receive care. Inevitably, there will be tests that have to be done, further tests, and coordination. If you have a patient who comes from Abu Dhabi, that patient will probably be given some help, but if you have an elderly woman from central California, how are we going to help her get around?" To make the process less daunting to patients, Dr. Yeh created a "help desk" resource. A phone line was created to help patients with any problem that they encountered. Dr. Yeh notes, "If you are a patient of ours, we will coordinate all your appointments on the same day so that you won't have to travel as often. If you get lost, you can call our number and we'll guide you around this huge campus. What I realized early on was that there were a lot of system problems that were too big for me to tackle as a junior professor. My goal, however, was to create a little bubble around my microculture so that things within our program could work the way I thought they ought to work."

Dr. Yeh is quick to point out that Endocrine Surgery patients are often fairly similar—young, outpatient, and technologically sophisticated. Because of those characteristics, Dr. Yeh reports, he has been able to leverage technology to ease access and speed recovery. Because much of the treatment involves monitoring endocrine function markers carefully prior to surgery, Dr. Yeh uses online technology to have patients send him daily results. Dr. Yeh reports, "By using remote technology and doing our homework up front, we can achieve the right diagnosis, find out exactly where the tumor is, focus down our operation, and treat you with medications to make sure the operation can be done safely. The payoff for you is a smooth, focused operation, and you stay at UCLA only a short time." Timely access to a variety of procedures through remote technologies and doing the detailed "homework up front" has allowed UCLA's Endocrine Surgery program to release patients more quickly compared to national averages.

This approach to viewing quality in the context of ease of access is echoed by Dr. Patricia Kapur, chair of the Department of Anesthesiology at UCLA. "As far as anesthesiology goes, we have been looking at a number of different ways to elevate the quality of our patient access across the many different venues where we work. Here in the hospital, we've been working on the preoperative patient experience because we have a large catchment area, and people travel great distances to be evaluated. Rather than making everyone travel to us with their medical records and complete an evaluation in person, we've used technology to significantly reduce the number of patients who need to make an additional presurgical visit. In the evaluation suite, we do a telephone and electronic screening in which the patients have the surgeon's office send over as much of the necessary information as they can by means of a fax server. The private MD or cardiologist sends in the patient's records in a similar manner. We review all that information, speak to the patient, and talk to the doctors' offices, and we've gradually gotten to a point where 80 percent of our patients don't need to make a time-consuming trip. Our goal is 90 percent. We'd like to make a connection without having the patient incur the cost and time expenditure to travel." Dr. Kapur acknowledges that there are patients with special circumstances who must be seen in person, but she indicates that providing high-quality care requires streamlining processes based on the level of contact needed, not based on the historical practice patterns of physicians, clinics, and other providers.

In addition to avoiding unnecessary travel in the preoperative evaluation, Dr. Kapur notes that the arrival experience of patients who require anesthesia has also been improved. "We've reorganized how we receive the patients here on the morning of a procedure and even before they arrive. Traditionally, the assigned anesthesiology person would try to call the patient the night before a surgery, but in approximately 40 percent of the cases, we weren't able to reach the patient. By trying to make contact so close to surgery, we ran the risk that some information would be missing and that we might want additional studies that could not be done unless we changed the surgery schedule. By switching to an electronic system, we are getting more information on patients earlier. On the day of the surgery, we have assigned the members of our house staff to the holding area and have positioned them in a way that addresses all the important transactional efficiencies that are needed to streamline the process for the patient. This has all taken a great deal of work, but high-quality healthcare isn't about producing excellent outcomes in a vacuum. Those outcomes must be delivered in a timely and empathetic manner." Throughout UCLA Health System, administrators, doctors, nurses, and line staff are looking for ways to deliver care in the timeliest manner possible. In the words of Dr. Kapur, it is not enough to offer high-quality outcomes if the patient's time is not valued in the process.

YOUR DIAGNOSTIC CHECKUP

What are some areas in which "this is the way it's always been done" thinking gets in the way of changing in the direction of timely customer-centric delivery?

━ How do you customize your service based on the
demographics (age, distance, technology skills, and
interests) of your customers?

━ Do you define quality in terms of timeliness of service or
product delivery?

━ Consistent with the work of doctors Kapur, Yeh, and
Steinberg, what have you done in your business to
address timely product delivery? What opportunities
for streamlined service continue to exist?

THE BETTER YOU ARE,
THE MORE DIFFICULT IT BECOMES

Despite all the progress that UCLA has made in creating ease of
access, the complexity of the cases treated and UCLA's specialized
care often create a "perfect storm" that decreases the efficiency of
the system. To understand the multitude of challenges faced in delivering care at UCLA, one need only talk to the mother of a pediatric cancer patient who was processed through the emergency
room efficiently, only to be housed in the Emergency Department
for hours while awaiting a bed on the pediatric oncology floor. Dr.
Mark Morocco of the Emergency Department notes, "Our problem is that we are at the top of a pyramid, and we are suffering from
the blessing of having a lot of incredible super-specialists, having
a lot of referral business, and being in a place where we are highly
visible. People send us their hardest cases. Doctors send us their
sickest patients. That pediatric cancer patient comes to us to be
treated by a specific super-specialist, and we are at the skinny end
of that funnel with only a certain number of beds available."

Dr. Morocco notes that once the Emergency Department
completes its evaluation and initial treatment, "Often we become
frustrated because we know where patients should go. We have
started them on their daily regimen. The appropriate specialist has

been involved in their care. We are doing the same things that staff members would do anyplace else in the hospital, whether it is an ICU room or a floor bed, but the patients are stuck physically in the Emergency Department. Patients don't recognize that they are in a bed that is as sophisticated and that provides the same level of care as an ICU bed. They just feel stuck." Dr. Morocco compares the Emergency Department to the front desk at a hotel. "There are certain things that should happen in each. People who arrive should have things happen relatively quickly and feel welcomed. Staff members should facilitate a set of services, and then guests should be sent elsewhere. You can read the paper, have coffee, and maybe have cocktails in the entry area of a Ritz-Carlton, but you should not sleep there. In hospitals, we are making people sleep in the lobby when they have to stay for extended periods awaiting beds. For us, it is simply a matter of having more referrals and many more patients than we have rooms."

Dr. Peter Viccellio, clinical professor, vice chair, and clinical director, Department of Emergency Medicine, Stony Brook University Medical Center, Stony Brook, New York, has advocated that patients who are being admitted to a hospital should be routed to their treatment unit as swiftly as possible, the logic being that a cardiac patient is better off being housed in the hallway of the Cardiology Department than in the hallway of the emergency room. Dr. Morocco notes, however, "In some states, there are actual laws against housing patients in hallways other than those in the Emergency Department because unit hallways are not licensable beds. So patients are left with the impression that they are waiting for care, while care is actually already taking place—just not on the unit where they want to be."

Dr. Lynne McCullough, associate professor of emergency medicine and medical director, Ronald Reagan UCLA Medical Center Emergency Department, notes, "Patients who are waiting for hospital beds in the ED certainly make our job more challenging, but those challenges should be invisible to our patients.

We should be tireless in our efforts to move patients through the system appropriately and to communicate with them constantly so that they have a realistic sense that progress is being made. At the same time, we have to execute to deliver a patient-centered experience at every level of need. In the end, patients in the Emergency Department have a great deal of staff interaction in a short period of time. Whether they are waiting for a bed or facing a life-threatening challenge, each interaction is important to them, and it is our job to get all of those interactions right."

When faced with the scenario of a pediatric oncology patient waiting for hours to be transported from a UCLA Emergency Department housing area to the oncology unit, CEO Dr. David Feinberg quickly responded, "That should never happen at UCLA, but it does all too often. I can tell you all the things we are doing to remedy the situation, like aggressively lobbying for more patient bed space, but none of that matters. If the hospital gets bigger, in time, those additional beds will be full, and we will be right back where we are now." Dr. Feinberg then offered a shocking solution: "The only way to deal with this is to be better. We have to take whatever knowledge we have that requires that child to be seen only by us, and we need to share that with doctors in our community so that the child can be seen closer to her home. Then we must push our expertise further so that we can treat more extreme cases. In an ideal world, I would like UCLA to push medicine to the point where very few cases will require any hospital care at all. Our goal should be to disperse knowledge so widely and advance treatment so rapidly that this hospital never has a shortage of beds."

As a consultant to many diverse businesses, I initially found Dr. Feinberg's words befuddling. He was essentially saying that he wanted to take his competitive advantage—extremely advanced medical care—and make it available to a lower tier of competitors. According to Dr. Feinberg, that would, in turn, drive greater innovation within his business and lead to a higher standard of service at UCLA. The endgame of this sharing would be to make hospital care significantly less common. At that moment, I began to re-think the wisdom of using a "world-class" healthcare provider as a standard bearer for business leaders. However, the more I thought about his words, the more I found genius in them.

Every competitive advantage you may enjoy has a limited timeline. Unless you are improving your product and service offerings, competitors will ultimately overtake you. Dr. Feinberg realizes that healthcare requires the sharing of knowledge to drive high-quality outcomes and save lives. Moreover, he understands that by UCLA's sharing advances, overall healthcare delivery improves. As the tide of healthcare rises, everyone benefits—including UCLA.

Prescriptive Summary

▶ Examine the value you provide given the formula:
Value = (Product Quality + Experience Quality) – Price.

▶ Determine the overall quality of your products or services
by assessing their safety, effectiveness, customer-centricity,
efficiency, and equity.

▶ Drive brand integrity by executing on your brand promise
in every interaction.

▶ Offer quality outcomes first, then streamline processes.

▶ Realize that in terms of customer experience, no amount
of amenities can make up for poor products or execution.

▶ Share knowledge.

▶ Elevate the tide, and you will benefit in the process.

CHAPTER 7

Quality for Less and for All

> *Continuous improvement is about removing the things that get in the way of your work. The headaches, the things that slow you down, that's what continuous improvement is all about.*
> —Bruce Hamilton

I f your family has health insurance and an insured loved one is in need of a medical procedure, does the cost of that procedure matter to you? If you are a healthcare provider and there are two treatment options available that are likely to produce similar outcomes, how much does the price of each option affect the one you choose? When it comes to health and/or lifesaving interventions, what role should cost play? Given concerns over maximizing the effectiveness of healthcare dollars and government debates about healthcare reform, healthcare quality is now being graded not only on clinical outcomes, but also on the cost efficiencies with which those outcomes are achieved.

Dr. Jan Tillisch, professor of clinical medicine and executive vice chair, Department of Medicine at UCLA, notes, "These efficiency concerns are not new to the people who have done health service research, but they are increasing in the public debate. People are talking a lot more about compared effectiveness research. In the federal government's economic stimulus package, more than $1 billion was allocated for compared effectiveness research." Dr. Michael Steinberg, chair of Radiation Oncology at UCLA, adds, "We live in a country where the demand for healthcare and technology is very high. You've seen the graphs; the percentage of U.S. gross national product allocated to healthcare is twice that of Europeans and Canadians. Our cost per capita is twice as much. Citizens in other countries have a much lower demand for technologically driven care. Some of these cost differentials are system-based, and some are cultural." From Dr. Steinberg's perspective, professionals in the U.S. healthcare system have not done a very good job of sitting down and explaining the trade-offs to patients. Specifically, Dr. Steinberg clarifies, "I'm not talking about money necessarily, but about having conversations like, 'Will this technology actually work?' We have some phenomenal devices. There is a robotic device for doing surgery on prostate cancer—the Da Vinci robot—and it tells a great story. It costs more than $2,000,000. You can magnify the surgical field three times larger. In a place where a human hand can throw about six or seven sutures, it can throw ten. When you go back and look at the outcomes, however, findings suggest that the results that the robot produces may not be substantially better than those from other surgeries. Now more than ever, quality has to come with questions like, will it work and is it worth the cost?" Increasingly, in all business endeavors, the issue of quality comes with the question, "At what cost?" Companies that deliver efficient quality wrapped in a maximized experience will enjoy a competitive advantage.

QUALITY AND EFFICIENCY

Insurance companies are certainly asking, "Is it worth the cost?" as they make determinations of healthcare quality. In Britain and shortly thereafter in the United States, some insurance companies began moving away from a fee-for-service model, where payments are rendered independent of high-quality outcomes or efficient service delivery. In a fee-for-service model, providers make money each time they perform a procedure, whether or not the procedure is necessary or even helpful. The healthcare reform debate in the United States has generated a great deal of discussion about how fee-for-service models coupled with costly malpractice exposure can create environments that are rife with excessive screening and defensive medicine. In these situations, tests are ordered to avert lawsuits, not chosen because of medical necessity. In a world in which healthcare needs are abundant and financial resources are limited, many third-party payers and healthcare reformers strongly advocate for "pay-for-performance" models. These concepts, which are sometimes referred to as "value-based purchasing," give providers incentives to meet pre-established targets efficiently in delivering healthcare services.

A pay-for-performance model offers incentives for physicians, medical groups, hospitals, and other healthcare providers when they meet performance measures on both quality and efficiency. By contrast, penalties are assessed and payment is withheld when costs rise above the guidelines or clinical outcomes fall below performance expectations. While large-scale pilot studies suggest that pay-for-performance scenarios can be successful in terms of improving clinical outcomes and efficiencies, there are many people in healthcare who view these approaches (including public scorecards of healthcare efficiency) as problematic. Concerns include the validity of quality indicators, how these guidelines affect patient and physician decision making (withholding possibly necessary procedures because of financial incentives), and how much these processes complicate already burdened healthcare administration.

As a business writer, I'm not attempting to endorse a pay-for-performance model as a key to healthcare reform. I am simply acknowledging the changing reimbursement trend, since third-party payers are linking outcome quality and efficiencies of delivery. Clearly, there is a somewhat confusing set of associations between healthcare expenditures and outcome quality. According to Dr. Michael Steinberg, chair of Radiation Oncology at UCLA, "In health services research, it turns out that when you look at the cost of care, quality goes up with cost, but then it starts to turn the corner. At some point, quality measures start to drop as cost continues to rise. The simplistic version of this reversal of trend is the thinking that at some point, extremely costly care causes iatrogenic problems. In essence, the costly fixes may be causing their own share of concerns. These issues are far more complicated than I can summarize in a few sentences, but the complexity indicates the importance of measuring the link between cost and quality and not assuming that spending more always leads to higher-quality outcomes."

Amir Dan Rubin, former COO, focused on the link between quality and efficiency long before the pay-for-performance model began to gain traction. Amir notes, "When I arrived at UCLA and began meeting new people, my first step was to ask about the quality of each person's department or area of expertise. Most people would tell me that they were delivering excellent care, and I would then ask, 'How do you know?' Often people had a hard time identifying metrics that they could point to that demonstrated both quality and efficiency. So I would say, 'No problem; let's find a way to track performance.'" Amir continues, "So the process of quality and efficiency management at UCLA started by asking people how they can measure those dimensions. Nowadays, UCLA uses metrics from a number of different sources—many that are specific to the hospital industry, some that are from the empirical quality literature, and others that are from external agencies that report and benchmark performance against others in healthcare. The challenge today isn't finding a way to measure quality and efficiency, but to position the data in ways that help people make the changes necessary to steward their resources so that they achieve the best possible outcomes."

While many excellent organizations collect and provide high-priority quality and efficiency metrics to managers on computerized dashboards, in many ways UCLA's reputation for efficient delivery of quality is a result of the extent to which UCLA tracks performance and the deep and detailed levels of measurement and analysis that its leaders provide. In essence, UCLA effectively and actively manages down into its "detailed dashboards." Given that UCLA is in a very complex and complicated business, it needs to look at processes in a highly detailed manner. CEO David Feinberg notes, "If we are not gazing both at the big picture and at the tiniest details of a process, we are missing opportunities." What is quite novel about performance management at UCLA is the depth and scope of the enterprise. As an example, Dr. Feinberg suggests, "We even look at quality and efficiency in an area like spiritual care. How do leaders in spiritual care know if they are doing a great and efficient job? You can't simply ask those leaders to track how many souls they saved today. However, you can track what percentage of the patients who wanted spiritual care received a visit in the first 24 hours of their stay. If we don't measure that, we will never know how efficiently and immediately we respond to our patients' spiritual needs." The delivery of these data is even more noteworthy in that the dashboards are not the byproduct of sophisticated technology, but rather reflect the engagement of leaders and staff members who make these data accessible through the manual creation of Excel spreadsheets.

Leaders at UCLA caution that data tracking and reporting are only part of the improvement journey. Additionally, leaders must use the data to provide flawless execution of operational objectives if they want to drive quality. Therefore, UCLA conducts a biweekly systems operations meeting at which managers put together their goals for the year. Those goals are then submitted to the managers' supervisors and placed in a binder that is shared with a Systems Operations team. That team consists of many senior leaders from across the health system and also includes several key physicians. Throughout the year, the COO and the Systems Operations team focus on particularly important goals that need to be addressed most aggressively. That operation team identifies various performance initiatives and engages the assistance of UCLA's Quality Improvement and Performance Excellence departments. The staff members in those departments facilitate projects and help the Systems Operations team look at large-scale process improvements that will decrease waste and increase efficiency.

The role of the Quality Improvement and Performance Excellence specialists at UCLA can best be described as being subject-matter experts in "lean thinking" approaches and catalysts to spread lean thinking throughout the organization. Lean thinking is a production management process that was derived largely from the Toyota Production System (TPS). In its most simplistic form, lean thinking represents the view that all expenditures of resources must be directly converted into value for the end user. Lean thinking looks to cut waste (expenditures that do not result in value) and increase efficiency by deriving more value from less expenditure. At UCLA, "lean thinking experts" are mapping out either the processes or the value streams. They then get people involved to find opportunities, build error-proof approaches, and standardize operations. They make sure that quality and efficiency happen every time. In a large place like UCLA, that means using a lot of process checklists. Whatever the industry, opportunities abound for value stream mapping and operational checklist development as part of a never-ending discipline of quality and efficiency management.

Doug Gunderson, executive director, Operative Services, and director, Performance Excellence, offers several examples of how lean thinking can positively affect both quality and efficiency. With regard to patient discharge times, Doug notes, "I can say that there are some natural inefficiencies. Since we are always full and patients are waiting for beds, we need to discharge patients when they are ready to be discharged. However, our data showed that most of our patients got discharged at 2 p.m. This 2 p.m. discharge was a function of how and when doctors do their patient rounds and was not necessarily based on consideration of what was best for the patient, optimal hospital flow, or the bottom line. In fact, from a patient-care and financial perspective, it would be better to have more discharges before noon." Doug adds that the 2:00 p.m. discharge phenomenon creates bed shortages and can both slow down surgeries and extend Emergency Department stays.

Since the timing of physician rounds was established in the 1950s at Johns Hopkins to assist in medical resident training, more than 50 years of tradition limit needed efficiencies. Doug notes, "To address this, we do cross-functional rounds where the nurse, the care coordinator, the resident, and the attending physician all come together to talk about the patient's care plan and how we can advance that care. We have streamlined that process, and now we do the resident teaching after rounds. We looked at this discharge challenge from a process perspective. The teaching aspect is very important, but if the patient is being discharged, orders can be written and tests or procedures can get done, and then the teaching can follow."

While established practice patterns can be difficult to change, Bonnie Millett, RN, MSN, unit director, Neurosurgical/Neuroscience/Stroke Unit, suggests, "We have developed a committee that is called Care Coordination. This committee meets every morning at 8:45 a.m. to talk about our neurosurgery patients. At 10:30 a.m., we talk about the strokes of our neurology patients. Since we are at over 100 percent capacity all the time, this effort focuses on getting all of the patients expeditiously placed in acute rehabilitation, a skilled nursing facility, or home physical therapy. The social worker attends these morning discharge rounds along with the interns and the nurse practitioner. The meetings help us clarify each patient's plan of care. What do we need for this patient? How can we facilitate transferring this patient so that the next person waiting for our service can come and be seen? We all work collaboratively, and if we know in the evening that a patient is going to be discharged, then the nurse practitioner or the intern will start writing the discharge instructions. They will talk to the charge nurse, and they will get the ball rolling so that family members can pick up their loved one first thing in the morning. We try to give families advance notice that their loved one is going to be transferred the next morning so that they can make their plans the night before or the day before. We try to have the staff nurse do as much teaching as possible prior to the time of discharge, so that medications, appointments, and the post-op discharge instructions can be handled swiftly. We try to have all of that paperwork done the night before so that in the morning, when the family member arrives, the nurse can sit down with the patient and the family member and go through the relevant discharge instructions. Our goal is to have the patient out by 11:00 a.m." This focus on increased care coordination, be it in a clinic or a hospital setting, holds great promise for deriving increased efficiencies in a manner that helps curb overall healthcare costs.

By expediting discharge and coordinating the time of busy professionals around shared communication functions for which their participation is needed (for example, allowing nurses to resume their nursing-care duties while residents are engaging in training processes), Doug reports improved efficiency outcomes. "When patients are medically ready to go home, we should get them home and not delay the discharge because of inefficient practices. Patients are better off at home. They want to be at home. It has been hard to shift this paradigm. We are so used to providing care for the person in front of us that it is difficult to remember that delayed discharges are costly to everyone, including the next patient, who is in the Emergency Department waiting for the bed. We don't want to compromise care, but when people are ready to leave, we want to get them into the place where they need to be. By tracking the data and adjusting processes, we are making discharge economically more efficient and improving the quality of the experience for patients who are ready to go home or who are waiting to get a bed."

To fully monetize the impact of encouraging lean thinking at UCLA, Doug offers insights into a $10 million annual savings achieved by a small team of UCLA professionals. According to Doug, a group of UCLA Health System operating room implant coordinators spent two years working on ways to reduce surgical-care expenditures. Operating room implant coordinators Jeff Rausch and Dennis Alfelor at Ronald Reagan UCLA Medical Center, Brian Sharkey at Santa Monica–UCLA Medical Center and Orthopaedic Hospital, and Craig Ross at Jules Stein Eye Institute developed processes that account more effectively for utilization and costs related to implants placed in procedures such as orthopedic, spine, cardiac, and eye surgeries. Doug shares, "At UCLA, we treat some of the most complex, highly acute patients in the nation, and we routinely use a high volume of very expensive implants. Prior to developing a team of operating room implant coordinators, we didn't have a consistent way to account or bill for these surgical implants. This team interfaced with all the stakeholders involved in surgical implantation and developed consistent processes for buying, tracking, and billing for devices. The efforts of the team resulted in $10 million in saved revenue in the first year alone."

The Operating Room Implant Coordination Team is a small part of a systemwide initiative to control supply costs. That initiative is overseen by a Supply Cost Steering Committee and a Value Analysis Team. Doug sums up efforts like expedited patient discharges or changes in the surgical implant tracking process by noting, "It is everyone's job to increase efficiency and cost effectiveness at UCLA. By doing so, we can serve more patients and improve more lives." Beyond profitability, efficiency management allows business leaders to be better stewards of their resources, thus allowing them to serve larger customer groups and sustain their long-term viability. Of course, quality guru Peter Drucker acknowledges that leaders must constantly be looking for ways to improve the efficiency of only those offerings that are worthy of being improved: "Efficiency is doing better what is already being done." However, Peter Drucker warns, "There is nothing so useless as doing efficiently that which should not be done at all." The art of efficiency management is deciding which processes are necessary, eliminating those that are not, and streamlining the remainder to eliminate waste and maximize value.

YOUR DIAGNOSTIC CHECKUP

- How would you best describe the reimbursement model involved in your business—"fee for service," "pay for performance," or a combination of the two? How would you think about quality and efficiency differently if your reimbursement model shifted?

- Consider asking all your direct reports how they assess quality and efficiency in their areas of influence. Follow up by asking, "How do you know?"

- How comprehensive is your performance management dashboard? Are you managing at the macro level, the detail level, or both?

- Are you utilizing "lean thinking" efficiency approaches? If not, what alternative strategies do you have in place to revise processes and standardize operations? Do you have cost steering committees and value analysis teams operating in your company?

QUALITY AND EQUITY

In most businesses, increased quality can be associated with a higher price, so that customers who can afford a lot more quality than others can get it. However, healthcare (like justice) must be blind to the economic status of the person requiring service. This is particularly true at UCLA, where the mandate for all-inclusive care is derived from both federal and state objectives. As a result, UCLA differs from hospitals that specialize in areas of care that draw larger reimbursements or from healthcare systems that fail to offer services that bring lower compensation. UCLA is not a healthcare provider that attempts to attract a higher-paying insured clientele by offering unique services such as cooking classes or health-oriented retail shops. UCLA's mission requires that it offer a broad scope of services to patients with varied levels of financial resources.

From an Emergency Department perspective, Dr. Mark Morocco notes, "What makes UCLA really special at the elite end of medical care is the people who staff this place. We are blessed in part by design and in part by serendipity. People like living in California, where the weather is good, but we also have people who understand the equal importance of every patient. I have never worked anyplace else that has the same level of excellence among the staff members, and by that I mean not just technical excellence, but also moral and personality-based compassion for each individual. My colleagues and team members at UCLA understand that what we do is a privilege. When a woman brings our team members her newborn baby, hands that baby to us hot to the touch, and says, 'Here is my child, my whole world; help me,' that's a privilege." Dr. Morocco suggests that there is no amount of money or anything else that a person could offer that could be more valuable than the trust that is offered to him—an offer that occurs hundreds of times every day in the Emergency Department and through out the UCLA Health System. Rather than feeling that customers should feel privileged to be treated at one of the premier facilities in the world, Dr. Morocco identifies humility and gratitude as essential characteristics needed to deliver care that equitably respects each patient. Strong business leaders look for equitable service delivery that demonstrates respect and gratitude to the customers who support them.

Dr. David Feinberg, CEO, suggests that the test of "equity" is ultimately the perception of those who are served. Do people feel that they are afforded the same level of respect, dignity, and high-quality care as someone with greater means or notoriety? Dr. Feinberg notes, "We have high-profile celebrities in our hospital on a regular basis. After an emergency room visit of one of those celebrities, I received two letters that essentially said, 'I was in the ER when the celebrity was brought into UCLA, and I felt that the entire team was focused on me, my care, and my family.'" Dr. Feinberg reflects that those two letters are very typical of the praise he hears from patients. They also reflect his expectation that staff members at UCLA care in a way such that "patients know they are treated to the highest-quality healthcare in a dignified, private, and equitable way. If we accomplish that with the next patient, they leave here as our ambassador. They will tell their friends, 'You never want to get cancer, but if you do, UCLA is the place you will want to go.'"

An example of one such "ambassador" for UCLA's equitable treatment is Donna Smith. Donna's account is based on her involvement in the care of a coworker named Jing Li. According to Donna, "Jing is Chinese, and her English is not very good. She kept telling me, 'I feel dizzy. Something hurts behind my ear, and it hurts when I chew.' So I took her to the dentist, and he said that there was nothing wrong with her teeth." Donna indicated that Jing's condition worsened, and that her excruciating pain affected her ability to work. It also prompted Jing's involvement in a pain management program. During the course of her ongoing medical care, an X-ray showed that Jing had a sizable tumor. She was being treated at another hospital, but her condition warranted a transfer to receive advanced care at UCLA. According to Donna, "Jing's transfer was denied by her insurance company. Jing knew about the quality of care provided at UCLA and wanted to be cared for there. UCLA agreed to take Jing despite the insurance denial and despite the uncertainty of whether it would ever be paid. UCLA's doctors knew how badly Jing needed their expertise." Donna continues, "The hospital Jing was in was in a bind, as it could not release her because of the liabilities it would incur, so Jing signed out of that hospital, and I put her in my car and took her to UCLA. As I was driving Jing to UCLA, she was vomiting out the window, but once I got her to UCLA, I knew she was in great hands, and the entire staff from triage to discharge cared for her like she was a VIP. Jing got the top doctor to do her brain surgery. She is back working and well because UCLA did the right thing for the right reasons." Donna's conclusion may be the best definition of equitable care, and it echoes the Agency for Healthcare Research and Quality (AHRQ) definition outlined in Chapter 6 —"doing the right thing for the right reason"—without considering extraneous factors.

As with many issues associated with quality, the subjective nature of "equity" can often create controversy. Such was the case at UCLA in 2008 when reports surfaced concerning world-renowned liver transplant surgeon Dr. Ronald Busuttil. Dr. Busuttil was the subject of media criticism for having performed transplants on four Japanese gang figures, including a Japanese gang boss. The news reports indicated that during the four years (2000 to 2004) in which these controversial surgeries were performed, "several hundred area patients died while awaiting transplants." Most of these reports failed to acknowledge that all UCLA transplant candidates go through a careful screening process involving committees of professionals who evaluate the medical appropriateness of patients being listed for transplant. More important, the media typically did not mention that Dr. Busuttil's transplants were performed under the stringent guidelines set forth by the United Network for Organ Sharing, or UNOS. The UNOS criteria ensure that transplant decisions are based on the severity of a patient's need and the ability of a recipient to be a good steward of the organ. The media reports implied that these four patients were "less worthy" of transplantation than those for whom a liver had not been secured, in essence suggesting that Dr. Busuttil should not have performed the transplant surgeries "equitably" based on individual treatment needs, but instead should have given preference based on country of origin or past legal status. The issue of "country of origin" is already factored into the UNOS guidelines, as noncitizens are allowed to receive a small proportion of organs (approximately 5 percent) to ensure that foreign-born residents continue to support organ donations (in southern California, for example, 20 percent of donors are foreign born). As for the issue of the "legal status" of the recipient, Dr. Gerald Levey, former vice chancellor of medical sciences and dean of the David Geffen School of Medicine at UCLA, said it best in an op-ed article for the *Los Angeles Times*, "Those who argue that criminals should not get transplants are on shaky ethical ground. Do we want to force caregivers to make a life-or-death decision based on whether a patient is a 'good' or 'bad' person? Dr. Ronald Busuttil's program has led to transplants for nearly 5,000 individuals, rich and poor alike. Without his team's expertise, they would have died. . . . But what a tragedy if, because of rumor, suspicion and a lack of understanding about the organ allocation process, people choose not to donate a liver—a consequence that would be seriously detrimental for everyone waiting for these lifesaving organs." Contrary to the meritless media-generated controversy, Dr. Busuttil's transplant practices continue at the highest levels of moral, legal, and professional integrity.

Dr. Juan Alejos, medical director of the Pediatric Heart Transplant/Cardiomyopathy Program and clinical professor of pediatric cardiology, suggests that in addition to all the oversight processes and guidelines on equitable organ distribution, physicians augment the assessment of organ utilization. According to Dr. Alejos, "Any time your phone goes off in the middle of the night or you get paged, you could be changing someone's life. You get that heart offer. There is no warning, and you've got to make a decision at that moment, 'Is that the right heart for this patient?' You make a calculated guess. This heart may be coming from Florida; that may be eight hours away, and I think my patient at home right now is better off waiting for a heart that is closer than taking a heart that is going to be affected by travel time. When you reject the offer, you pray that another heart will come along. Sometimes another heart offer isn't received, and your patient decompensates and dies. It's an assessment that can't be taken lightly."

Dr. Alejos further notes that issues of fairness go beyond those awaiting an organ. "I talk to the parents of potential recipients, and I tell them that I have two very distinct jobs. I have my work to make sure that their child gets the very best possible care she can receive. My other job is to be an advocate for the donor. I must make sure that the heart we are offered goes to the very best possible family. That heart is an incredible gift. So when I begin to ask my potential recipient's family questions about who is going to give the child medications and who is going to drive her to appointments, they understand my obligation. It is not because I want to be nosy or to deny them an organ, but I must also protect this donor. I know that if the recipient does not take care of the heart, it is not fair to either the donor or the person who didn't get the heart because the wrong recipient received it."

Unlike a heart donation, which occurs upon the death of another person (a cadaveric donor), issues of fairness to living donors are often poignantly entangled when someone offers an organ to someone in need. Suzanne McGuire, RN, kidney transplant living donor coordinator, notes, "We work very hard to make sure that people who want to offer the gift of an organ fully understand the impact of that decision. Most of our living donors and recipients work through this process together very well. Many of them are pairs in some way, such as husband and wife. There are a few best friends, but there are a lot of spouses and a lot of parents and children, with either the child donating to the parent or vice versa. Given the strength of many of these relationships, organ donation is a foregone conclusion. By contrast, the dynamics can be pretty profound when someone makes a cavalier statement at a party like, 'I'll help you. I'll give you a kidney.' There are recipients who really get their hopes up and then are devastated when the donor backs out. That tends to happen more with an acquaintance than it does with someone that they are close to."

Suzanne notes that when a prospective donor is close to a recipient and then withdraws his offer, it can be a very difficult time for all parties. "There have been cases where the prospective donors felt mistreated by the family because the family felt that the donor should have gone through with the process. Sometimes we know the reasons why donors can't follow through, and sometimes they can't share that with us. It doesn't matter what the reason is; if they don't want to proceed, our job is to back them." For the entire system of living donations to work, donors must be medically compatible and psychologically able to give consent freely. It is only fair that UCLA helps donors work through this most personal decision. While fairness is ultimately a subjective variable that is determined by the consumer, business decisions must factor equity of access and the needs of diverse stakeholders into their calculations of quality.

CUTTING-EDGE TECHNOLOGIES AND PRODUCTS

Unless you are an advanced scientist, a highly specialized treatment provider, or a healthcare administrator, it is difficult for you to appreciate the state-of-the-art technology that is available at UCLA, some of which has been created by scientists at UCLA (more on this in Chapter 8), much of which has been purchased at great expense, and still other components that are available only to "the best of he best." Dr. Edward R. B. McCabe, former physician-in-chief, Mattel Children's Hospital UCLA, points out, "Given that we are the largest solid organ transplant program for children and adults, meaning hearts, lungs, livers, liver/small bowel, and everything but bone marrow transplantation, we are given access to the latest technologies and immunosuppressive molecules from the drug companies. Those cutting-edge products enable us to provide outcomes that are better than most, and for some organs better than anyone else. We gain access to the most innovative technology, in part, because of the volume of patients we treat in those areas and because of the quality of the outcomes that we traditionally achieve." Dr. McCabe's point demonstrates the symbiosis between technology and quality. Advanced technology without competent talent to fully deploy it is a misspent resource. On the other hand, having talented people without cutting-edge technology denies these people the opportunity to reach their fullest potential. Clearly, the leadership at UCLA has the task of securing technology that attracts and retains the best talent. In turn, that talent creates and attracts technology that allows UCLA to be the "best today and better tomorrow."

As an example of this synergy between human talent and technology, renowned UCLA brain surgeon Dr. Nestor Gonzalez highlights the advantages that patients derive from UCLA's advanced surgical suites. "The spaciousness of the design accommodates our large teams of specialists and our absolutely modern equipment, things like highly advanced microscopes and endoscopes. I would not be able to resect a malformation in such delicate places without these visual tools. My surgeries involve more than my hands. They require my eyes being aided by very powerful instruments. In addition, our operating rooms have a very special way to engage the entire team, even those who can't necessarily look into a microscope during the procedure. To achieve their involvement, we have large screens upon which everyone can see what I'm doing. I think those screens are important because they allow everyone to participate in and understand what is going on. The nurses are engaged in my process, even if they don't participate in all the technical aspects of the surgery. Finally, if I need anything in the way of equipment and instruments, they are available for me. When you have the best talent equipped with the best technology, you have extraordinary surgical outcomes." Often quality reflects a leader's investment in finding extraordinary talent and providing that talent with technology that enables those talented people to collaborate with their peers and grow their abilities further.

Dr. Gerald Levey, who served as vice chancellor, Medical Sciences, and dean of the David Geffen School of Medicine from 1994 to 2010, knows the responsibility for stewardship of UCLA's vast human and scientific resources. Dr. Levey was largely responsible for securing funding to make the Ronald Reagan UCLA Medical Center possible and solidifying a $200 million endowment from David Geffen on behalf of the medical school. Dr. Levey looks through the lens of history to examine the relationship among talent, technology, and quality. "Very few medical schools took off as rapidly as UCLA. I think that over the years, the culture developed around a commitment to science, teaching, and attracting the best staff members and the best students. We maintained that commitment as we recruited and kept the best scientists and physicians we could find. Our first hospital exemplified a commitment to quality because when it opened in 1955, it quickly became known as a place where you received the best of care and where the staff was very much committed to your personal satisfaction. I think that when that culture becomes ingrained during the first 10, 15, or 20 years of an institution's life, it can last a lifetime."

While maintaining patient-care quality, Dr. Levey notes, "We began to suffer based on challenges posed by our physical plant. The original hospital was built in an era when you could have hallways that were 75 yards long. You can't do that anymore. Medicine is too intense, and you need to be closer to observe and create efficient care delivery."

In support of his drive to make the new hospital a reality, Dr. Levey shares, "Given our run-down, damaged building, we needed to elevate our environment to match our talent. So we conducted focus groups before the new hospital was constructed to determine what patients, families, nurses, and others who work in the hospital environment wanted in the new building. We asked, and they answered uniformly. Whether it was a patient, an orderly, or a physician, everyone wanted a setting that reflected life and vitality. They wanted a sense of spaciousness, and they wanted families to be able to sleep in the patients' rooms with them. People wanted better food and better food delivery. When we met with the great architect I. M. Pei and told him that we wanted a sense of space and a sense of smallness at the same time, and we wanted people to know that they were in southern California from the light that streamed into the building, he brought all that together alongside some of the world's most amazing technology."

Dr. Levey is quick to point out that great leaders create organizations in which talent is prized and then seek to secure technological resources to allow that talent to flourish. Using his decision to hire CEO Dr. Feinberg as an example, Dr. Levey suggests that selecting the best talent not only reflects well on those who make the selection, but also establishes the sustainability of quality and excellence. "I love people who are young, extremely bright, and extraordinarily talented. My mentor in Pittsburgh, Dr. Thomas Detre, always said that he considered himself a talent scout. I think that is the job of leadership: to scout for and support talent. Thanks to the talents of Dr. David Feinberg and his senior leadership team, I have left a legacy and set up the UCLA Health System to continue its greatness for decades to come." Dr. Levey's comments suggest that the greatest leadership talent is the ability to identify, develop, and secure resources that support the talent of others.

YOUR DIAGNOSTIC CHECKUP

Even if you are in a business in which people can experience different levels of quality based on how much they are able to pay, how do you create an environment in which some customers don't feel that they are receiving inferior product or service quality?

- What inequities exist in access to quality in your business? Can you or should you work to minimize them?
- What is the balance between your talent and your technology? Which is stronger? Which needs to be augmented?
- What do you do as a leader to take care of technology resources and to be a "talent scout"?

Dr. Feinberg sums up UCLA's constant journey to "make the best better" in this way: "We hold people's lives in our hands, and with that privilege comes a great responsibility. That responsibility means that no matter how good we are today, it isn't good enough. Everything we do must be of the highest quality, and we have to be in a relentless pursuit of constant quality assessment and enhancement. I am pleased with where we are today. We have a bedrock foundation of excellence in research, medical education, and patient care that helps this all move forward. However, each day I think about one thing: what can I do as a leader to make sure that our quality of care is the best it possibly can be—you guessed it—for our next patient?"

In the next two chapters, we will examine how Dr. Feinberg's vision for dramatically changing healthcare delivery (minimizing the need for hospital care) and incrementally improving the experience for the "next patient" is being realized at UCLA. Those two chapters will address our fourth leadership principle, "create the future."

Prescriptive Summary

▸ Ask your people to offer subjective assessments of the quality that they provide. Then ask them to support those assessments through the follow-up question, "How do you know?"

▸ Measure, measure, measure!

▸ Create dashboards for your metrics (manage via global and detail dashboards).

▸ Infuse lean thinking.

▸ Where possible, create equitable service delivery.

▸ Consider the impact of your decisions, not only on the customer in front of you, but also on stakeholders who are less visible.

▸ Be a talent scout.

▸ Source your talent through technology.

▸ Build a legacy through talent acquisition and the steward-ship of resources. Create the quality experience for your most important customer—the *next one.*

CREATE
THE
FUTURE

CHAPTER 8

High-Value Innovation— Leveraging the Risk of Excellence

> *Innovation distinguishes between leaders and followers.*
> —STEVE JOBS

The battlefield of business competition is littered with the remnants of once-great companies that failed to adapt or innovate. For example, many of the companies profiled in Tom Peters and Robert Waterman's classic book *In Search of Excellence* were no longer viewed as front runners in their industry as early as two years following the book's release, and some had closed their doors. In fact, in a November 1984 issue of *BusinessWeek* magazine titled "Oops. Who's Excellent Now?" it was observed that of the 43 "excellent" companies surveyed by Peters and Waterman, approximately one-third had experienced financial difficulties. Notable among these were businesses such as Atari, Data General, DEC, Lanier, and Wang Labs. Some of these once-revered brand names became complacent and produced a fairly unimaginative and narrow array of products. By contrast, other "excellent" companies maintained their premier position in the marketplace by both maintaining product quality in their core offerings and taking the risks necessary to position themselves for excellence in the future. In the preceding two chapters, I examined how the leaders at UCLA Health System addressed product excellence in the delivery of day-to-day healthcare quality.

This chapter will look at cutting-edge research at UCLA, which consistently generates breakthrough knowledge, diagnostic innovations, and treatment technologies. It reflects the spirit of innovation presented in one of Stephen Covey's *7 Habits of Highly Effective People*, namely, "beginning with the end in mind." This is the type of purposeful innovation that starts with the question, "If I could accomplish anything, what would it be?" Once a destination has been defined, this approach reflects a tireless journey toward that goal.

A historical example of this aggressive form of innovation was President Kennedy's declaration in 1961 that the United States would be the first to put a man on the moon. While the technology necessary to achieve this outcome was rudimentary at best, the declaration of the objective led to innovative advances that realized the objective some eight years later.

In this chapter, you will see examples of UCLA doctors and researchers who clearly had an "end in mind" when it came to a treatment breakthrough or some form of technology that would change the future of medicine. The journeys of these researchers through setbacks and successes are illustrative of the outcome-based vision that is critical to dramatic change. Dr. David Feinberg, CEO of UCLA Hospital System, notes, "In order for our doctors and researchers to produce revolutionary results, we must have a healthy risk tolerance, particularly when it comes to inventing the new technology and implementing it. It is more entrepreneur-like, and our organization has to be able to respond with an entrepreneurial spirit." Dr. Feinberg adds, "We experience risk taking on two different levels. There is the risk necessary from the academic research perspective, and at some level that risk is funded by grants and the ability to compete for those grants and donations. Our greater risk as a hospital system comes with regard to funding new treatment interventions for clinical care because our margins are too small to set up endless laboratories to test new clinical interventions. We have to make difficult decisions that allow us to make the best use of our resources in areas that are most likely to revolutionize patient care.'"

Whether one is dealing with personal finance or the development of corporate strategy, it is important to determine one's risk tolerance and set timeline objectives. A balanced portfolio of higher-risk/higher-return and lower-risk/lower-return options should be built into your strategic innovation plan. The higher-risk elements can be viewed as "revolutionary" change, and the lower-risk approaches as more "evolutionary" growth.

While this chapter will look at the type of revolutionary research-based breakthroughs that are common in academic medicine and, for that matter, are critical to gaining substantial advantages in business, the next chapter will focus on a more evolutionary process. Specifically, in Chapter 9, I will examine processes, programs, and initiatives championed by UCLA staff members that have improved on the best practices of other businesses or that have piloted incremental approaches to change.

It's been said that it is easier to attain greatness than to maintain it. In these two chapters, I offer key insights from UCLA on achieving sustainable excellence through pure innovation, imitation, and even relevant modification.

MISSION POSSIBLE

If you look at the mission statements of most businesses, you'll seldom find references to the future. Mission statements often talk about being the "best" at some type of service for some target audience. But at UCLA, future innovation is mission-centric. Dr. Edward McCabe, former physician-in-chief, Mattel Children's Hospital UCLA, notes, "One of the important things about UCLA departments in general, but pediatrics in particular, is that we are in the top 10 nationally when it comes to receiving National Institutes of Health (NIH) research dollars. We are an outstanding research institution, and our research in pediatrics is top-notch. We also know that we can't simply be an 'ivory tower' research institution. We need to translate that basic science research into improved healthcare. So we see our job in the Department of Pediatrics and the Mattel Children's Hospital UCLA as being to improve the health of today's and tomorrow's children. That is our mission. We want to take the best possible care of the child who walks into our front door today, but we also have a mission to improve the quality of care for the future through research and education." One of the key words in Dr. McCabe's comments is "translate." Whether it is medicine or business, the objective of innovation should be to translate knowledge into practical solutions that serve the current and future needs of customers.

BIG VISION/BIGGER IMPACT

At the core of high-impact innovation is often the question "What if?" What if we were to apply this knowledge in a different context to address a problem other than the one to which the knowledge was originally applied? Dr. Michael Phelps, chair of UCLA's Department of Nuclear Medicine, faced one of these "what-if" scenarios. Essentially, he asked, "What if we could better understand the health or pathology of various human cells not by looking at anatomical changes (size or shape), but by looking at how those cells consume energy?" That question, which offered the prospect that cellular metabolic changes could be imaged in a helpful way, led UCLA scientists Dr. Michael Phelps and Dr. Edward Hoffman to invent PET (positron emission tomography) scanning and produce the first PET scanner. According to Dr. Johannes Czernin, professor, Molecular and Medical Pharmacology, and director, Nuclear Medicine, at UCLA, "At that time, no one else had the PET. It was a completely novel system because it departed from the idea that one looks at various disease processes anatomically and instead changed the perspective to look at disease from a metabolic point of view. How much glucose does this mass consume or how many amino acids does this tumor eat? What is the lipid synthesis pathway that we can see in tumors? The reason why this is important is that changes in the metabolic pathway created by therapy are much more sensitive markers of responses than just looking at the size criteria. The concept was really completely unknown at that point."

While these breakthrough studies of PET scanning were important, the technology's full potential began to be realized as research focused on the diagnostic advantages of PET. Dr. Czernin notes, "The great hope for the technology was always that it would offer information about cellular changes long before we could detect a medical problem through traditional anatomical imaging. You need a lot of time before you can see a tumor form, so the idea was that metabolic changes would precede the anatomic level of abnormality. One was looking for changes in cellular metabolism that could be detected early and that would be very sensitive to treatment changes, such as the introduction or termination of chemotherapy."

Thanks to ongoing research at UCLA, the applications of PET scanning technology spread to cardiovascular viability, the treatment of pediatric epilepsy, and improved diagnosis of Alzheimer's and Parkinson's diseases. Researchers used PET to determine whether poorly functioning heart tissue would recover from bypass surgery, thus averting the need for unnecessary heart transplants. The work on PET brain imaging helped pediatric specialists identify seizure-producing areas of the brain, isolate those areas for removal, and subsequently offer many children seizure-free lives.

Not only did Dr. Phelps's and Dr. Hoffman's "what-if" challenge produce a revolutionary breakthrough, but they, like most great innovators, solicited the ideas and skills of colleagues from diverse backgrounds to help them expand the application of this technology, and in the process, UCLA became the center of excellence in PET scan research. Much of the early work on PET scanning came through a wide variety of departments at UCLA. In the early 1990s, computational capabilities were improved through UCLA physicist Dr. Magnus Dahlbom. Dr. Dahlbom developed protocols that allowed him to acquire whole-body PET images. Those protocols reflect the widening interdisciplinary approach to knowledge acquisition, as Dahlbom analyzed enormous amounts of data that depended on high-level computational capabilities and mathematics. Once whole-body imaging was available, PET scans were used in oncology to examine tissue throughout the body.

PET scanning began to give important information about tumor behavior well before structural changes could be detected. PET scanning is now also used to measure the effectiveness of chemotherapy treatment and to determine whether chemotherapy should be discontinued in favor of alternative approaches, such as surgery or radiation.

The journey of the PET scan at UCLA offers many teachable lessons for business innovation. First, examine the current technologies or benchmarks in your industry. Conceptualize a desired outcome and ask "what would happen if" you applied unrelated existing technologies to achieve your goal. In the case of Drs. Phelps and Hoffman, the outcome was to use cellular metabolism to gain early indicators of cellular pathology. Methodologically, they then developed the technology or innovations to make that outcome possible. A final teachable lesson is to solicit the talents of colleagues from diverse backgrounds to help you refine the accuracy of your technology or expand its applications.

PET scan breakthroughs at UCLA are typical of countless newsworthy advances by UCLA researchers each and every week. In fact, synopses of media interest in UCLA innovations are reported on a weekly basis (www.uclahealth.org) and normally list 20 to 30 UCLA research findings that have captured media attention.

These articles include such things as "Commercials Are the Culprit in TV-Obesity Link," "Mediterranean Diet May Help Prevent Dementia, Study Says," and "Visual Processing Plays Role in Body Dysmorphic Disorder." While 20 to 30 UCLA research findings are found newsworthy in any given week, one can only speculate on how many medical breakthroughs occur at UCLA that fly beneath the radar of media interest or understanding.

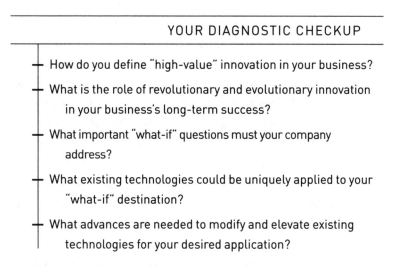

YOUR DIAGNOSTIC CHECKUP

- How do you define "high-value" innovation in your business?
- What is the role of revolutionary and evolutionary innovation in your business's long-term success?
- What important "what-if" questions must your company address?
- What existing technologies could be uniquely applied to your "what-if" destination?
- What advances are needed to modify and elevate existing technologies for your desired application?

DEFINE THE TECHNOLOGY NEEDED

While PET scan technology is a tool that interfaces directly with patients (customers), some forms of technology are developed to deal with the needs of the doctor (or service provider). Dr. Neil Martin, chair of Neurosurgery at UCLA, notes that in his department, innovation not only is mission-centric, but requires a proactive tools development mindset. "The mission for UCLA neurosurgery is to invent the future of neurosurgery. When we see problems, we are looking for solutions. We are not waiting for someone else to solve the problems. We were probably one of the first places in the country to have the clinical ability to look at all of a patient's images and medical data on our cell phones. We developed that right here. We ultimately commercialized it, and it was acquired by another company."

Dr. Martin relates that the technology was pioneered because neurosurgeons have to make immediate triage treatment decisions around the clock. "You have to decide for someone with a brain hemorrhage: does she go to the operating room immediately, do we monitor her with CT scans to see if the problem is getting worse, does she go to the ICU because it's not something we can operate on, or is it so bad that all hope is lost? No radiologist can tell you the answers to those questions from hearing a description of the scan. You have to see it for yourself. An X-ray is worth a million radiology words. Some doctors have access to that level of imaging on their home computers, but before the cell phone technology we pioneered, if you were at Dodger Stadium and you got paged about a patient with a brain hemorrhage, you'd say good-bye to your family, get in the car, and drive through LA traffic to come look at the scan. That could take 45 minutes." Dr. Martin continues about how the UCLA Neurosurgery Department drove the development of mobile technologies to benefit all involved. "In the old days, while you were heading to the hospital, other professionals were waiting for you before they could initiate the right course of action. So what you would have said on the phone was, 'I will come to look at the scan. Wait until I get there.' Today, with the information available on your cell phone, you ask your team to give you a minute. You dial in and look at the scan and say, 'This is not an operative case. Have the patient admitted to the ICU; call Dr. Vespa, the neuro-intensive care specialist, and I will see the patient in a few hours.' Or, 'This is an emergency operation. Call the OR, tell the anesthesiologist, get the room ready, and I will meet you in the operating room.' So instead of 30 to 40 minutes of wasted time, the ball is rolling. You are already moving in the right direction. In a critical case, every minute that goes by, brain cells are dying, and we can now make a difference."

Rather than waiting for a medical IT firm to provide the software, Dr. Martin shared, "We turned to a team of great programmers who had been extracting information from the hospital systems in support of our head trauma and stroke research for almost a decade. I had a Palm Pilot, and I told the guys that I wanted this imaging information on that portable device. Two months later, they were showing me X-rays on the Palm Pilot. Granted, those first attempts were pretty grainy, but they were real CT scans of the head. Within a year, we had high-quality images on mobile phones. As we started getting further and further into this process, we found that there was already technology available that could revolutionize how we administer medicine; it just needed to be adapted to what we do." Dr. Martin later led a research study that demonstrated that the mobile phone images were equal in quality and readability to traditionally delivered images.

To provide further evidence for the importance of adapting existing technology, Dr. Martin talks about a robot used by the neuro-intensivist Dr. Paul Vespa, FCCM. "We are the first ICU in the world to have a robot for patient surveillance, patient monitoring, and face-to-face discussions. The robot was being advertised as a way for families and doctors to see patients in nursing homes, where doctors seldom go. In the advertisements, one doctor was talking about making his rounds in one of the three hospitals where he went as a surgeon, but nobody was talking about it in an ICU at that point. We saw the robot and said that this was what we needed for immediate access to our patients."

Dr. Martin continues, "In a medical crisis, when Dr. Vespa is in his office, he can now drive the robot at Santa Monica because Santa Monica doesn't have a neuro-critical-care specialist like him. He is also providing contract services to a local community hospital that is 40 miles away and doing the same sort of thing. Part of our job in a place like UCLA is obviously to heal people, and the key part of that is treating the patient right and making sure that he is satisfied. Rather than using technology to replace personalized care, Dr. Vespa's robot is used to extend his specialized care in a remarkably personal way. It is face to face. Patients would rather talk to their own doctor through the robot than talk to a doctor whom they don't know in person. The face-to-face thing is key because when the patient locks eyes with Dr. Vespa through the robot, she forgets that she is talking to a robot. She is just talking to her doctor. It is anthropomorphic. The robot walks up to you. Its head turns and moves up and down. I know some people might say that this is just another way in which doctors are going to remove themselves from interacting with patients—that they are going to insert another technology layer. That is totally opposite from the way we use it. We still make rounds every day, and we still go see the patients. But when a patient is crashing at 2:00 a.m., it is not a phone call. It is a world-class doctor seeing everything he or she can right from the bedside."

CEO Dr. David Feinberg notes that the decision to purchase the robot was a matter of using technology for connectivity and leveraging high-quality patient care while taking a step into the future. "Dr. Vespa used to get called all night long. So he was taking care of 26 patients, seven days a week, 24 hours every day, even when he was away. Now, with the robot (at home or on the road), he has a laptop with a joystick, and he drives the robot around into the rooms and you see his face on the screen. He checks on all of his patients before he goes to bed. This means that he doesn't get called as frequently during the night. His wife said that the robot saved his marriage." According to Dr. Feinberg, the connectivity of the robot to the patients is reflected in the fact that as the robot is moving from patient room to patient room, Dr. Vespa might drive the robot past a room because the patient doesn't require him to check in. "In those cases, you will often see family members come up to the robot and say, 'Dr. Vespa, aren't you going to check on us tonight?' They're talking to a robot. And he'll say, 'Oh, your husband is okay, but let me come take a look.' It's technology leveraging specialized connectivity—getting the right doctor or the right nurse to the right patient at the right time with the right information. That's all it is; it's people. When you think about surgeons, they use their hands once in a while, but most of the time doctors are using their brain to make decisions. We need to use technology to provide intelligent people with information and get them to the right place. Medicine is about buying brainpower. Should a surgeon operate or not? What medicines are you taking? What's wrong with you? If something happened to my brain, I would want Dr. Vespa taking care of me. The robot extends his scope and connects with more of his patients."

Both the mobile phone imaging technology discussed by Dr. Neil Martin and Dr. Vespa's robot are examples of service providers looking for ways to maximize the use of their knowledge to revolutionize efficient service delivery. How much are you driving technology or applying existing technologies to increase your connectivity with your customers?

IT DOES TAKE A VILLAGE

Most of the significant breakthroughs at UCLA are the result of collaborative partnerships. To some degree, this concept has already been demonstrated by the multidisciplinary research on the PET scan and Dr. Martin's partnership with IT professionals to achieve the needed technological advances. However, Dr. Jean DeKernion, chair of the Department of Urology, articulates the critical nature of interdisciplinary team approaches to innovation most succinctly: "You have to understand that progress in many things in medicine cannot be accomplished by one specialty. Cancer is one example. Somebody who is studying the genetics of cancer in a lab may not have a full understanding of how to apply that knowledge in a clinical setting or may not be aware of the real problems that patients experience. The key to innovation in cancer, then, is to bring people together so that you can identify the important questions, try to answer those questions, and bring possible answers back to the patient."

Dr. DeKernion has been instrumental in creating a number of treatment programs in areas such as prostate, kidney, and bladder cancer that were the result of bringing the right people together. Dr. DeKernion shares, "You often need to knit together many players who share your vision for integrated innovation. In the case of our Institute of Urologic Oncology, we sought a partnership with the Jonsson Cancer Center, which was very helpful in identifying people and helping with funding. You need faculty partners like Dr. Arie Belldegrun, who helped me champion the idea to the dean of the Medical School at the time, Dr. Gerald Levey. Dr. Levey shared our vision and provided the initial funding from the dean's office. You need partners in the community, like former patients, to help you provide seed money to elevate research to the point where major grants can be secured. For us, all of these efforts led to our Institute of Urologic Oncology. That institute connects surgeons, medical oncologists, radiotherapists, radiologists, pathologists, molecular imagining people, statisticians, outcomes specialists, and quality of life researchers here at UCLA."

Dr. DeKernion also notes that he is eager to support enthusiastic UCLA physicians who partner with professionals outside of UCLA, such as Dr. Jeff Veale. Dr. Veale was the first physician in the West to perform a kidney chain transplant and to encourage donor-centric improvements in the kidney chain process. Dr. Veale explains, "Say you want to give a kidney to your mother, who is on dialysis, but your kidney donation would be incompatible with your mom. Maybe she is an A blood type and you are a B blood type. In the past, your mom would have had to stay on dialysis potentially for years until she received a deceased donor kidney. Now, suppose I am in the same situation with my mom, but I have an A blood type and my mom has a B blood type. With this innovative program, you and I can swap kidneys for our parents. I could give a kidney to your mom, and you could give a kidney to my mom. We performed our first chain transplantation in July 2008 here at UCLA, and my contribution was to help donors recover in their nearby hospital and not have to travel to the location of the transplant. To that end, I thought it would be a good idea to ship the donor kidney, and for the first time we sent a living donor kidney unaccompanied on a commercial airline, just in a box of ice. Now I am quite proud that exchanges and chains are becoming quite common around the country, and that essentially all kidneys are being shipped to the other recipient rather than having the donor traveling to the other city or the recipient's hospital."

As a result of these collaborations through the Urology Department at UCLA, breakthrough technologies are moving from basic research science to real-world clinical applications. Dr. DeKernion notes, "A simple example of how all this comes together is the collaboration we are doing with the UCLA School of Engineering. That collaboration is producing a tool that will detect bacteria in urine, tell a physician which type of bacteria are present, and offer guidance on what drug to give within about 20 minutes in the doctor's office. Currently, the process for making those determinations takes more than two days. This breakthrough was a matter of interdepartmental collaboration between our department and Biomedical Engineering. Strategic collaboration is a concept of innovation that is gaining wider acceptance. You have to facilitate working relationships for all the people who could possibly weigh in on a problem and try to get them to figure out how to best approach resolving that problem using their particular areas of specialty knowledge." Has this innovation approach of harnessing a diversity of knowledge gained traction and wide acceptance at your business?

YOUR DIAGNOSTIC CHECKUP

- How can you leverage the diversity of your organization to build on your breakthrough innovations and achieve a "center of excellence" for your specific area of innovation?
- What opportunities to merge technology-focused individuals (for example, IT or engineering) with basic or applied researchers exist in your organization?

┬ How are you using technologies to increase your connection
│ with your customers?

┬ How do you bring together all the people who could possibly
│ weigh in on a problem? How can you help them figure out
│ how best to resolve that problem using their particular
│ areas of specialty knowledge?

PERSISTENCE IS ELEMENTAL

Writing in *The Scientist* in 2005, David Morris notes, "'No pain, no gain' is an American modern mini-narrative. It compresses the story of a protagonist who understands that the road to achievement runs only through hardship." This is particularly clear in the path traveled by UCLA's Dennis Slamon. Dr. Slamon has been described both as a "hero" and as having a "murderous resolve." He has been played by Harry Connick, Jr., in the Lifetime movie *Living Proof* and has been the focus of Robert Bazell's book *HER-2: The Making of Herceptin, a Revolutionary Treatment for Breast Cancer*. Dr. Slamon is the director of Clinical/Translational Research and the director of the Revlon/UCLA Women's Cancer Research Program at the Jonsson Comprehensive Cancer Center. He is also a professor of medicine, chief of the Division of Hematology/Oncology, and executive vice chair for research for UCLA's Department of Medicine. Dr. Slamon also serves as director of the medical advisory board for the National Colorectal Cancer Research Alliance, a fund-raising organization that promotes advances in colorectal cancer.

Dr. Slamon went from relative obscurity as a cancer researcher to being one of the world's most respected oncologists as a result of a Homer-like odyssey that was rife with highly political medical battles, unruly egos of detractors, and a withdrawal of research funding. When a drug company terminated funding for his research, Dr. Slamon enlisted the aid of philanthropists such as Ronald Perelman and Lilly Tartikoff. His research then continued as a result of an initial donation from Perelman's Revlon charity and ongoing funds raised by the "Fire and Ice Ball" organized by Tartikoff. Ultimately, drug company research dollars resumed, and Dr. Slamon created the drug Herceptin to treat the HER-2 positive subtype (representing approximately 25 percent of cases) of breast cancer. By 2010, it was estimated that his breakthrough had resulted in saving well over 400,000 lives.

Dr. Slamon noted in an interview for standup2cancer.org that, "You go from the outside to the inside pretty quickly if you're fortunate enough to be involved in a success like Herceptin. So the fact that it worked so well in metastatic disease, and ultimately in early disease, means that a lot more people believe our ideas than when we started in 1986. The problem is, we needed the help back then. The drug could've been and should've been available to patients seven years before it was, and if it weren't for donor money, it would've been another five to seven years beyond that."

Dr. Slamon's unwillingness to give up despite a lack of funding speaks to his willingness to take a risk to achieve excellence and his appreciation that the best ideas aren't always easily accepted. Furthermore, he acknowledges that incremental change is often safer to embrace than revolutionary change, although safe bets often offer limited returns. According to Dr. Slamon, "The Revlon funding made all the difference in the world. Had we had to depend on federal funding, we'd never have been able to get it done. The process by which grants are submitted, reviewed, approved and funded is incredibly long, and it reduces ideas to lowest common denominator approaches. Approaches that are innovative frequently don't get funded."

The impact of Dr. Slamon's treatment breakthrough can be palpably felt from comments left by women on Web sites that chronicle the development of Herceptin. One reader writes, "As I watched this movie *Living Proof,* of course I cried, but I also learned new facts about how Herceptin was created, and it was amazing to watch the struggle Dr. Slamon went through to get this drug approved. I have the utmost respect for those brave women who helped with the clinical trials to get Herceptin FDA approved. I also look at the company Revlon in a new way. Just when Dr. Slamon was down and out and almost out of money, Revlon donated over 2 million dollars to help him continue his amazing work. . . . Without Herceptin I don't know where I would be today. If I was diagnosed 20 years earlier, what would my outcome have been? . . . When I was first diagnosed, the doctors asked if I wanted to participate in clinical trials, and I was like NO WAY! That would be just too scary for me. But without the brave people that do participate in clinical trials, we would be nowhere. So thank you to all who try to help these amazing doctors."

Another blogger notes, "I just finished watching *Living Proof* for the fourth time. The first three times were when it originally aired. I watched it three nights in a row. I was diagnosed with stage 2 HER-2 positive breast cancer in July 2005 when I was six months pregnant with my daughter. Shortly after my surgery, I found out that I was . . . HER-2 positive. I thought I was going to die. My doctor told me that I was lucky. Herceptin was approved only last month for use in treating my type of cancer. I can't tell you how blessed and lucky I feel. I had 52 Herceptin treatments along with chemo and radiation. I have been cancer free for three and a half years. This movie was so emotional for me to watch. I sat and cried several times and I feel so thankful for all the time and energy put forth to make this drug a reality for women like me." Herceptin use has now expanded beyond breast cancer into areas such as gastric cancer, where the hormone HER-2 is overexpressed in around 20 percent of all gastric cancer cases.

The story of Herceptin is only one in a sea of similar advances by UCLA researchers. In fact, Dr. Kathryn Atchison, vice provost, Intellectual Property and Industry Relations, and associate vice chancellor for research, UCLA professor, UCLA School of Dentistry and School of Public Health, notes, "We see such spectacular things here, whether it is the innovation of the nicotine patch for smoking cessation, brain coils for stroke patients, or technologies to create a portable dialysis belt-pack. My office, which helps UCLA researchers translate their innovations into usable consumer products, reflects growth income that is in the neighborhood of $22 million annually. We also have additional revenues to help with patent costs. For example, the School of Medicine alone received from this technology transfer mission almost $9 million that they were able to use in 2010."

In addition to the financial benefits of medical research innovation, Kat Fibiger, JD, UCLA copyright officer, indicates, "We have intellectual properties that may not result in a patent or a profit but that become commercial products. For example, Dr. Patricia Ganz, a pioneer who developed the concept of cancer survivorship care, created a video that deals with what to do once you have completed your cancer treatment. You are not really going back to being treated by your regular primary-care physician; you are in this interim stage where you are not 100 percent fine, and you may have lingering effects from either your chemotherapy or your radiation treatment. Dr. Ganz is not at all interested in profiting from the video, but she wants it responsibly licensed and distributed so that as many cancer survivors as possible can benefit from it. She has also worked with outside partners to develop treatment planning software that patients can download free of charge from the Web site www.JourneyForward.org. This type of breakthrough intellectual property is common at UCLA."

Whether research innovations produce profits, copyrights, or patents, UCLA and healthcare as a whole benefit from the perseverance of the UCLA research community. The "no pain, no gain" approach of individuals like Dr. Slamon and his Herceptin breakthrough will change the future for literally millions of cancer patients. When faced with resistance, funding shortfalls, and conservative thinking, Dr. Slamon and colleagues like him continue to pursue their vision tenaciously. While not every corporate innovation can or should be pursued with this level of aggressiveness, it is essential to dedicate a portion of a business's resources to research and development in potentially high-payoff areas.

YOUR DIAGNOSTIC CHECKUP

- What "high-value" innovation strategies are you deploying in your business?
- What percentage of your innovation dollars are dedicated to potentially high-gain research projects?
- What are the most common barriers encountered in seeing "high-value" projects through to fruition?
- What innovative legacy do you want to leave for your business? How dedicated are you to achieving this legacy?

A MATTER OF PASSION

While I have suggested that all business is personal, could that possibly be true for research innovation? In a word, yes! Even research that can appear to be dispassionate, linear, and analytical is often sparked by the personal passions of the researcher. Imagine being in the third year of your medical residency when your mother is diagnosed with breast cancer. Such was the situation that faced Dr. Linda Liau, neurosurgeon, cancer researcher, and UCLA professor. Her mother had strongly supported Dr. Liau throughout her life, and the news of the diagnosis affected Dr. Liau greatly. Unfortunately, her mother's cancer metastasized to her brain, and her condition worsened to the point that she was hospitalized at UCLA. Dr. Liau's sister had to accelerate her wedding plans so that her mother could participate in the wedding. The expedited wedding occurred with a UCLA chaplain presiding over the ceremony and with nurses as bridesmaids.

Shortly thereafter, Dr. Liau's mother died at the age of 51.

Dr. Liau cites her mother's death as the motivation that expanded her career path beyond that of a highly accomplished neurosurgeon and into the realm of being a world-renowned researcher. Dr. Liau has served as the editor-in-chief of the prestigious *Journal of Neuro-Oncology* and is developing custom-tailored vaccines designed to avert the recurrence of a patient's brain cancer after a brain tumor has been removed. These vaccines, which are in the final stages of clinical trials, are showing extremely promising results with patients, adding months and years to outcome expectations.

Dr. Liau works with patients who travel great distances for her to perform brain surgery to painstakingly remove cancerous tumors. In some cases, these patients return on a regular basis to receive experimental vaccines. Those vaccines resulted from Dr. Liau's applying to brain tumors a technology that her colleagues at UCLA were exploring for use with melanoma and lung cancer. In describing her innovation, Dr. Liau humbly notes, "It was certainly not a eureka moment. It was more just a question that came to me. If it could possibly work for lung cancer and melanoma, why not brain cancer?"

For patients like Dominic Bakewell, the intervention that produced life-enhancing results was strictly surgical. In 2006, Dominic, a singer-songwriter, was in his home with his two-year old son when he experienced a seizure. When he regained consciousness, he found blood on his pillow. Upon being diagnosed with a brain tumor, Dominic and his wife, Sarah, researched brain surgeons and selected Dr. Liau for the procedure. Dr. Liau, assisted by a team of professionals at UCLA, painstakingly mapped Dominic's brain using electrophysiological studies. Further evaluation of functional areas of Dominic's brain occurred during his six-hour surgery.

Given the location of Dominic's tumor (left frontal, with the tumor pressing against speech and motor areas), and also given that Dominic's profession was closely linked to both motor and speech functions, Dominic underwent an awake craniotomy. That surgery, which is done only at a limited number of medical centers, involved Dominic's being placed under anesthesia for the process of sawing through his skull and exposing his brain. His anesthesia was then lightened so that Dominic could provide verbal responses as Dr. Liau systematically used a wand to electrically probe his brain tissue and determine functional aspects. Once the neurosurgery was complete, Dominic was placed back under full anesthesia to have his skull cap reattached, and he awaited a recovery that is typically fraught with multiple complications. Given the intrusion into his brain tissue, these complications could include bleeding, infections, stroke, seizures, paralysis, allergic reactions to medication, and loss of feeling.

Three years after his surgery, singer-songwriter Dominic Bakewell remained on antiseizure medication and visited UCLA for routine follow-up. He had resumed driving and was an engaged husband to Sarah and an active father to his son Julian. Dominic also released an album of children's songs. He views Dr. Liau as being responsible for saving his life.

Despite the precision of the types of surgeries that Dr. Liau performs, in some cases tumors return. This is particularly true for aggressive tumors, where the lethality results from the speed at which the tumors grow and how they generate microscopic offshoots into different brain areas. That's where Dr. Liau's research vaccine comes into play. Her vaccine is created by extracting proteins from a patient's tumor and then loading those proteins into dendritic cells taken from the patient's blood. Once those modified dendritic cells are injected back into the patient, they instruct the lymph nodes to activate the immune system and kill the cancerous cells.

Scott Burk, a patient of Dr. Liau, had a type of tumor that required more than surgical intervention alone. Scott and his wife, Andrea, travel from their home in Cincinnati to UCLA every three months to receive Dr. Liau's vaccine booster. In 1999, at the age of 33, Scott had a seizure while jumping into a swimming pool and was rescued by his wife. After he was diagnosed with an oligoden-droglioma, Dr. Liau performed brain surgeries on him in 2000, 2004, and 2008. Scott's condition qualified him for Dr. Liau's vaccine in 2004.

Scott Burk understands consummate surgery and research skills, since he is an M.D., Ph.D., Harvard-trained ophthalmologist, and molecular biologist. While some of Dr. Burk's abilities have waned during his 10 years in Dr. Liau's care, he is grateful for the gift of life that the surgeries and vaccine have afforded him. While Dr. Burk can no longer perform the 10 cataract surgeries a day that he conducted prior to the onset of his tumors, he continues to see patients in his practice, parents his children, and enjoys his marriage. This is all quite remarkable for a man who was given a very grim prognosis early in his disease process.

Dr. Liau's research career was inspired by her mother's metastatic brain cancer. She is now seeking the ultimate vaccine to wipe out primary brain cancer after surgery. Her dogged pursuit of her goal is reflected in the fact that she averages four hours of sleep per night.

Like Dr. Slamon and his Herceptin breakthrough, Dr. Liau reports that the greatest challenge of her innovative journey is the absence of money for her research. Since there are only about 20,000 new patients diagnosed with primary brain cancer annually, there isn't that great an incentive for drug companies to invest in her vaccines. According to Dr. Liau, "Most companies want to find the next blockbuster drug," and her individualized, costly vaccine does not meet the profile. In fact, Dr. Liau suggests that a great deal of important innovation does not rise to the level of "blockbuster" status and that small steps are needed in pursuit of significant outcomes.

Dr. Liau's work is an example of much of the research that is currently taking place at UCLA. It is innovation that is inspired by passion, exhaustively pursued, to create a series of small breakthroughs that can take what is untreatable today and offer hope, provide quantity and quality of life interventions, and ultimately eradicate disease. Dr. Liau's work highlights key aspects of innovation in any course of endeavor:

- An emotional interest in the innovation outcome

- A willingness to target important intermediary goals (life extension or quality of life for tumor patients) en route to your long-term objective (disease eradication)

- An ability to take prior advances and apply them to a unique set of needs

- An appreciation that important breakthroughs often occur on roads that are less traveled because they lack mass consumer appeal

- A willingness to be actively involved in the process of editing, publishing, and facilitating discussions of breakthroughs with peers and colleagues

Great business leaders take the time to learn the passions of their people and help their staff members pursue answers to business questions that relate to their areas of greatest interest. Furthermore, those leaders attempt to remove barriers that may impede their staff members' progress in pursuit of their dreams. Essentially, extraordinary leaders unleash the greatness within their people by adhering to the wisdom of the German poet and dramatist Hegel, who once wrote, "Nothing great in the world has ever been accomplished without passion."

BREADTH AND SCOPE

Innovation and the advancement of medicine have been key aspects of UCLA since the medical school opened its doors to students in 1951. The culture of research anchors itself to relational breakthroughs of the types outlined in this chapter. Through human clinical trials, laboratory outcomes are translated into viable treatment technologies that literally change the future of medicine.

From CEO Dr. David Feinberg's perspective, "At the hospital and clinic level, it is incumbent upon us to make sure that the scientific method permeates everything we do. We must do our fundamental background research, form a hypothesis based on best practices, try new approaches at all levels of care, measure our outcomes against our hypotheses, and share our knowledge with one another and with those outside our institution. If we do this consistently, we can't help but change the future of medicine and the process of care as well."

In the chapter that follows, you will see how UCLA's leadership has effectively infused this spirit of innovation and the scientific method into quality improvement practices such as unit practice councils at the nursing level. You will also see incremental improvements made across a wide range of patient-care services, including the involvement of pets and music, as well as innovations that affect the quality of training for medical students and the overall well-being of employees.

Revolutionary breakthroughs are an element in the success of most businesses. Therefore, UCLA is an excellent example of how to facilitate the environment of determined, passionate, multidisciplinary research that results in financially and socially beneficial advances. UCLA's leadership should also inspire you to constantly stir the research passions of your people and facilitate the essential ingredients necessary to drive innovation in the core of your business enterprise.

Prescriptive Summary

▶ Examine the role of innovation in your business.

▶ Determine the degree to which "high-value" innovations are necessary if your business is to thrive.

▶ Articulate the innovation legacy you wish to leave.

▶ Set priorities for mission-critical innovations.

▶ Define the percentage of innovation investment that you will earmark for "high-value" exploration.

▶ Perseveringly stay the course through the "pain" of exploration.

▶ Participate in discussions of research breakthroughs.

CHAPTER 9

Transformative Evolution

> *The innovation point is the*
> *pivotal moment when talented*
> *and motivated people seek the*
> *opportunity to act on their*
> *ideas and dreams.*
> —W. ARTHUR PORTER

While sitting in the cafeteria at Ronald Reagan UCLA Medical Center, a patient's family member shared, "We have been involved in care across the UCLA system—in clinics and at both hospital campuses. I have to say that I have never seen a more dynamic organization. It is one that is constantly evolving to serve the needs of patients and reflects a great deal of positive leadership influence." In their book *Launching a Leadership Revolution*, Orrin Woodward and Chris Brady suggest that "leadership influence" is a critical aspect of business success and can be quantified as a function of the effort of the leader multiplied by the scope of those he affects. To achieve maximum influence, leaders must not only exert extreme effort but also gain broad buy-in for their initiatives. When it comes to the influence of UCLA's leaders on the organization's innovation practices, both effort and scope are maximized.

In this chapter, we will look at the processes and outcomes of incremental innovation—evolutionary steps that are changing the future of medicine. This chapter also shows how leaders drive innovation into their corporate DNA. It points out the benefits of increasing service diversification and of maximizing staff empowerment.

OFFERING STAFF MEMBERS TOOLS FOR INNOVATION

In my career as a corporate consultant, I have seen many well-intentioned leaders beat the drum for staff innovation. In these businesses, staff members know that innovation is important to the long-term future of the company, but they are essentially clueless and lacking in tools when it comes to starting the innovation process. Often leaders fail to distinguish between invention and innovation. They don't make it clear that innovation involves ideas that benefit customers and invention refers to a great idea without a definable customer market or interest. To offer guidance for incremental quality improvement, consistent with the evidence-based nature of medical best practices, UCLA's leaders have offered structure and process to front-line workers. One example of this innovation structure comes in the form of process improvement nursing teams. These teams, which are based at the unit level, are integral to a major nursing certification that UCLA attained.

UCLA was selected by the American Nurses Credentialing Center (ANCC), the world's largest and most prestigious nurse credentialing organization, for Magnet Recognition in 2005. The Magnet Recognition Program® was created to acknowledge health systems that provide nursing excellence. Magnet Recognition is considered the premier benchmark for consumer confidence in the quality of nursing care that can be attained and is one of the factors considered in the *U.S. News & World Report* rankings of hospitals. The process of achieving Magnet Recognition involves lengthy applications, written documentation verifying the implementation of key nursing procedures, site visitation, and ongoing monitoring. A key pillar upon which the certification is built is the creation of organizational platforms that ensure nursing empowerment. While the organizational structures required by the Magnet Recognition Program are quite extensive, a couple of examples of the ACAA empowerment criteria are

> There must be an established nursing council/committee in which representatives from all component entities participate in shared decision-making and developing strategy for system-wide nursing initiatives.
> The component entities must demonstrate how nurses participate in shared decision-making.

A strategy deployed by UCLA, not only to meet the Magnet criteria for shared decision making, but also to achieve the leadership's objectives for practical innovation, is the nursing Unit Practice Council (UPC). The UPCs operate within a shared governance model that gives nurses direct input into work processes that affect them and affords all nurses across the system active representation. The structure of the UPC is provided by the nursing administration, utilizing best practice tools from outside vendors. The tools essentially address things like how members of a UPC are selected, the frequency of meetings, the evidence-based objectives of the UPCs, process guidelines for the work of the UPCs, and administrative oversight of the recommendations generated by these work teams.

Tamara Jean Gavilan, RN, Acute Care Pediatrics & Pediatric Hematology/Oncology Units, chair of the Acute Pediatric Unit Practice Council, shares, "UPCs are designed to enable unit nurses to empower themselves to make changes in the hospital that will meet their patients' needs. The number of representatives on a Unit Practice Council is based on the size of the unit. For example, in Pediatrics, we have 10 representatives for acute care because we have 160 staff members. Each UPC participant is directly responsible for bringing information to the council meetings that reflects the input of each of the staff members he represents. Conversely, the representatives are responsible for communicating the results of the UPC efforts back to their nurses. Representatives are selected by their peers, and we develop charts and diagrams on our communication boards so that everyone knows who represents them." When asked about the focus of the committee, Tamara notes, "We receive great training and support from nursing administration to take an evidence- and relationship-based approach to identify ways in which we can constantly innovate improvements in the patient experience."

Martha Lusk, RN, charge nurse, Liver Transplant Unit, shares one of the innovations that emerged directly from the work of her unit council. "Our UPC began looking for ways to increase communication with our patients, particularly given our patients' long lengths of stay. We did a comprehensive literature review on best practices for humanizing and connecting during extended inpatient care. Based on that research, we coordinated ideas with all of our nurses and came up with tabletop frames that we place near each patient's bedside. The frames display information gathered from patients and their families. It is our way to ensure that all service providers get to know interesting aspects of the person that go beyond her medical condition."

According to Martha, in addition to having each patient's picture in the frame, "We also place information that we gain from asking the patient what he prefers to be called, where he grew up, information about his occupation, his interests, the television programs he enjoys, and much more, including his goals after hospitalization. That last question helps us remind the patient of those goals and that he does want to get out of bed, because we are working toward getting him back home to spend time with his family." Jennifer Do, RN, director of the Liver Transplant ICU, stated, "We wanted to ensure that staff members were not only providing patients' medical care, but also getting to know them on a personal level with holistic and compassionate care. This UPC project has been a team effort."

The team innovation efforts of the UPCs are replicated over and over again in the clinics throughout the UCLA Health System and on units at both the Ronald Reagan UCLA Medical Center (RRUCLA) and the Santa Monica–UCLA Medical Center and Orthopaedic Hospital (SMUCLA). To demonstrate the unified commitment to customer-centric innovation, I will offer examples from the Birth and Delivery units at each of the UCLA campuses.

Fiona Angus, assistant unit director of Women's and Children's Services at the BirthPlace at SMUCLA, shares how evidence-based, patient-focused interventions change nursing behavior for the better. "Our nurses conducted research and presented it at an annual conference here at UCLA. The conference showcases findings of UCLA teams, such as our nurses' 'skin-to-skin' initiative. There had already been a great deal of evidence on how early skin-to-skin bonding postdelivery helps babies initiate breastfeeding and sustain it for up to three months after birth. We thought we were doing a really good job with skin-to-skin practices on the unit, but we went back to the basics and started collecting additional data. To our surprise, we found that some members of our staff had a knowledge deficit on the magnitude of research supporting skin-to-skin contact, plus we had practical barriers as well. Nurses knew intuitively that offering skin-to-skin contact between a parent and the newborn was the right thing to do, but they were busy, and they had considerable computerized charting responsibilities immediately after delivery. In some of those cases, nurses might facilitate a little bit of skin-to-skin bonding, but they felt pressure to keep things rolling. Our nurses' research actually showed that if you set up skin-to-skin bonding correctly from the outset, you save nursing time overall."

Innovations and improvement of the skin-to-skin initiative at the BirthPlace at UCLA's Santa Monica campus offered many benefits (breastfeeding, bonding, and more efficient use of nurse time) and ultimately led to implementation of a "golden hour" and "nesting time." Assuming that the mother and baby are stable, the "golden hour" has been designed to give couples an hour of un-interrupted time for skin-to-skin contact with their baby imme-diately after delivery. Similarly, postpartum couples are afforded an hour of daily "nesting time" with their newborns. In the case of both the "golden hour" and "nesting time," signs are placed on pa-tient doors to ensure that nursing, housekeeping, and food service staff will respect this important bonding function.

Over at UCLA's Westwood campus, a "breastfeeding task force" was created to offer a weekly discussion of current practices and evidence-based approaches to aid breastfeeding support for staff members in birth and delivery functions. The efforts of the task force positioned UCLA to participate in the Birth and Be-yond California (BBC) Quality Improvement Project. That project offers technical assistance, on-site education, help in developing breastfeeding resources, and training for hospitals to help mothers breastfeed their infants for six months. At the end of this quality improvement project, the Baby-Friendly Hospital designation awaits. While achieving awards is important to any organization, Dr. Isabell Purdy, N.P., Ph.D., director of the NICU High-Risk Infant Follow-Up Clinic, suggests, "Our ultimate goal is to have new mothers and fathers leave UCLA feeling competent and con-fident that they can take care of their baby and that they have re-ceived consistent information about breastfeeding from all their caregivers."

UCLA's UPCs, annual research conferences, and interdisci-plinary task force strategies are example of the wide array of par-ticipatory innovation structures that have been deployed by the organization's leaders. By adopting these types of organizational structures for your business, you will inspire customer-centric, evidence-based innovations. In turn, these formal processes will empower and revitalize your talented and passionate staff mem-bers to seek solutions that often elude well-intentioned managers who are not close enough to the customer to know where the solu-tions live.

YOUR DIAGNOSTIC CHECKUP

- How important is incremental innovation to the success of your business?

- Can your staff members articulate the importance of this innovation and communicate a "line of sight" between their functions and innovation opportunities?

- What structures (such as UPCs, research conferences, or multidisciplinary task forces) do you deploy to systematically drive incremental innovation?

- If someone wanted to write a book similar to this one about your business, what stories would they share in a chapter like this?

A GOOD IDEA EXPLORED

A lot of great innovation results from simple trial and error. Leaders who encourage the members of their staff to look for opportunities to make a difference for those they serve often end up with the greatest competitive advantage. These leaders typically examine the business case for taking steps in the direction of a staff member's idea and then offer direct nominal resources or limited trial opportunities to test the viability of the concept. If the concept fails to meet expectations, the effort can be scrapped, and if it exceeds expectations, the idea can be nurtured until it is self-sufficient. This "let's give it a try" approach has led to some impressive programs at UCLA. As with the cases discussed in the previous chapter, examples of "front-line" trial innovation efforts at UCLA are so diverse and prolific that you will be provided with only a few examples of this innovation approach in action. Unlike the breakthrough technologies and blockbuster drug innovations featured in the previous chapter, however, this chapter's "soft breakthroughs" have more to do with customer care program development.

TREATING THE WHOLE PERSON

People-Animal Connection

In 1994, UCLA was among the first hospitals in its area to explore the possibility that the presence of animals could have positive benefits in a hospital environment. According to Jack Barron, Jr., director, UCLA People-Animal Connection (PAC), "It started with a fish tank and, later on, a dog visit on the cardiac care unit." Anecdotally, the presence of animals seemed to reduce heart rate, improve respiration, and lower blood pressure for patients who were awaiting a heart transplant. Jack notes, "For the moments that the dog was on the patient's bed, that person was not thinking about surgery or the prospect of a transplant."

But anecdotal findings would not necessarily sustain a novel program at UCLA, so the original director of PAC, Kathie Cole, RN, MS, CCRN, set out to explore the empirical benefit of the human-animal bond. According to Kathie, "What compelled me to pursue the research study itself was the attitude conveyed to me and several others before and during the development of the current People-Animal Connection program at UCLA Medical Center. The concept of doing a 'dog visit' was considered 'nice' or 'cute,' when in fact it was much more than a thoughtful gesture. I believed that it was important to establish scientific evidence to show specific psychological and physiological effects."

To that end, Kathie and Anna Gawlinski, RN, DNSc, and director of Evidence-Based Practice at UCLA, embarked on a study that involved 12-minute visits between dogs and patients to discover what effect those visits had on the patients' blood pressure, heart and lung function, anxiety, and stress levels. Seventy-six hospitalized patients suffering from heart failure were included in the study. These patients were randomly assigned to have either a visit from a human volunteer and a dog, a visit by a human volunteer only, or no visit at all. In the group that received the visits from a human volunteer and a dog, the dogs would lie on the bed so that the patients could touch the animal while interacting with the volunteer and the dog.

The researchers then measured the patients' hemodynamics (blood volume, heart function, and the resistance of blood vessels). These measurements were taken repeatedly just before the 12-minute visit, 8 minutes into the interaction, and 4 minutes after the visit. Researchers also evaluated epinephrine and norepinephrine levels at each of these three points and provided a test of anxiety before and after each intervention.

Results of the study showed that dog visits improved lung and heart function, reduced harmful stress hormones, and decreased anxiety by 24 percent. The research validation of PAC coupled with the obvious emotional delight of patients has fueled UCLA to create one of the premier animal-assisted therapy programs in the country.

UCLA's PAC has been given national recognition in *Newsweek*, *Los Angeles Business Journal*, and the *Los Angeles Times*. It also has been featured on NBC's *Today* show, and a video about PAC was nominated for a News Emmy. Several PAC teams have been the recipients of special awards for their work at UCLA. The Joint Commission on Accreditation of Healthcare Organizations (JCAHO) uses PAC protocols to advance animal-assisted therapy on a national and international basis, and PAC has been a benchmark that has assisted the development of many other animal-assisted therapy programs.

On a day when I was following a PAC team, I watched a treatment-resistant patient completely reverse course and engage in care once she saw that a dog would be involved. Subsequently, the same team was dispatched to a staff area to offer comfort to nurses who had just encountered a stressful patient situation. Jack Barron notes, "The PAC teams are of service to the staff members and patients alike. I get calls all the time. Most are for patient visits, but some request visits for nurses, interns, or residents because of certain situations. Dogs are here for the staff, too. We need to spend time with people, especially those who are reaching out and asking for visits. It improves their day, even if it's a 30-second or a one-minute encounter. They tell us all the time, 'Thank you for sharing your dog with us, because I've had a horrible day.'"

Kit Spikings, a former trauma patient and volunteer coordinator for the patient liaison program, suggests that PAC delivers on its mission for patients and staff members alike. "I e-mail Jack every week with comments from patients and doctors. For example, I was holding the hand of a woman who had been in an awful auto accident. She was lonely, scared, and frightened, and then one of Jack's dogs came in. This woman had been moaning and groaning for six hours. The dog got up in the chair and starting licking her face, and everything was okay. She stopped experiencing pain, as the dog brought her pleasure. A lead ED doctor came by and simply said, 'Unbelievable.' That dog did what morphine and two other drugs had not done, and in the process lifted the moods of all of us who worked with the patient."

The teamwork between the owner and the dog is obviously integral to engaging patients. Jack notes, "PAC volunteer-dog teams offer companionship and warmth to more than 500 critically ill children and adults each month, plus dogs form instinctive bonds with patients of all ages, cultures, and socioeconomic levels. I think we have the highest standards, and I am very protective of this program. We have a lot of very ill patients in our hospitals, and I really want to have the best volunteers and the safest canines that I can get to come in and do their job."

To increase the lasting impact from the animal visit, the human volunteer offers to take a Polaroid picture that can be left behind. However, even something as simple and important as a photo memento requires ongoing innovative considerations in a hospital setting. According to Jack, "We are still using Polaroid cameras, and there is still a little bit of Polaroid film out there. Unfortunately, Polaroid shut down part of its division, and that poses a challenge for us. A highlight of the visit for the patient, besides the fact that they got to have that dog in the bed, is that Polaroid keepsake picture of them. If we run out of film and we don't find something else that is acceptable to replace it, the patient will be denied that special memory. Finding a replacement is not as easy as you might think, given HIPAA requirements. A Polaroid stays in the room, can't possibly be replicated, and is for that patient only. Digital photos and most other options don't meet those criteria." Jack continues, "While issues like a Polaroid picture may seem like a small thing to some, this is an important issue for us. Sometimes a patient will stop me on the street years later, and he will recognize me and say, 'Look what I have here, my Polaroid of your dog Joey on my bed back in 2003.' It's amazing that people would carry that picture with them years later."

Despite the success of the PAC program, it must run on its own merits and live as a result of the tireless work of the PAC volunteer teams. Moreover, its operating budget is fueled exclusively by donations. Jack concludes, "Some of our greatest innovations involve finding funding streams to keep the PAC work moving forward. We have come a long way since 1994, but we are always hustling to avoid extinction. We can always use the support of those who believe in our cause."

PAC is an excellent case study in saying yes to an idea, encouraging validation of the outcomes promised in the concept, building a leading program around the successful concept, and helping the business unit to make the transition to being fully independent and financially sound. Extraordinary leaders are slow to say no; they listen to staff suggestions, seek additional data at times, and give a rationale when ideas do not seem viable. In cases where a concept has promise, those leaders gently support the idea, at least on a trial basis.

MASSAGE THERAPY

Ross Scales and his massage therapy services at UCLA are an example of this same "yes, we will test it out" leadership mindset. Ross was a unit support assistant who went to massage school on his own. He saw the tired, scared families in the ED, and he asked Chief Nursing Officer Heidi Crooks for permission to offer massages to these people on his off hours. Upon receiving support from Heidi, Ross also collaborated with an oncology nurse supervisor, Mark Flitcraft, to use massage to assist cancer patients with pain management. The success of those trial efforts expanded to collaboration with yet another supervisor, Ellen Wilson, and a formal massage therapy program was created.

Ross's program has now been expanded systemwide, and he travels to offer massage services at different campuses. Ross reports, "The process of building this program was simply amazing. At UCLA, if you have what you think is a good idea, it gets heard. This program is my baby, and I have an ownership stake in its success. My manager, Heidi Crooks, really got the ball rolling, and she was a major part of the program's launch. She fell in love with the idea and championed it from there. Other leaders were open to this possibility, and because of their receptivity, we have opened up the benefits of massage to patients, family members, staff members, and leaders."

From the staff perspective, massage has been integrated into the UCLA Wellness Program, and when Ross comes to a staff lounge to offer a chair massage, he sees "people who give so much getting a little bit of something back to revitalize them." When patients and families receive a massage, Ross indicates that they react fairly uniformly. "They are typically excited and look for nurturance and relief. Family members are often stressed and worried, and our time together becomes not just a massage, but a catharsis of sorts. They come in and talk while I am massaging. Sometimes they'll cry at little bit and let some of that anxiety out. It's a very rewarding personal experience."

In addition to the financial viability, profile, and popularity of the program (for example, massage therapy services are listed in the patient admission manual), the leaders have gained a helpful nurturing tool in the face of service breakdowns. Coupons for massages from Ross's program are a standard part of the service recovery kit available to managers throughout the UCLA system. Managers can offer those coupons (among other things) to patients and family members who have experienced a service issue at UCLA. Ross's program went from a trial offering to a systemwide resource for patients, families, staff members, and leaders. Often strong ideas from staff members come full circle. At first they rely on the leaders to serve those ideas, and in the end the ideas turn out to serve the entire organization, including the leaders.

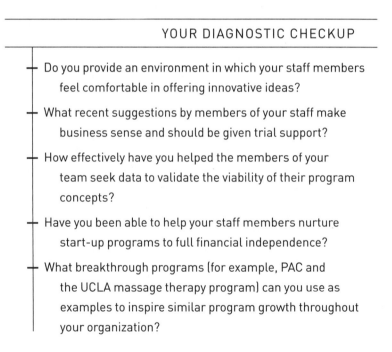

YOUR DIAGNOSTIC CHECKUP

- Do you provide an environment in which your staff members feel comfortable in offering innovative ideas?
- What recent suggestions by members of your staff make business sense and should be given trial support?
- How effectively have you helped the members of your team seek data to validate the viability of their program concepts?
- Have you been able to help your staff members nurture start-up programs to full financial independence?
- What breakthrough programs (for example, PAC and the UCLA massage therapy program) can you use as examples to inspire similar program growth throughout your organization?

SPIRITUAL CARE

Unlike PAC or the massage therapy program, the story of pastoral care services at UCLA is not about taking an entire program from the idea stage to broad prominence. According to Reverend Karen Schnell, director, Department of Spiritual Care, "We are very well integrated into the hospital. We've had a professional chaplain program here for more than 20 years, and the staff members expect us; they call us, and we're well blended with interdisciplinary rounds." Reverend Schnell continues, "At UCLA, we have a high vision— our vision is healing humankind one patient at a time, improving health, alleviating suffering, and delivering acts of kindness. I think that vision elevates our call as healers, whether the healer in question is a chaplain or a doctor or a nurse. In my view, our society is specialized in such a way that you have different people who are offering this healing in different forms. Because of that, integration of healing services is key. We no longer have a single holistic healer, as they did in indigenous communities. So our strength and our innovation challenges must relate to finding ways to bring the many healers together through multidisciplinary teams and also customize our offerings to the unique needs of those who are receiving care."

Through the years, providers of pastoral care have developed innovative ways to position themselves as part of the team of healing professionals at UCLA. They make chart entries in the medical record, communicate their assessment of the patient's spiritual needs, and work with other members of the team to collaborate in providing spiritual assistance. Rabbi Pearl Barlev, Jewish chaplain, shares, "We are always looking for ways to do what we do better and to be flexible enough to adapt to the changing needs of those we partner with and those we serve. Often the most innovative things we do in pastoral care emerge from simply being present with people. I was recently called to the Surgery Department early in the morning as patients were being prepped. The patient I was called to see was a Catholic who wanted to make a confession. Well, he got the rabbi at 6:30 in the morning, so I took his confession. Of course, I didn't have the authority of the Catholic Church to absolve him of his sins, but by my being present for his need, he experienced an important catharsis, and that was a privilege for me.

The innovation is often a matter of improvising to find our commonalities and the strength of the human spirit."

That improvisational approach is also reflected in pastoral care's creation of a "Shabbat box." Rabbi Barlev notes, "The Shabbat boxes are part of our volunteer program for Jewish patients. Friday night is the Jewish Sabbath, and to many people it's deeply meaningful, and it affords tremendous opportunities for spiritual healing. Our volunteers pack up all the goodies to celebrate Shabbat, and we give them as gifts to the patients who would like to have them. As much as I would love to visit with every Jewish patient on a Friday afternoon, it's not possible. Given that we have a limited budget for religious supplies, we've had to be creative about getting individual items and putting them together in what we call the Shabbat box. So we incorporate candles, the challah, grape juice, and other items, and it has become a model program for other hospitals in the area." Reverend Schnell notes that the innovative idea for the Shabbat box came from the hospital's previous Jewish chaplain, Rabbi Micah Hyman. "Rabbi Hyman observed that while we offer Shabbat service at 4:30 every Friday, many patients realistically can't get to our service, so we need to take the service to them." Much of great innovation is nothing more than observing how to make products and services more accessible, more portable, or easier to use. Innovation for ease of access has propelled many companies to greatness.

Music Therapy

As was the case with innovation in pastoral care, professionals like music therapists often find themselves innovating patient care approaches based on giving attention to the unique needs of an individual at a given moment. UCLA Music Therapist Vanya Green shares, "I'm often looking for opportunities to make positive connections while I am on a unit. For example, I noticed a girl who was really upset because she didn't want to have a procedure done. So I asked a nurse about her situation, and it turned out that she and her family had a limited understanding of English. There wasn't a staff member that spoke the family's language around at that moment, so I asked if I could go over and interact with her. As I brought my guitar out of my bag, the patient's eyes were totally set on it. She calmed down and was curious. I started playing softly, and the patient and her family were engaged. I didn't sing any particular words, but I found out that they were from the Middle East, and I used my background in music to play in modes that would be familiar to them. The girl was totally hooked and was able to focus and calm down and make the connection. We started out with things that were more familiar to her—music from her background that she connected to—and then we broadened out the music that we shared. So when we sang a song like "A Whole New World," the theme of the song connected as much as the activity of doing the music together. Almost every interaction with a patient should be improvised to connect and break down barriers."

Beyond the momentary ad hoc improvisations, Vanya has embarked on innovating music recording for patients at UCLA. Vanya shares, "We've gotten a few grants, and a few agencies have made donations to us, so we decided to set up a small recording studio housed in one of the playrooms. Here we have a laptop, an interface, a small hard drive to record onto, and software to do the recordings. Children who are able to come into the playroom and can interact together can choose from a variety of instruments, including electronic drums and a Midi keyboard that produces thousands of sounds. Even kids without musical skills can participate, thanks to the technologies we have available. We are seeing terrific results from the recording studio. Children are connecting and being motivated by a technology that matters to them, and in the process they are using more of their brain and broadening their skills. Patients also make gains in rehabilitation goals that have to do with movements, such as playing drums, and in psychosocial goals relating to their self-esteem or to their level of involvement or interaction."

While creating a "recording studio" in a hospital playroom may not be a commonplace healthcare offering, it reflects the constantly evolving innovations that enrich patient experiences. At its core, innovation in customer care is often about improvising to break down barriers and finding creative ways to make the customer connection.

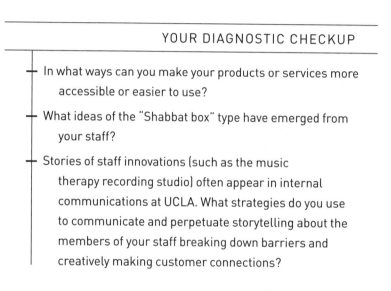

YOUR DIAGNOSTIC CHECKUP

- In what ways can you make your products or services more accessible or easier to use?
- What ideas of the "Shabbat box" type have emerged from your staff?
- Stories of staff innovations (such as the music therapy recording studio) often appear in internal communications at UCLA. What strategies do you use to communicate and perpetuate storytelling about the members of your staff breaking down barriers and creatively making customer connections?

INNOVATING ON BEHALF OF STAFF MEMBERS

While some patient-directed innovations result in benefits to staff members (for example, People-Animal Connection and the massage therapy program), some innovations can work in reverse. A classic example of a novel improvement at UCLA that was initially staff-focused is the UCLA Lift Team. Not only does the evolution of the Lift Team offer important teachable lessons about program innovation, but it also demonstrates how innovating on behalf of staff members often results in direct benefits to customers.

UCLA was one of the first hospitals to develop a trained team of professionals to handle the physical transfer and repositioning of patients. Ellen Wilson, director of UCLA Therapy Services, comments on this innovative approach, referred to as the Lift Team. According to Ellen, "The concept of a Lift Team was relatively new back in 2004, and we started it to reduce the injury rates for our nurses. Our injury rates were high, and nursing satisfaction was less than what we wanted, so I was approached by individuals who were responsible for workers' compensation costs, and we began to examine the possibility of a Lift Team. We had heard about a lift team concept that had been started out in San Diego, and we met with several consultants to develop the program from the ground up, using a lot of intuition. We talked about piloting the program and doing things with equipment in the meantime, but we decided to just go for it." Ellen adds, "Within a three-week period, we had the program designed, the policies written, and the staff hired, and training was starting. I think the total implementation probably took about two months." According to Ellen, the cost of doing nothing outweighed the risks that were being taken in developing and implementing the lift team concept quickly. "The Lift Team members have varying levels of training and expertise. A lot of the Lift Team members had no hospital experience. The biggest cost was salary, and that investment was warranted given expenses of more than $30,000 per injury plus lost time, replacement cost, and so on. Within the first year, our injury rates went down 75 percent. We went from a high of 40 nursing physical movement and patient handling injuries per year to about 11 in the first year of the program alone."

Ellen cites "early communication with all stakeholders" as the key to the Lift Team's successful launch. She shares, "Our team met with every single unit director to see what needs they had, how they thought the Lift Team could best help their nurses, and when their peak times were so that we could structure how the members of the Lift Team did their rounds. We consciously involved all of the nurse managers, even ones that we thought might resist the program, in helping to plan it. There was already buy-in and a lot of anticipation when the program started because everyone had already given input. We had our share of growing pains for sure, but there were no major mishaps. Mostly we faced the fear of the unknown, as these strong Lift Team members dressed in black would come onto an ICU to move a fragile patient, and nurses had to let it happen. We partnered with nursing and ensured that nurses had to be present when the Lift Team members moved their patient. The nurse's job has shifted from transferring or repositioning the patient to watching the lines and monitors to make sure that nothing pulls out and everything goes fine."

Ellen articulates that the benefits of the Lift Team go well beyond a reduction in workplace injuries. "The Lift Team not only makes nursing safer, but helps make nursing easier. In addition, patients are deriving outstanding benefits. For example, there is the potential for a reduction in pressure ulcers because patients are being turned more frequently. Patients are getting out of bed more because the Lift Team helps them, so there is the potential for a reduction in respiratory complications as well. There are a lot of important medical benefits that come from this intervention, not the least of which are emotional connections with patients. Since the team members make their rounds every two hours on their assigned floors, they have multiple and meaningful contacts with patients daily. We receive many cards and letters of praise from staff members and patients on behalf of the endearing care given by our Lift Team."

Grandvell Taylor, a Lift Team member, notes, "I can't tell you how gratifying it is to help nurses and patients avoid injury and increase activity." Teammate Steven Arnold added, "I'm glad the leadership took the chance on the Lift Team. It has given me a rewarding career, and I know it has made a difference throughout our hospital system."

Not only did the UCLA leaders take a calculated risk by creating the Lift Team, but they did not overanalyze the concept before making a full commitment. Benchmarking, consultation, intuition, soliciting buy-in, and including possible detractors early in the planning phase were all integral steps in creating a program that is a model for hospitals around the country. Staff members notice when leaders practice disciplined innovation strategies on behalf of their teams. Those employees typically appreciate and emulate leaders who innovate for them, and in turn, those staff members increase their focus to create measurable benefits for customers as well.

INNOVATING IN EDUCATION

While innovations in patient care and research are critical to the UCLA Health System's mission, CEO Dr. David Feinberg is quick to point out, "We would not exist as a hospital if there were no medical school. We do not need to be in the hospital business; we are here for the medical school. My job is to make dreams come true for the School of Medicine; our hospitals are its main teaching facilities. As a result of that, we have to help facilitate innovations in education as well as in treatment and science."

Dr. Neil Parker, senior associate dean for Student Affairs and Graduate Medical Education, David Geffen School of Medicine at UCLA, shares, "In order for us to be among the top 10 medical schools with one of the most diverse student bodies, we have embarked on a very innovative curriculum. We are teaching at the bedside; learning about patients in our doctoring program starts in year one. So, in your first year of medical school, you will be involved in small-group problem-based learning. This is very different from medical school training in the past, where year one was normal anatomy and year two was pathology. In those days, you would sit in a lecture or do dissections early in your training, and you didn't necessarily see doctors and patients interact until you were called upon to function as a doctor on a medical unit in year three. Now we are engaging in small-group discussions of real cases. It's not textbook learning and then real life. It is textbook *and* real life." Dr. Parker adds, "Many of these small groups are run by two people, and often a mental health person is part of the teaching team to help students see the totality of the human medical experience."

In line with this practical and holistic approach to medical education, Dr. Angelika Rampal, assistant professor of pediatrics, notes that sometimes breakthroughs occur through listening to and building on great ideas that were attempted elsewhere. According to Dr. Rampal, "Some of our new initiatives come from our students. For example, I was approached by a medical student who said that some medical schools are piloting programs in which a medical student partners with a pediatric patient. The goal of that partnership is for the student to gain greater empathy for the patient's experience and to be a mentor to him. That medical student asked whether we could consider such a program here at UCLA." Dr. Rampal then went to Amy Bullock, director of UCLA's Child Life Services, to assess the viability of the concept, and also further solicited support from Dr. Parker at the medical school. Dr. Rampal adds, "We positioned the learning opportunity not as a class but as a 'selective,' something that is not required, but that can be selected as part of one's training."

Dr. Rampal and her colleagues assessed medical students' interest in this mentorship program by having them fill out applications that included written essays. This process ensured a high level of commitment on the part of the medical students. In the first year of the program, after screening the applicants, 12 very engaged students were connected with children who were coping with diverse medical conditions. For example, the pediatric patients served included two liver transplant recipients, along with children with posttraumatic stress disorder, depression, anxiety, chromosomal abnormalities, visual impairments, and a whole spectrum of chronic illnesses. The medical students were paired with patients based on their interests and backgrounds. The program leaders facilitated the introductions and afforded guidelines for forming a mentoring relationship.

Dr. Rampal adds, "It's been amazing to watch how each side of those relationships grows through contact. One of the patients was on dialysis, and her medical student mentor met her on occasion in the dialysis unit. In one incident, the dressing on the patient's catheter was being changed, so the nurse asked the student to step aside. The patient, however, said, 'No, no, no. Let her look. She needs to learn how to do this stuff if she's going to be a doctor.' It is touching for me to think about how the patients and medical students are mentors to each other. The medical students often act as cheerleaders and role models for the patients, and the patients, who are often quite experienced in healthcare, have a great deal that they want to share with the students."

Innovations in methods of training delivery are vital to all business enterprises. Traditional classroom training programs have to be adapted to the changing needs, attention spans, and learning styles of today's employees. Mentorship and experience-based learning innovations are central to a dynamic learning organization.

INVOLVING PATIENTS IN CREATIVITY AND INNOVATION

While examples of patient involvement in innovation at UCLA are rampant, space limitations allow for only one example, from Amy Bullock, director of UCLA's Child Life/Child Development Services department. Since many of these children require extended hospital stays, the Child Life department embarked on an approach to soliciting parent involvement to make improvements in the overall patient/family experience. Amy notes, "We decided to implement a Parent Advisory Council concept. For approximately 4½ months, our staff members talked about which families we thought would be best to invite into the council. We were looking for the mix that would offer the most comprehensive, diverse group that we serve here." Amy's team then explored best practices for creating patient councils, developed a volunteer interest form, established ground rules for the council, and invited the identified candidates. Amy notes, "About 95 percent of the candidates said, 'Great; sign me up!' When we met for the first time, we collectively set expectations and defined the participants' role, and we have been making improvements ever since."

Jennifer Fine, one of the parents involved in UCLA's Pediatric Parent Advisory Council, notes, "A significant difference between our council and other similar types of programs is that our focus is on improving the experience not just for current patients, but predominantly for future patients." Jennifer continues, "Since the hospital setting we are working to improve has a specialty chronic-care population, one of the things we began working on was a care package that can be given to parents when they arrive; it includes a toothbrush, mouthwash, shampoo/conditioner, deodorant, and things to get you through the first day or two. Nobody goes to the hospital with their child thinking, 'I'm going to be here for a month.' The first time you go, there is something acutely wrong, and you don't even process that you could be living at a hospital. You don't bring an overnight bag. The last thing you want to do is leave your child. It's a very traumatic experience, so this care package can help get parents through those first days and give them a chance to breathe until they can get their own things. This care package is provided free to families that are coming in for the first time. We are also putting together a binder that includes information about resources at the hospital and in the community. For example, it has information on the fact that UCLA is a teaching hospital, so you have residents, fellows, and attendings, and it offers insight into the functions of the members of each of the teams. When you come in, you have no concept of this; all you know is that you have doctors coming in again and again. The binder explains the process. It also has places where you can write down all of the medications that your child is going to be taking. It has calendars so that you can plot out your child's treatment plan. It has tabs where you can keep all the paperwork the hospital gives you—and it gives you *lots* of paperwork. There is also information on support and how to see signs and symptoms of depression and posttraumatic stress."

Another member of the Pediatric Parent Advisory Council, Lisa Beck, notes, "I am pleased to be a part of this process to help innovate on behalf of other families. I was overwhelmed with the volume of information I received when my daughter Miranda was in the hospital, and I am very proud to be part of a program that is creating resources that make the experience of the patient and the family more manageable."

YOUR DIAGNOSTIC CHECKUP

- How are you focusing incremental innovation strategies to improve your staff members' experience?
- What innovative approaches have you used in the delivery of your training programs?
- How have you involved your customers in your innovation processes?

Innovation is a concept that seems daunting for some business leaders. They often find themselves tactically responding to their day-to-day management challenges and struggling to look to the horizon of necessary business growth. In the end, innovation often comes down to ideas that are tested in action. While UCLA's leaders enjoy an environment in which intellectual inquiry is celebrated and ideas are richly shared, all of us can benefit from the importance that UCLA places on creating business structures for encouraging staff input. It is those structures (shared governance, unit practice councils, task forces, research consortiums, participatory educational structures, and so on) that contribute to most of UCLA's staff-generated breakthroughs. Albert Einstein emphasized the role of structured processes in creating breakthrough inventions when he said, "Innovation is not the product of logical thought, although the result is tied to logical structure." Once solid ideas surface, great leaders adopt an entrepreneurial spirit that views those ideas as opportunities and looks to identify the best of the possible options.

In the upcoming chapters, you will look at the results UCLA enjoys as a result of adhering to the business principles to which you have been exposed. By executing on "commit to care," "leave no room for error," "make the best better," and "create the future," UCLA has built a well-respected international brand that is known for its excellence. It has also enjoyed financial and social benefits from its revolutionized service experience, and as such appreciates the notion that "service serves us."

Prescriptive Summary

▶ Consider your leadership influence to be a function of effort multiplied by scope.

▶ Evaluate the degree to which you have emphasized the importance of incremental innovation for long-term business viability.

▶ Empower employees by providing them with tools and organizational structures that create shared governance and sanctioning processes for idea generation and program development.

▶ Consider using the "yes, let's give it a try" approach more consistently when presented with reasonable business suggestions.

▶ Encourage staff members to validate the viability of new programs and to swiftly move those programs to financial independence.

▶ Focus some discussions of customer experience improvement on concepts of accessibility or ease of use.

▶ Develop strategies for consistently communicating customer-centric innovations.

▶ Distinguish between invention and innovation.

▶ Encourage improvisation in the direction of breaking down barriers and increasing customer connection.

▶ Realize that innovation must also be directed toward staff needs and that training methodologies have to adapt to accommodate changing learning styles.

▶ Create systems to engage customers in the innovation process.

SERVICE SERVES US

CHAPTER 10

Service Experience—More than Just Pretty Words

> *There is one word which may*
> *serve as a rule of practice for all*
> *one's life—reciprocity.*
> —CONFUCIUS

A t this point in the book, I expect some readers might be thinking, "Okay, so let's say I innovate cutting-edge solutions that change the future of my industry, increase service consistency, enhance customer experiences, develop a safety culture, and even practice continual quality improvement. How will all this affect customer loyalty, my business's bottom line, and its sustainability?" UCLA's fastidious efforts with regard to product and service innovation have generated numerous positive economic and business-related outcomes. As a result, UCLA's "high service" approach serves as a case study for investing in customer experience excellence.

Many leaders think that enhancing the customer experience is an important value proposition, but many also have an inflated sense of the quality of the experience that their companies are currently providing. Some studies suggest that 80 percent of CEOs think that their business is offering an exceptional experience, although only 8 percent of customers come to the same conclusion.

That distortion notwithstanding, most leaders at least think about enriching their service environment. In essence, who wouldn't want to deliver the best possible experience for their customers? Even senior leaders in companies with a customer-centered mystique like Simon Cooper, CEO of the Ritz-Carlton Hotel Company, talk about helping their people continually strive for the "ultimate customer experience" and set a new gold standard for "how good *good* can be."

Unfortunately, for a consultant, hearing a CEO say, "I want to improve the experience for our customers" is somewhat like hearing a beauty pageant contestant suggest that she wants to "create world peace." Both are noble, omnibus, cliché phrases that will not draw overt resistance from anyone. Who would vocally oppose peace or better service delivery? The problem arises in execution. Ultimately, many of those well-intentioned leaders fail to deploy effective service strategies because they do not believe that investing in customer experience enhancement will result in compelling deliverables for their business. These leaders essentially acknowledge that elevating all contact points in the customer journey is an admirable pursuit, but they can't reliably predict that the cost of those improvements will produce outcomes such as increased revenues or organic growth. The two chapters that cover this principle, "Service Serves Us," will build a business case for taking a high experience value approach to your business. Using UCLA as an example, I will offer insights into what I will call ROE, or return on experience. UCLA has invested extensively in providing improved service consistency and an enriched patient experience, and this chapter will explore the following benefits (ROEs, if you will) that UCLA has received from those investments:

Greater profitability

Improved customer loyalty and increased referrals

Team mobilization toward a common goal

Positive staff morale, retention, and recruitment benefits

Strong community support for UCLA's programs

Chapter 11 will offer a discussion of additional ROE benefits associated with international brand equity, sustainability, and
brand significance that UCLA enjoys and that are available to your
business.

I vividly remember a heated exchange early in my consulting
career between a mission-focused hospital executive and a fiscally
conservative businessman who sat on the hospital's board. The
hospital executive was making a case for investing in a systemwide
customer experience mapping and intervention project and appealed to the board for approval. The request was framed largely on
the argument that improving the patient experience would help the
hospital achieve its stated service mission. Tersely, the board member fired back a phrase that I have since heard frequently, "There is
no mission without money." So in words inspired by a Tom Cruise
movie, let me first "show you the money" as the foundation for the
ROE.

SERVICE ECONOMICS—PROFITABILITY
AND CUSTOMER REFERRALS

As early as 1981, Morris B. Holbrook and Elizabeth C. Hirschman
wrote about the importance of emotional experiences in the marketing and sale of products and services. The concept gained a
wider audience in 1999 when James H. Gilmore and B. Joseph
Pine authored a book titled *The Experience Economy: Work Is The-
atre and Every Business a Stage* (Harvard Business Press, 1999). As
that title implies, Gilmore and Pine declared that we had entered
a new economic era. Just as agrarian economies gave way to the industrial age, Gilmore and Pine suggested that we had moved from
a time when customers sought transactions or services to one in

which customers crave emotionally relevant experiences. Using the company I wrote about in my book *The Starbucks Experience*, Gilmore and Pine demonstrate the increasing revenues that businesses can achieve when they move from a service orientation (coffee served in a convenience store for $1 per cup) to staging experiences in a living room environment (a $4 per cup price point for coffee presented in an emotionally engaging setting).

Despite the economic theory and anecdotal examples advanced by Gilmore and Pine, scientific research was somewhat slow to support the existence of consistent economic benefits as a result of adopting a high-service business strategy, let alone a high-experience strategy. Initially, many case examples were available showing that improved brand differentiation and substantial profits were linked to service consistency and the creation of relevant customer experiences. Later, empirical findings from wide-ranging sources validated the concepts of customer experience theorists. Some of the findings that are most relevant to corporate decision makers include

- Even in difficult times, 50 percent of consumers will pay more for a better service experience.

- Only 14 percent of customers report that they leave a business for product reasons.

- A full 68 percent will sever a customer relationship because they were treated poorly by a staff member.

- Companies that are successful in creating both functional and emotional bonding with customers have higher retention rates (84 percent vs. 30 percent) and greater cross-selling ratios (82 percent vs. 16 percent) compared to companies that are not.

- The average value of a customer is 10 times his initial purchase.

- The cost to attract a new customer is 6 times the cost to save one.

- Low-service-quality companies average 1 percent return on sales and lose 2 percent market share per year.

- High-service-quality companies average 12 percent return on sales and grow 6 percent per year.

Similarly, Steve Downton, Hillbrand Rustema, and Jan Van Veen, authors of the book *Service Economics*, report on three years of research funded by Oracle analyzing the service industry. The goal of the research was to uncover and understand productive service and experience strategies and examine whether excellent service environments really do produce tangible financial rewards. According to the authors, companies that successfully execute a high-service-value strategy enjoy annual growth rates of 20 to 40 percent. By broadening the role that salespeople play and functionally enabling them to serve as trusted advisors (not transactors of sales), businesses on average enjoyed a 20 percent sales increase. Companies that effectively made improvements in the customer experience and gained a 5 percent increase in customer loyalty consistently derived profit increases of 25 percent or more.

The body of research amassed on service and experiential economics suggests that it is wise and prudent to invest in customer experience enhancement. Some analysts, however, have argued that the economics of customer experience enhancement do not apply to healthcare. John Goodman, BS, MBA, vice chairman, and Dianne Ward, BS, MA, senior account manager for TARP Worldwide, writing in *Patient Safety and Quality Healthcare*, explain the distinctions that are commonly cited between the healthcare and nonhealthcare sectors: "Most industries have readily accepted that improved customer service will lead to increased customer loyalty, increased revenue, and an enhanced bottom line. However, the healthcare industry has lagged in accepting this concept for several reasons:

Customers are not loyal in the traditional sense because they usually wish to avoid using the healthcare system except when necessary, and most executives believe they go to the health facility to which their physician sends them.

Most customers are insulated from price due to health insurance, and often fail to care about cost, only wanting the best, newest procedures.

Clinical care is often viewed by physicians as completely separate from traditional customer or administrative service (which is viewed as the admissions, billing, and 'hotel' aspects of a medical encounter).

Clinicians believe great medicine will gain forgiveness for poor service (reinforced by television shows such as *House*)."

Goodman and Ward go on to disprove these alleged differences by analyzing TARP Worldwide's research regarding healthcare delivery. Most notable among these findings are conclusions that the patient experience delivered by physicians *is* as important as the experience provided by other staff members when it comes to determining patient loyalty.

Patients' word-of-mouth reports about their healthcare experiences has as much impact on potential patients as it does on physicians who make referrals. In fact, TARP Worldwide research shows that referring physicians were greatly influenced by the reports of their patients regarding the way they were treated at the facilities to which they were referred. In essence, referring physicians had more loyalty to their patients than to the physicians to whom referrals were made. Additionally, Goodman and Ward note, "It is possible to quantify the revenue and risk reduction impact of improved experience in a manner that both the chief financial officer and clinicians will accept and appreciate. Eliciting and more effectively addressing complaints from patients and their families can lead to double-digit improvements in patient satisfaction scores and re-ductions in risk costs."

UCLA's journey to large double-digit improvements in patient satisfaction scores and commensurate increases in profitability vali-date the findings reported by Goodman and Ward and support Gilmore and Pine's views of the experiential economy. Whether it is healthcare or a non-healthcare-related business, customer satis-faction is fundamentally connected to profits and to the long-term success of your company. It's time to examine your likely ROE.

A MULTIFACTORIAL UPSURGE— WITH SERVICE AT THE CENTER

At the departmental level, Brenda Izzi, RN, MBA, UCLA's chief administrative officer for the Department of Radiology, clearly sees a connection between service and profits. "We are experiencing our best financial years and are trending upward. We've seen a number of the private imaging centers fold in the last five years, while our volume has grown. I attribute our success directly to improving the patient experience and creating better access. Obviously, we are also always improving our product, but we have a fundamental awareness of the importance of service in our setting. Enhancing the patient experience garners support not only from our patient base, but from referring physicians as well. Part of our service focus is demonstrated through our desire to offer education not only to our own people, but also to individuals who might come into con-tact with a medical radiology environment in an emergency situa-tion, such as firefighters. Our department is part of annual training for such people. We are also answering our phones more quickly and reducing call abandonment rates. We are listening intently to customer needs, and when we identify a unique customer opportu-nity, we try something new. If our new approach fails, we go back to the old way. From a leadership perspective, we realize that we have to get out of our comfort zones to create relevant customer experiences." The Department of Radiology reflects a positive connection between enhanced patient experience and unprecedented financial results, but are those trends demonstrated throughout the UCLA Health System?

UCLA's chief financial officer, Paul Staton, believes that a commitment to service has significantly contributed to positive economic growth throughout health sciences. "You have to be careful in ascribing cause when there are so many factors that affect financial performance, but a passion for elevating service certainly seems to be one important factor. If you go back to the early 2000s, we were operating in the range from breaking even to making a slight profit at UCLA. It was a very difficult time for the medical center. When senior management turned over some years later, a whole different set of strategies was brought into play. Those approaches included fiscal elements like controlling cost structures and evaluating staffing needs more effectively, but a central element was improving customer care and satisfaction. Those efforts put us on the road to a better financial future." Paul indicates that while cost controls were an important aspect of UCLA's increased profitability, "Improving customer care and enhancing patient experiences lead to positive satisfaction scores and enthusiastic patient reports. Improvements in customer satisfaction, coupled with high-quality outcomes and cost control, translate directly into favorable contract conditions when we negotiate with insurance companies. Engaged customers strengthen our reputation and build the best type of referral business—word-of-mouth recommendations." From Paul's perspective, organic business growth is sustainable by building an effective cost-control infrastructure, exceeding the service expectations of your existing customer base, and driving referral business through high-quality outcomes and emotionally connected experiences.

CEO Dr. David Feinberg understands the difference between correlation and causation, but he is convinced that the simultaneous occurrence of service enhancement and UCLA's increased profitability is more than coincidental. "I know that if we graph our dramatic improvements in patient satisfaction, where patients are acknowledging that they got the right treatment at the right time and that our people communicated well, it's the exact same graph as our increased profitability. Increased service and satisfaction are paying for themselves more than 8,000 times over. Beyond that, our efforts to emotionally connect and deliver patient-centric care are strengthening our referral business and providing us with new customers. But even with the achievement of the highest patient satisfaction scores for academic medical centers, there is more room for us to wow every customer every time. If we achieve that, I'll stop all my marketing because patient and family referrals are better than any marketing we can do."

Increased focus on both service and customer-centric experiences has contributed to substantial elevations in customer satisfaction and parallel increases in profits at UCLA. Comparative outcome data regarding safety, quality, and patient satisfaction (which are currently available online) will become more readily accessible to consumers. Performance on these quality and patient experience measures should play a greater role in the way healthcare facilities are reimbursed. Given these trends, the link between consumer choice, profits, and reported satisfaction levels will increase.

As is the case with businesses in non-healthcare sectors, more than 40 percent of consumers already research healthcare services online, and 60 percent report using the information they gain from that research to make a decision on a healthcare provider. Twitter, Facebook, and consumer review Web sites are increasingly presenting healthcare tweets, posts, and customer opinions that are considered by prospective patients. Ultimately, if you want to know whether service matters in your business, you need only ask online prospects who are making purchase decisions based on reports of customers who are blogging about the service they received from you.

YOUR DIAGNOSTIC CHECKUP

- How do Gilmore and Pine's views on the "experiential economy" relate to your business? What insights can you draw from the research supporting the link between service and experiential economics?

- In what ways is your business delivering "service" rather than "experience"?

- If you could identify the emotionally relevant experience that you wish to provide for all your customers or for specific customer segments, how would you articulate the "ultimate customer experience"?

- In order to measure your ROE (return on experience), what outcome measures would you target—revenues, organic growth, customer retention, cross-selling?

- Do you accept that the growth of your business is dependent upon your building an effective cost-control infrastructure, exceeding the service expectations of your existing customer base, and driving referral business through high-quality outcomes and emotionally connected experiences? If so, which of these areas in your business are most in need of improvement?

TEAM MOBILIZATION TOWARD A COMMON GOAL

When you focus your staff members on the importance of service and the need to create positive experiences for others, that outward focus can have the beneficial, albeit unintended, benefits of unifying team efforts and ameliorating petty bickering. Dr. James Atkinson, senior medical director of Clinical Operations and chief of Pediatric Surgery at Mattel Children's Hospital UCLA, understands the positive outcomes that emerge from helping staff members give service the priority over personal agendas. "I was asked to step into a leadership role in making the transition from our old hospital to the Ronald Reagan UCLA Medical Center. Extremely intelligent and motivated physicians, staff members, surgeons, department chairs, and hospital leadership surrounded me. Collectively, we were looking forward to our new hospital with great trepidation. A lot of people thought, 'I can't possibly fit my program into the new building.' Or 'I can't work in that space; it is too far from the recovery room or the operating room or the nursing unit.' Some thought that there wouldn't be enough storage space for supplies or that there were going to be irresolvable problems with getting food to the patient rooms. Many people suggested from the very beginning of the design process that the building was too small, despite its being 1.2 million square feet."

In the face of this resistance, Dr. Atkinson began explaining the customer-centric components that had been built into the hospital's space utilization and design. "I think what some leaders didn't initially realize was that we had invested so much of the efficiency of the building in the comfort of the patients, with single-family rooms, separate public and private quarters, and many lift devices so that families and staff members didn't have to wait for an elevator. All that design focus on customer care took away from the greater personal and service provider space that we had enjoyed at the old hospital." To deal with the emerging turf battles and perceptions of personal inconvenience, Dr. Atkinson called upon hospital and medical leaders to align with the shared purpose of creating the optimal patient experience. Dr. Atkinson notes, "As people rallied behind that common objective, they moved away from their personal discomforts. They started thinking about what could be rather than what used to be. We could then build processes and flows that leveraged the new building to make the service that we had provided in our old hospital even better." Dr. Atkinson continued to keep the patient experience at the center of design discussions with the 500 physicians, nurses, and patients whom he involved in the planning process. Those discussions forced people to look at their practice patterns and challenge assumptions about the processes that had been in place in the older facility. As Dr. Atkinson put it, "While I would not recommend such a large-scale undertaking (moving from one hospital to another) to derive the benefit we enjoyed, I think it shook up stale practice patterns and forced us to reconsider patient-centric alternatives. Just because we were comfortable with our processes didn't mean that they were best for patient care. Our comfort meant that our processes worked best for us. Looking at processes from the perspective of how they can better facilitate service and care led to both disruption and advancement."

The actual patient move ran ahead of schedule, lasting a total of seven hours and involving the transportation of both critical- and acute-care patients by mobile intensive-care units, shuttles, and ambulances. The efficiency of this team service effort was reflected in the fact that on average, one patient was moved every two minutes. The humanity of the move is indicated by the way the patients experienced the transition. The first pediatric patient to be transferred to the new hospital was 11-year-old Miranda Beck. Miranda, wrapped warmly in a UCLA sweatshirt and donning a surgical mask, was accompanied by her mother, Lisa. Miranda and her mother arrived at the new hospital via ambulance. Lisa Beck notes, "The attention to detail and the kindness of the staff during the move was totally consistent with the way Miranda was cared for during her entire 18 months at UCLA." Miranda summed up her reaction to the move by succinctly saying, "Wow."

When patients can be "wowed" and staff members can be flawlessly coordinated during a massive undertaking like planning and carrying out the transition to a new facility, the merits of championing a customer-centric service mindset seem obvious. Effective leadership rallies teams to greatness by aligning them with a cause that is bigger than themselves. Every business leader has the opportunity to make that uniting cause be the care and comfort of the business's customers.

FOCUSING ON SERVICE PAYS DIVIDENDS IN STAFFING

A great deal of time, effort, and money have been spent on demonstrating that customer satisfaction depends largely on the degree to which an organization's leaders create an environment in which their staff members are satisfied and engaged. Books like *Human Sigma: Managing the Employee-Customer Encounter* (Gallup Press, 2007), written by John H. Fleming, Ph.D., and Jim Asplund of the Gallup Corporation, show that companies that build a critical mass of employee engagement grow earnings per share at 2.6 times the rate of companies that do not. Fleming, Asplund, and their colleagues at Gallup also indicate that this earnings trend is generalizable across multiple industries throughout the world.

While most business leaders understand this link between employee engagement and profitability, they often fail to appreciate the role that "service" or "experiences" play in securing the engagement of their employees. Using the Gallup metric of employee engagement (the Q12) as the benchmark, many of the components that have been empirically shown to drive employee ownership behavior are directly related to the way in which leaders serve employees and the benefits that employees gain from serving customers. For example, items on the Q12 focus on the employee's perception of the degree to which her supervisor takes an interest in her, whether the employee's opinions seem to matter, and the scope of opportunities that employees are afforded to learn and grow on the job. Reflecting back to Chapter 3, these dimensions can be translated into how much the supervisor adheres to the "caring processes." For example, employee engagement can be thought of, in part, as the degree to which supervisors practice the service behaviors of knowing, maintaining belief, and enabling on behalf of their direct reports.

An additional element of employee engagement defined by Gallup is the degree to which employees feel that their contribution is substantive. In the Q12, this is stated, "The mission/purpose of my company makes me feel my job is important." By helping to serve others well, employees often report a connection to the purpose of their organization and increased emotional engagement in their work. Dr. Lori Baudino, PsyD, ADTR, dance and movement therapist at Mattel Children's Hospital UCLA, puts it this way: "When service is championed as central to the success of a business, as it is at UCLA, it allows staff members like myself, who feel a deep passion to serve, to see how we fit into something larger. We sense a match or fit and connect with the power of the organization to amplify our efforts."

Pam Hoff, Outpatient Radiation Oncology Clinic clinical social worker, notes, "There is nothing better than meaningful service to keep you connected to your work and to have the healthcare team you work with share the same values and work ethic. I have been at UCLA for more than 20 years, and I have seen how a positive staff morale not only benefits the care of patients, but also has an impact on the overall spirit of the department. Every single person in our clinic strives to create a caring atmosphere for our patients and works hard to encourage them and help them through the treatment process. For example, patients with tongue, tonsil, and throat cancer have to go through a challenging treatment regimen of chemotherapy and radiation. Our physicians have pointed out that nationwide, many of these patients do not complete their course of care. Our staff does everything we can to communicate with, care for, and comfort those patients through this difficult therapy. It is a team effort, involving not only our department, but the collaboration of different specialties within UCLA, working together to encourage these patients to complete their treatment. It is this group effort of respect for one another, as well as putting the patient care needs first and foremost, that makes me proud of our team and our goals of excellent patient service."

Myrtle Yamamoto, RN, manager in Quality Resources at UCLA, reports that the service mindset of an organization also has an impact on those who provide support functions. "Not all of us at UCLA have responsibility for the direct clinical care of patients, but a lot is done behind the scenes to promote high-quality patient care founded on evidence-based medicine. I get to work with incredibly compassionate physicians, administrators, nurses, pharmacists, and other staff members. Together we strive to deliver the best patient care."

Michael P. Richards, administrative specialist in Radiological Sciences at UCLA and a volunteer patient liaison for the Ronald Reagan UCLA Medical Center Emergency Medicine Department, believes that "service in action" can even attract like-minded people to come to work for a company. "My day job is basically clinical faculty administration, where I prepare dossiers for faculty advancement or work on arranging travel, expenses, and so on. But in my volunteer function in the emergency room, I get to work with patients, the patients' families, and staff members who are committed to making a difference in the lives of those patients. If you are a service-oriented volunteer, family member, or patient, you can't help but want to be working in that kind of a service community. For example, Kit Spikings is a manager for UCLA Alumni Travel and supervisor of liaisons in the Emergency Department. Kit is one of the most empathetic, caring people you will ever meet. Her sensitivity to patient needs and preferences is extraordinary. She is right there with patients, asking, 'Would you like regular water? Would you like iced water? How do you want your coffee?' When Kit is serving, you would think you were at a Ritz-Carlton. I know this will sound a bit like a cliché, but people like Kit serve as my motivation, and I greatly look forward to helping our staff members give our patients the best care and the best service. The entire service environment is infectious."

In response to praise from her colleagues, Kit Spikings simply notes, "I am such a rich person. I've gone through a lot in my life, like we all have. Where I am in my life today, the richness, is what I get back. If we could only get more people to serve others, the lives of both those who are served and those who are serving would be so much better." Kathy Deutsch, a registered nurse who had let her nursing license lapse, understands the rewards of volunteering in an environment of service like UCLA's emergency rooms and adds, "What makes me feel so gratified is that almost every single time I'm in the ER, I feel as though I've made a difference for a few people. Because of my volunteer experience in the ER, I decided to renew my nursing license. Perhaps I will work as an RN again one day. For now, I am loving my volunteer job, and I plan to stay." Service experiences draw people into a business and forge relationships where volunteers and prospective employees find a job that they can "love" and where they, like Kathy Deutsch, make "plans to stay."

UCLA's investment in service experience creation is paying clearly identifiable mission-centric dividends in one of its most important assets—its human resources. Data on employee satisfaction and engagement are also trending upward at UCLA, consistent with improvements in relationship-based care and customer satisfaction scores. Customer experience–based businesses enjoy an ROE that is somewhat difficult to quantify, but very real, in the form of employee engagement, team cohesion, staff retention, and even attracting possible future employees to your service environment.

YOUR DIAGNOSTIC CHECKUP

- How can you focus on service experiences to rally conflicting work groups toward a common goal?
- Have you examined the relationship between the intrinsic rewards of serving and overall staff morale?
- How are you using stories of patient experience excellence to reinforce and engage your workforce?
- Have you strategically looked at driving service excellence as an approach for recruiting like-minded individuals who encounter your brand?

SERVING COMMUNITIES PRODUCES LOCAL SUPPORT

People who are genuinely committed to service believe that positive outcomes will ultimately follow from that service. However, if they find that their acts of service are not reciprocated and that, in fact, advantage is taken of their kindness, those individuals will target their efforts in a more productive direction. In essence, most people understand the distinction between servitude and service professionalism. While a service mindset can result in abuses by recipients, in most cases service professionals derive benefits commensurate with the service they extend.

The same dynamics of service and reciprocity are at play for organizations. Companies that authentically encourage individual and corporate acts of giving typically reap outstanding rewards in the form of the support that they receive from the communities they serve. At UCLA, the care that is given to patients is often reciprocated by the volunteer efforts of those patients or their families.

Betsy Korbonski, pet therapy volunteer for Santa Monica–UCLA Medical Center and Orthopaedic Hospital, acknowledges that the compassion that was shown toward her family contributes to her volunteerism. "I spent a lot of time in UCLA hospitals with various family members. I had a grandson with a congenital heart defect who made many trips to the hospitals in both Westwood and Santa Monica. Ultimately, my grandson died at UCLA Santa Monica at four months of age. Despite that sad outcome, I am so grateful for the care that my family and I received, so volunteering at UCLA was an obvious choice for me. Additionally, the opportunity to be of service enriches both my life and the lives of my animals."

Some forms of repayment offered to UCLA for the compassionate care provided by staff members come in the form of referral business. Joi Edwards, patient and physician liaison, Department of Radiology, notes, "Part of our mandate at UCLA is to educate, and we take that mission very seriously. To that end, we have a

'Specialist in the Community' lecture series that was started back in 2004. The program was implemented to allow physicians to gain continuing medical education credits, the CME credits that they require if they are to maintain their license. We hold the dinner lectures four to six times a year, and we focus on new advances in the attendees' areas of specialty. Sharing the knowledge of our researchers and physicians with community doctors typically results in a win/win situation, as those physicians often show their gratitude for the knowledgeableness of our doctors by making referrals to our service." Doing the right thing for customers and helping them achieve success or realize their dreams often results in their helping you achieve your own.

Beyond volunteerism and referrals, UCLA often sees its commitment to service returned in powerfully personal ways. For example, 12-year-old Cameron Cohen spent a considerable amount of time being treated for a tumor on his leg at Santa Monica–UCLA Medical Center and Orthopaedic Hospital. During that period of care, Cameron created an application for the iPhone and iPad. Subsequently, he donated a substantial portion of the proceeds from the 99-cent application, called the iSketch, to UCLA. On his Web site (www.cccdevelopment-llc.com), Cameron notes, "Inspired by the care I received at Santa Monica–UCLA Medical Center and Orthopaedic Hospital, I have dedicated a portion of my iSketch proceeds to purchase entertainment and electronic items for Mattel Children's Hospital UCLA's Child Life/Child Development programs in Westwood and Santa Monica so that pre-teens and teens will have additional age-appropriate options available to them during their hospital stays." From the mouths and minds of babes, there is no greater testament to the principle "Service Serves Us" than a 99-cent iSketch iPhone application and the donated revenue that flows back to UCLA programs.

Similarly, Lisa Beck (whose daughter Miranda remarked "Wow" after being the first patient transferred into the Mattel Children's Hospital UCLA from the former facility) has established the Miranda D. Beck Pediatric Cancer Research Foundation in the name of her daughter, who passed away in October 2008. Lisa notes, "Miranda was diagnosed with leukemia in January 2007, and a few days later, after she was admitted to UCLA, we found out that she had an additional complication that they call a positive PH or Philadelphia chromosome. This meant that Miranda had to have a bone marrow transplant; otherwise, she would never get rid of the leukemia. We started our journey with that, and she did her chemotherapy. In June 2007, Miranda had her transplant from an umbilical cord that came from the Italy bank. It was very exciting for us, and we hoped that everything would turn out well. Unfortunately, Miranda had a lot of complications after the transplant. Because of all the problems, she was not able to walk and had to participate in physical therapy. She was transferred from UCLA to another hospital for that extensive therapy. While she was there, Miranda caught an infection and passed away. Sometimes I wish she had died at UCLA, because we really didn't know anybody at the other hospital." Lisa shares the strength of the bond she and Miranda formed at UCLA, "Miranda and I made UCLA our home for 18 months. She was in the hospital most of that time."

Lisa adds, "Because of my experiences at UCLA, my husband and I have made it our passion to continue to support the hospital and its researchers in every way that we can. Many people don't realize how expensive pediatric cancer care really is and how many children cancer affects every day. So it's our goal to increase awareness that children do get cancer, enlighten people on different types of pediatric cancer, and raise funds for UCLA's research in the area." Miranda's foundation is but one example of widespread donor support from passionate families and patients who repay service excellence by partnering to further UCLA's service, research, and treatment mission. When thinking about the benefits derived from creating engaging customer experiences, leaders should consider measuring the energy and gifts returned to the business by current and past customers.

YOUR DIAGNOSTIC CHECKUP

— How are you offering service to your customers and referral
sources beyond the walls of your organization?

— Beyond the products and services that you sell, in what ways
can you add value to your customers through education or
other forms of assistance?

— Other than through the bottom line, how can you see a return
of community support in response to your commitment to
service?

LOOKING FOR TANGIBLE AND
INTANGIBLE RETURN ON EXPERIENCE

UCLA's commitment to patient-centric care has contributed to departmental and systemwide revenue growth—an important objective for any business. In addition, the customer experience journey continues to offer benefits that are desirable, albeit less easily monetized, such as improved employee satisfaction and pride in service. Much like UCLA's, your investments in customer experience enhancement are likely to result in increased staff engagement, a greater ability to attract and retain service talent, improved team function, and increased support from the communities you serve.

The great theologian and philosopher Albert Schweitzer once said, "I don't know what your destiny will be, but one thing I do know: the only ones among you who will be really happy are those who have sought and found how to serve." As it relates to business, I will take the liberty to modify Schweitzer's words to suggest, "I *do* know your destiny. Your success is proportionate to the degree to which your organization has sought and found how to serve."

Prescriptive Summary

▶ Advocate for customer experience by using a combination of likely financial and interpersonal outcomes.

▶ Be alert to research on customer experience design and the effects of customer experience on organizational profitability.

▶ Look for trends in your revenues and customer experience elevation efforts.

▶ Consider excellence in customer service as a possible driver of employee engagement, attraction, and retention.

▶ Look for non-revenue-generating ways to assist your customers in achieving their goals.

▶ Start with service and watch for reciprocal returns. If returns are not forthcoming, adjust the target of your service.

▶ Appreciate that there are both tangible and intangible ROEs (returns on experience).

▶ Track the intangible as well as the tangible returns!

Sustainable Success through Service without Bounds

*A life is not important except in
the impact it has on other lives.*
—JACKIE ROBINSON

n business, leaders often compartmentalize the groups that they serve. They use a wide range of labels to distinguish among those groups, such as employees, customers, prospects, leads, board members, and stockholders. On occasion, there are natural tensions that emerge between these constituencies. For example, the pursuit of return on the shareholders' investment can lead to compromises in the customers' experience. While competing interests do surface, great leaders understand that business success can often be reduced to "profiting people through people." UCLA's commitment to profiting a wide cross section of people is reflected in the first two words of its service vision: "Healing humankind." While some businesses create different levels of care for employees and customers and even provide varying levels of care based on a customer's ability to pay, UCLA is seeking to care uniformly so that it can heal all of humankind. Thus, the vision statement does not begin: "Healing our highest-paying customer segment." By casting the net of service to the entirety of humankind, UCLA's leaders have pushed the traditional boundaries and achieved pervasive impact within their community, throughout the United States, and even globally.

Dr. Feinberg puts it powerfully, "For us, it's about serving people, not about diseases, payer classes, employment status, or even your country of origin. If we care well for people—all people—great things happen, and there is no limit to what is possible at UCLA." This chapter gives you the opportunity to reconsider the distinctions that you may be making concerning service, and, by extension, it previews the benefits that you may receive if you widen your service perspective. The chapter should challenge you to think about the boundaries that confine your concept of service and whether those boundaries are disadvantageous, worthy of reconsideration, or completely consistent with sound economic and social decision making. As suggested by Dr. Feinberg, this chapter should cause you to consider what business you are in, which "people" you are serving, and the ideal local, regional, or even international scope of your service area.

SERVICE SERVES STAFF MEMBERS TODAY AND INTO THE FUTURE

Today

Some business leaders make distinctions between internal (employee) and external (customer) service; however, UCLA views service for employees and patients identically. In practice, patients and staff members are often one and the same. Alison Grimes, head of the Audiology Clinic and clinical professor of Head and Neck Surgery, sent a letter to the leader of her organization, CEO Dr. David Feinberg. That letter had nothing do to with her employment, but instead reflected on the service that her family had received at UCLA. In that letter, Alison noted, "My mother died at UCLA on Friday. . . . I am writing to let you know that, in spite of the sadness of the experience, how wonderful UCLA was throughout her entire stay. Mom entered the hospital through the ER. I had been alerted that she was on her way via ambulance and even before her arrival, I was treated with amazing and wonderful courtesy, concern, and efforts on my behalf to connect me with Mom. . . . She was transferred to the 7th floor Medicine unit. Again, her physicians, nurses, care partners, were simply amazing. In the morning, a nurse named Staccy comforted me in a way that I so badly needed as I watched my mother fail. . . . When Mom was transferred to the MICU, again, her nurses and physicians were concerned, attentive, and expert. The resident who handled most of her care, Dr. Edward Lee, was amazing. He helped me, and my brother and sister, make difficult decisions about her end-of-life care, and he bent over backwards to talk with (not to) us about our desires and what my mom might have wanted. He exemplified the very best in a caring physician, and we were immensely fortunate to have had him as our guide."

Alison adds, "Everyone, from the people who cleaned the room to the care partners, nurses, physicians, and respiratory therapists—everyone—embodied the very best in patient care. I, of course, expected no less, but my brother and sister were amazed, and relieved, that everything was handled so efficiently and empathetically. When it came time to say the final good-bye, spiritual care was so helpful in creating an environment in which this could happen. My mother's last nurse, Roman, was attentive and empathetic to the end, and informed us that she had passed. This truly was the 'Best Patient Experience,' in spite of the sad ending. . . . I am thankful to the myriad of professionals who tended to her, and to us. UCLA is truly the best!"

Cynics might suggest, "Of course Alison's family would get great care. Since she is a prominent UCLA manager, her mother would probably have been be flagged for VIP treatment." That cynicism, however, indicates a lack of understanding of what it takes to create a customer-centric business. At the heart of a customer-focused company is the assumption that everyone will be treated as a very important person—so much so that care is individualized based on the recipient's unique wants, needs, and desires.

While medical assistant Roxana Vargas doesn't have a management title and technically is not a patient at UCLA, she reports that she received VIP treatment from a social worker on her unit. Roxana shares, "Pam Hoff, our clinical social worker, has always been my encouraging force. . . . This has not been my best year; I have endured a lot of turbulence, especially with my niece Ashley being diagnosed with GI cancer. . . . Pam guided me and my niece's mother through the next steps when everything else seemed so dark and gloomy. Pam actually gave us hope and holds a very special place in our hearts, with lots of love and appreciation toward her." Pam's care of Roxana is probably consistent with the care that Pam provides to the patients on her unit. When service comes through a desire to meet the needs of the recipient, it is authentic. Otherwise, service behavior can appear contrived and will fail to connect with the person receiving that care.

In order to make the authentic connection, UCLA's service revolution has highlighted empathy. Whether it is a coworker in need, a staff member beside the bed of an ailing family member, or an ill and frightened stranger, compassion and empathy guide UCLA's delivery of care. Jeanne Durrant, office manager at the UCLA Medical Group Practice office in Malibu, notes, "Our staff members see broken bones and other urgent-care needs all day long, so it becomes routine. However, for the person who has just broken a bone, it is a significant life event. We are constantly working to refresh our perspective, to fully connect with the experience of the person in front of us, and to get out of our own frame of reference."

Delia De Sasia, RRT, respiratory therapist for the Liver Transplant Unit, points out that the true test of empathy occurs when a patient becomes difficult to manage. "In those cases, I have to take a deep breath and think about how I would want to be treated if I were stressed and sick. I can't expect people to be at their best when they are hurting or frightened, but in response, I can expect my treatment of them to be at its best." Gene Loveland, RN, UCLA Emergency Department, highlights just how challenging service can be in an environment in which people sometimes want the opposite of care. "A trauma patient was brought in with a self-inflicted gunshot wound. He wanted to die, and he didn't expect to survive his suicide attempt. When the paramedics rolled him into the Emergency Department, he was yelling and screaming about how he didn't want to be helped, he wasn't paying the bill, and he didn't want to be in the ED. That's when you kick in an extra gear of empathy to treat him the exact same way as you would a family member. It might seem like a bit of a stretch, but we are all family. We're all human, and we all have our issues. I just do the best I can in those moments."

The more leaders champion high-quality service for all who enter their businesses, the more likely employees will be to patronize that business. Great leaders understand the value of converting employees into customers. In fact, this was a consideration when Henry Ford began paying his employees $5 a day in 1914, essentially doubling the compensation for auto workers. Henry reasoned that he needed to pay his employees enough to enable them to buy his cars. Hopefully, your employees would choose to be customers of your business if they were in a position to purchase from you. If they would not, you may want to think about what distinctions or service shortcomings on your part might cause them to buy from a competitor.

The Future

Just as service distinctions between customers and staff members often occur, similar distinctions between seasoned staff and trainees sometimes take place. In some businesses, staff members are treated differently based on their status or perceived value to the employer. Managers in these companies may in fact create formal and informal standards of care based on seniority or other distinguishing factors. In these cases, a new hire might be placed in a position where he would "pay his dues." For example, many television programs depict medical residents as being treated in rather inhumane ways, almost as if they are enduring an unkind rite of passage. Dr. Mark Morocco, FACEP, UCLA associate residency director, associate professor of Medicine/Emergency Medicine, and former medical supervisor/staff writer for the hit television series *ER*, notes, "The image of residents enduring disrespect and a lack of care may be an artifact of another era of medical training. I can assure you that residents are valued and cared for here at UCLA. In Emergency Medicine, we realize that they are the future of our vision, and UCLA's leaders, from individual program directors up to the systemwide leadership, promote and protect this belief in all departments. If UCLA is about 'healing humankind,' we have to demonstrate the best of humanity for our healers and our healers in training. You have to realize that most of these residents will practice medicine around the world, and each one of them will represent UCLA as she goes forward. Added to that, some of them will join our staff here at UCLA, and that inextricably links them to our future. Serving students and residents well not only is our duty, but it is good for us all."

Similarly, Reverend Karen Schnell, director of the Department of Spiritual Care at UCLA, notes, "We see our Clinical Pastoral Education internship and residency training as an opportunity to nurture the development of our program participants, and in the process our staff members are given the opportunity to work with extremely talented religious leaders from around the world. I look at the training as a conversation, where these students reciprocally enrich us in our ability to deliver our services today and into the future. For me, the greatest empathy builder and testament to caring for your students is the realization that many of us were sitting in the chairs where these students sit today. I did the majority of my CPE and supervisory training here at UCLA. We were fortunate enough to train Reverend Yuko Uesugi. She is now the director of our ACPE Clinical Pastoral Education program and the associate director of our Spiritual Care Department. So when I look into the eyes of our interns, I am enlivened. Caring for them is the same as caring for the future."

Unfortunately, business leaders can develop rather short timelines for success. The pressure to make quarterly numbers can lead to service messages that produce unintended segmentation of customers or differential treatment of inexperienced staff members. The pursuit of profit can at times lead to mistreatment of people, with resultant customer churn and staff defection. W. Edwards Deming is quoted as suggesting that companies are in business not to make a profit but to "make a customer." It is through customers that profits are made. At UCLA, the term "customer" is extremely inclusive. In fact, it is synonymous with "humankind."

While every business leader wants to think that his company's employees and customers are being treated equally, it is clear that in some businesses, the leaders give the care of customers priority well beyond the care of employees. Under those circumstances, it is unlikely that those employees would feel a desire to spend money that benefits those leaders. Similarly, while most leaders hope that all staff members will be treated in fairly equal ways, they have not spent time talking with people at all levels of their organization to assess how well employees are treated across their business landscape.

YOUR DIAGNOSTIC CHECKUP

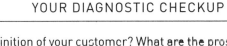 What is your definition of your customer? What are the pros and cons of expanding that definition?

Do your employees purchase products or services from your company? If the nature of your business makes this implausible, would they buy from you if they could?

Is there a different standard of care for employees as opposed to customers?

┬ Do some customers get a higher level of care than others?
│ If this difference exists, is it by design (a strategic
│ segmentation) or by default?
┬ Is the employee experience consistent, or are the leaders
│ treated differently from the front line?

SERVICE THROUGH HUSBANDING RESOURCES

Broadening a service vision or expanding the definition of "customer" has its share of complications and challenges, not least of
which is the ability to husband one's resources as needed to maximize care. Helen Contreraz, director of admissions for UCLA
Health System, notes, "We have had a lot of challenging cases, and
we have many groups to serve with a finite pool of resources. These
groups include patients, citizens of California who are stakeholders, insurance providers, doctors in training, and our scientists.
One way we monitor our treatment resources is through a High
Dollar Committee that I chair. This multidisciplinary committee
works to identify and proactively plan care for patients with needs
that are probably complex and costly. For example, our committee
addressed the case of a gentleman and his wife from China who
were visiting their daughter here at UCLA. They were meeting at
a Starbucks in Westwood when a car careened out of control and
pinned the man against a wall. His injuries required a field amputation of his legs. The unlicensed driver had apparently suffered a
seizure, and it was clear that there would be limited resources available to assist the victim. Our committee got involved very early in
what turned out to be a six-month hospitalization for the patient.
We looked at all the barriers to his care, discharge planning needs,
and other posthospitalization considerations. We involved our Pastoral Care and International Relations representatives to help the
patient's wife deal with the situation and assist in her husband's
medical care. We reached out to the Chinese community to get

housing resources for him after his discharge. His daughter lived in a second-floor apartment, and the patient needed to be discharged to ground-level living, given that he had had a double amputation at the hip. After discharge, the patient experienced kidney malfunction, so our team had to be very creative in the way we contracted with an outpatient dialysis unit to secure those services. We even addressed the fact that the patient would not be repatriated to China because of his medical needs and the limitations of his small village. The committee was very proactive with this case, and we knew from the onset that we would need to partner with others and be as resourceful as possible."

In addition to anticipating and reacting to the needs of specific patients, Helen's committee also addresses large-scale resource challenges. Helen notes, "The care of the homeless is an issue for us. To address this, we started an initiative in Santa Monica where we partner with a vendor who helps us with coverage for unfunded patients. Working with that vendor, we started following these homeless patients to assist them to qualify for social security disability. The process of qualifying for disability benefits is usually 2 to 2½ years. Within the first 2½ years of our pilot program, we have qualified 136 people who otherwise would not have received benefits to which they are entitled."

Dr. Feinberg notes that all cost-oversight procedures are important to the viability of programs at UCLA. During a time when the state of California was in the midst of a severe financial crisis, Dr. Feinberg shared, "We enjoyed our second-best year ever. And we did that despite the terrible economy. While other hospitals struggled, we were successful and maintained a favorable patient mix. Again, this is because we take excellent care of our patients and treat them the way we would want ourselves or our family members to be treated." Dr. Feinberg also explained that despite generating $50 million in profit that year, the leaders had to be very conscientious about the organization's resources. "About half of our profits go to the David Geffen School of Medicine at UCLA and provide support for the clinical leadership that we receive, for teaching, and for development of the clinical facilities needed to support our physicians' work on behalf of our patients. The remaining net income that year was used to pay for equipment and improvements to our physical plant. We also have an obligation to the community to help care for the uninsured and underinsured. To that end, UCLA Health System spent approximately $52.4 million during that fiscal year to provide uncompensated care and to offer free screenings, information at local health fairs, lectures, fitness programs, and classes." Despite UCLA Health System's profitability in a down economy, its leaders had to manage system-wide furlough and salary reduction options as part of the state of California's declared "financial emergency" and the impact of that emergency on the University of California system as a whole.

The average business leader working outside of healthcare probably has not had to wrestle with issues of providing services to uninsured, underinsured, or homeless customers while generating $50 million in profits and operating in a situation requiring mandatory pay reductions and furloughs. Every leader, however, does face questions of how to husband her service resources for both the maximum financial outcome and the greatest overall social good. For example, a large wireless U.S. phone company made headlines in 2007 when it "fired" customers who made a large number of calls to the company's customer service line. A representative of the company was quoted in a Reuters's article as saying, "These customers were calling to a degree that we felt was excessive. [We took this step because] we're working very hard to improve customer service. That's our number one priority." In essence, that phone company's leadership took the approach that the company could serve the majority of its customers better if it selectively severed relationships with those who placed large demands on service resources. Husbanding of resources comes in many forms, and decisions as to the scope of service must be financially prudent, practical, values-based, and mission-centric.

At UCLA, the High Dollar Committee is one example of a mission-centric approach to identifying cases that may stretch the organization's resources and creatively collaborating with outside agencies to generate favorable service outcomes in a cost-conscious manner. In the end, business margins put pressure on leaders to do more with less. Effective executives find ways to do more with less and still serve their customers well. They develop mechanisms to address high demands for service in the context of their resource allocations, and they do so in accordance with the company's mission, vision, and values. They are also looking for strategic partnerships that allow them to pool resources to maximize positive service impact.

INVOLVEMENT IN COMMUNITY—FROM LOCAL TO INTERNATIONAL

As evidenced by the High Dollar Committee's work to secure disability benefits for homeless patients, UCLA's leaders explore ways to address the varied needs of the patient groups in its local community. Hala Fam, Patient Affairs and Interpreter Services manager, suggests, "In Los Angeles, we serve people from diverse cultural backgrounds and with many language interpretation needs. As a result, our medical interpreters speak several languages, and we solicit qualified volunteers from our student body to assist us as well. Those volunteers must pass language skill tests and engage in training. The opportunity to volunteer actually turns out to be a service to the volunteers, as many of them are premed students who want to have patient contact and secure references for medical school. Through our combined efforts, we tailor our service to the language needs of our patients."

One way to serve communities that support your business is to craft your services to meet the communities' unique needs (for example, securing staff members or volunteers who can deliver service with cultural sensitivity or in the preferred language of a particular population segment). Another approach is to encourage and facilitate your staff members' involvement in community volunteerism. Hal Bookbinder, director, IT Finance, Administration, and Mainframe for UCLA Health System, indicates that the leaders are actively involved in expanding the definition of service to include community volunteerism. "Our leaders and employees care about people, whether they are our patients or not. . . . Being in Information Technology, I don't directly interact with patients. But I am extremely proud of what UCLA health professionals do to save and improve lives and our patient-focused cultural shift over recent years. For the past eight years, I have been volunteering at the Midnight Mission here in Los Angeles and with its sister organization, the Midnight Mission Family Housing Facility. I lead a program that trains individuals who are in recovery in job interviewing skills, assisting them in their transition. Until the recent recession, we were achieving more than 80 percent success (that is, in gaining targeted employment). This has dropped a bit with the recession. But the graduates of my program continue to be far more successful in achieving employment than those who leave the mission without this training. Recidivism among people with a history of addiction is distressingly high. And if they move on from a recovery facility without the grounding of a job, recidivism is almost guaranteed. The program at the Family Housing Facility (which caters primarily to women and their children) is focused on job success skills, helping the residents move up the ladder from low-paying, entry-level positions. The women there are generally working, but often in positions that may not even cover their expenses for themselves and their children. Often, they have no clear vision of how to improve their situation. This program helps them clarify their goals and provides them with tools for better achieving these objectives. Quite a number of current and former UCLA Health System staff members have served as volunteers in this program, both as instructors and as mock interviewers." Hal goes on to note that this is just a single example of countless volunteer programs supported by UCLA leaders and staff members.

Publications directed toward UCLA Health System staff members are rich with stories of the community involvement projects of their peers. Headlines from just a few issues of these internal communications are representative of the diverse community involvement of UCLA healthcare professionals:

- "UCLA Volunteers Bring Free Medical Care to Thousands"

- "SMUCLA Physicians and Nurses Volunteer at Marathon"

- "Reaching Out Staff Support Adopt-a-Family for the Holidays"

- "UCLA Health System Heart Walk Team Raises Funds"

- "UCLA Physician Helps Students Deliver Care to the Homeless"

In the same way that the UCLA leadership has broadened the definition of "customer," it has also expanded the concept of "community." Dr. David Feinberg notes, "Our patients come to us from well beyond the boundaries of Los Angeles County, so our community support has to extend outside of our local catchment area." Jeff Fujimoto, director of rehabilitation at San Antonio Community Hospital and chair of the patient handling committee at Casa Colina Hospital, has benefited from the willingness of the UCLA leaders to be of service to those outside of Los Angeles: "I was looking for a program to benchmark for us to create a successful lift team at our hospital. I chose UCLA as the program that I wanted to visit because of its reputation, what I had read about it, and how it integrated the lift team with nursing practice. When I went for the visit, the UCLA leaders exceeded my expectations. I got to meet the director of the program, Ellen Wilson, who was fantastic. She spent a lot of time with me, and I was also introduced to the supervisor of the team and two team members. I got to see the team in action and witnessed how the team members worked in different situations on a critical-care unit. UCLA's willingness to generously share its staff members' time and wisdom definitely helped me reconceptualize aspects of the program that we are putting in place."

In addition to supporting site visits, the UCLA leaders leverage technology to serve patients, physicians, and other hospitals. For example, the UCLA Telestroke Network Partner Program allows UCLA stroke experts to use live video technology to help doctors at other hospitals quickly assess acute TIAs (transient ischemic attacks) and other strokelike presentations.

While UCLA has no obligation to offer support to patients, hospitals, or physicians in distant locations, the leaders see this as an important part of UCLA's business. CEO Dr. David Feinberg states, "You can't heal people in a vacuum. Sharing knowledge is a two-way street. We teach and we learn. For example, our chair of Neurology, Dr. John Mazziotta, had just been to New York-Presbyterian Hospital, where his mother was receiving care. While he was visiting her, Dr. Mazziotta saw nurses picking up trash from the ground and experienced people coming up to him and saying, 'How are you doing?' He also noticed that when he spent a great deal of time talking in medical terms about his mother's condition, the head of the intensive-care unit would say something like, 'I don't want to talk only about how your mom is doing medically—how are you doing? Do you have somewhere to eat? Do you have a place to stay?' Based on those reports, I took 20 people to New York-Presbyterian to benchmark its approach to care. In business, what goes around, comes around."

In a highly connected world, opportunities to share information and service well beyond one's geographic area surface regularly.

UCLA's leaders perceive themselves to be part of a healthcare "community" and believe that through service to that community, they too will be served. Obviously, leaders have to take care of their primary service functions before they can address more remote requests. However, when business leaders say yes to service opportunities outside their local neighborhood, they often extend their brand reach and increase their reputation as service leaders.

INVOLVEMENT IN INTERNATIONAL CAUSES

Dr. Juan Alejos, medical director of the pediatric heart transplant program at UCLA, said yes to community service opportunities by expanding the definition of "community" to international proportions. According to Dr. Alejos, "I initially went to Lima, Peru, to offer talks on pediatric cardiology. Soon thereafter, I took a trip with two of my colleagues, and our mission trips have grown from there. As many as 15 UCLA staff members evaluate children, provide cardiac catheterization, offer echo surgery, and work alongside Peruvian doctors. Today our organization, Hearts with Hope, www.heartswithhope.org, is completely run by volunteers, but in the early days, it was just me. I used to start working on this after my regular workday, normally around 7:00 p.m., and I'd spend the rest of the evening on the project. A couple of private companies made donations, and people helped the program grow. Each year we spend three weeks on the medical mission. Two weeks are cardiac surgery and cardiac catheterization, and one week is electrophysiology, such as ablations and pacemakers. Everyone who goes with us does so using her vacation time. There are so many people that want to go that I feel like I am taking all of the cardiologists from UCLA. Now referring cardiologists join us, taking time from their private practice. Many of those doctors trained at UCLA. I don't ever want to deprive anyone of the opportunity to serve, but I make the schedule for our division, and I have to ensure that everything is covered at UCLA when we are in Peru."

Dr. Alejos shared that he has many motivations for serving internationally. These driving forces include the opportunity to elevate care, the ability to address significant needs, the chance to offer substantial service at nominal cost, the ability to train young doctors in socially responsible medicine, and a mission to build goodwill across national borders. Dr. Alejos's Hearts with Hope program, like many other similar efforts championed by UCLA healthcare professionals (for example, medical relief teams after the earthquake in Haiti and UCLA pediatric anesthesiology professor Dr. Samuel Wald's work with Medical Missions for Children, providing cleft lip repair in Rwanda), has effectively achieved the objective of strengthening relationships between people in other countries and the UCLA brand.

Maged Matta, international patient coordinator for the Middle East, appreciates acts of service performed by UCLA health professionals and sees how they often have unintended benefits in elevating UCLA's brand presence and reputation worldwide. "Many of my Arabic-speaking patients learn about us through media stories about our doctors, come to us through word-of-mouth referrals from patients, research exceptional clinical outcomes on the Internet, or have their care sponsored by their government." While international patients often present with additional needs, Maged sees the service provided to them as a win for the patients, a benefit for the countries that sponsor the care, and a boost for UCLA. According to Maged, "The patient gets extraordinary care and is afforded access to treatment that can't be secured in his own country. But I look at the social benefits of this care as well. When those patients go home, having had a caring experience, they become ambassadors for the United States within their cultures. I see patients go back home and spread the word—and not just that they were treated well medically and the outcome hopefully was good; they also talk about the humanity, kindness, and attentiveness that they received at UCLA. UCLA becomes like a small town, and it represents America to these patients."

When international patients have a compelling need for the services offered by UCLA but cannot afford care, philanthropic considerations are made on a case-by-case basis, just as they would be for any domestic patient. The circumstances surrounding Marwa Naim's need for medical assistance availed her compassionate care at UCLA. During the U.S. invasion of Iraq in April 2003, nine-year-old Marwa was in her home when a bomb exploded, killing her mother, destroying her right thumb, and essentially removing her nose from her face. U.S. aid agencies appealed to UCLA and the hospital's chief of plastic surgery, Dr. Timothy Miller, to offer her care. Providing services at no cost, Dr. Miller and his team at UCLA were not able to repair the damage to Marwa's hand, but they successfully rebuilt her nose. Seven months later, Marwa returned to Iraq. Working through the Palestine Children's Relief Fund and the Campaign for Innocent Victims of Conflict, Dr. Miller and his team were able to bring Marwa back to the United States to put the finishing touches on the surgery that they had originally performed. Theresa Moussa, patient coordinator for UCLA's Patient & Guest Services, offered comfort and logistical support for Marwa, and noted, "I am blessed to work with a lot of patients in need, and I love what I do, but when you have the chance to give of yourself for someone like Marwa, you know your life matters."

As might be expected, Marwa's care generated considerable media attention throughout the world. Kurt Streeter, writing for the *Los Angeles Times*, poignantly encapsulated the significance of UCLA's involvement with Marwa in the following words: "Marwa Naim has her face and life transformed by an American surgeon. It was shrapnel that brought her to Los Angeles. Hot and sharp, it pierced her legs, her stomach, and her right hand. It mangled her face around her deep brown eyes, and it tore off her nose. . . . The University of California, Los Angeles (UCLA) Medical Center and its chief of plastic surgery, Dr. Tim Miller, offered to restore her face—for free."

Even in difficult economic times, leaders know that they must make service decisions that transcend the corporate bottom line. Carefully considering the company's mission and vision (in the case of UCLA, "healing humankind, one patient at a time, by improving health, alleviating suffering, and delivering acts of kindness"), these leaders must initiate the right action at the right time and trust that positive benefits will someday follow. Leaders at UCLA and physicians like Dr. Miller appreciate that not all worthwhile pursuits result in money. These leaders focus their charitable acts on the underserved and those that the leaders feel will gain the greatest benefit from the care.

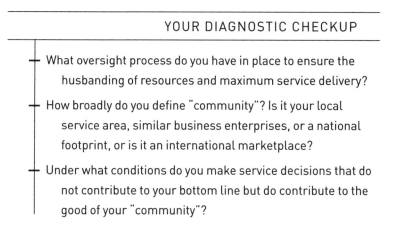

YOUR DIAGNOSTIC CHECKUP

- What oversight process do you have in place to ensure the husbanding of resources and maximum service delivery?
- How broadly do you define "community"? Is it your local service area, similar business enterprises, or a national footprint, or is it an international marketplace?
- Under what conditions do you make service decisions that do not contribute to your bottom line but do contribute to the good of your "community"?

SERVING THOSE WHO SERVE US ALL

Given that there are so many worthwhile community needs, some business leaders and owners make decisions about which causes to support from a purely tactical perspective. Leaders or marketers identify the issues that are most relevant to their prime customer groups and position corporate giving and marketing efforts in those defined areas. These strategic corporate responsibility initiatives can prove unsustainable in periods when budgets are tight because of a lack of authentic interest or the absence of a champion to fight for funding. Social giving programs that gain traction at UCLA typically emerge from leaders who have a genuine, heartfelt passion for a given area of concern. Those leaders, in turn, partner with like-minded individuals within UCLA and the community.

A classic example of this impassioned collaboration is the UCLA Operation Mend program. Ronald Katz, a successful inventor in the automated call-center industry and a Ronald Reagan UCLA Medical Center board member, saw an opportunity to enlist the skills of talented medical professionals at UCLA to support medical-care efforts on behalf of soldiers who had been wounded in Iraq and Afghanistan. Mr. Katz's idea was readily embraced by senior leaders (people like Dr. Gerald Levey, then dean of the Medical School, and CEO Dr. David Feinberg), as well as other leaders and medical professionals throughout UCLA. Ron, whose Katz Family Foundation helps cover a portion of the costs associated with the program, describes Operation Mend as "an extraordinary collaboration between the surgeons and staff of UCLA Health System and Brooke Army Medical Center."

Primary among the surgeons recommended by Dean Levey to Ron Katz was Dr. Timothy Miller, chief of plastic surgery at UCLA, the same plastic surgeon who was involved in the care of Marwa Naim. Dr. Miller shares, "The program started thanks to an identified need by Ron Katz, a true philanthropist. He saw a Marine corporal who had sustained some very serious burns to his face and hands. He subsequently approached the dean of the Medical School, Jerry Levey, and I got a call asking if I would be willing to operate on some Marines and soldiers who had been injured in Iraq and Afghanistan. I immediately said yes." When asked why he was so quick to embrace this cause, Dr. Miller notes, "I had done a fair amount of reconstructive work on firemen, burn patients, and skin cancer patients, but primarily I was making a living doing cosmetic surgery. As a Vietnam veteran, this cause mattered to me. I wanted our wounded soldiers to receive the best care possible and experience a level of support that was not present when I returned from Vietnam. These young men and women have given a great deal and have put themselves at tremendous risk on our behalf. We owe them, and Operation Mend was a unique opportunity for me to give something back as a plastic surgeon. I jumped at the chance, and it has been the most rewarding thing I have ever done in my career."

For many of the patients in the Operation Mend program, the care they receive at UCLA restores hope and a sense of normalcy to their lives. Marine Corporal Aaron Mankin, the first patient treated in the UCLA Operation Mend program, shares that his war-related injuries were beyond anything he could ever have envisioned. "When you are headed into combat, you kind of think, 'All right, I don't want to get hurt, but it's a possibility.' I even thought about what I could live without. I could lose an arm and I would be okay. I could do without a leg. Man, you don't think about losing your fingers or your face. But that is in fact what I lost." Corporal Mankin goes on to share how a television appearance led to the start of the UCLA Operation Mend program. "After I got wounded, I was sent to the burn unit at Brooke Army Medical Center in San Antonio and got a natural feel and mix to my facial skin. Later, I became the patient media liaison because I had public affairs training and knew how to give and conduct interviews. When Lou Dobbs came to do a story, I did a short interview with him and a little standup. One set of questions he asked was, 'What is next for you? What can you expect?' I made some jokes about how the Army just needed to make me pretty again. Ron Katz and his wife, Maddie, saw me on television and reportedly thought, 'Why don't we do this? Why don't we get involved?' Ron jumped in and started making things happen, and UCLA Operation Mend was created. I was the first patient to partake in this new venture."

Shannon O'Kelley, associate director of operations in Clinical Services, explains the steps taken by UCLA's leaders to turn Ron Katz's idea into an actual program that was ready to accept Corporal Mankin and others. "A team from UCLA, including a group of surgeons, flew down to Brooke Army Medical Center in San Antonio to talk to officials there. The Army was initially uncertain whether our services were needed, given the military's internal resources, and it expressed concern for the well-being of these men and women if they were to travel to Los Angeles. Upon returning from Texas, I worked with our team to operationalize a unique way to manage every aspect of the care of these individuals. We designed a patient care flow process that ensured seamless service from the arrival of these special patients through to their departure." As a result of Shannon's efforts in the early stages of Operation Mend, he was nominated for a Hospital Hero of the Year award. While processes in Operation Mend are far more established, Shannon's Hospital Hero of the Year Award nomination noted that he "personally met soldiers at the airport arrival gate, and made himself available around-the-clock to answer any of their questions or allay concerns. He escorted them to appointments, and he dug into his own pocket to pay expenses. He forms a personal relationship with each soldier that continues after the soldier leaves UCLA."

Operation Mend patients such as Army Sergeant Richard (Rick) Yarosh value the willingness of people like Shannon to meet their needs. Sergeant Yarosh notes, "I am so grateful for the entire team that serves me at UCLA. I am 60 percent burned, with the only parts of my body that aren't burned being my chest and my back. In terms of my face, my ears were burned off, as was half of my nose. My surgeries at UCLA are focused on reconstructing my nose and helping me loosen up the scars around my lips because the scars on my face tighten. I wanted the UCLA Operation Mend program to do these things, and it came through for me and then some. UCLA didn't need to step up to the plate, but it did." Marine Corporal Oyoana Allende adds, "This is a life-changing program. You notice the care here at UCLA, and the speed with which you recover from surgery is amazing. Plus UCLA has built an experience that is completely supportive and efficient. Beyond the amazing surgical outcome, I am grateful to the Buddy Family program. My husband couldn't be there for two of my surgeries, as he is an active-duty Marine, and other members of my family were also not available. Fortunately, my Buddy Family was here for me and made sure I wasn't alone."

Dana Katz, the Buddy Family coordinator for Operation Mend, describes this important social support component. "As part of UCLA's efforts to assure complete care and comfort for the program's participants, my father-in-law, Ron Katz, had the idea for the Buddy Family Program and asked my husband and me to be the first host family for Aaron Mankin. Aaron was coming for his initial procedure with his wife and their daughter, so we sought to be their family support away from home. We have been constantly refining the Buddy Family Program ever since, but for Aaron, we started by greeting the members of his family when they arrived at UCLA Tiverton House and having them over to our home for dinner on their first night in town. From there, we focused on anticipating and meeting the needs of Aaron and his family at every point along their care journey."

Marine Gunnery Sergeant Blaine Scott appreciates not only the surgical services he has received at UCLA, but the care offered to his family as well. "UCLA Operation Mend has done so much for me. I just wanted my mouth fixed and my eye taken care of, but they went the extra mile to give me a new nose and even helped with my ankle. Better yet, the program staff members take care of my family so that we don't have to worry about anything while we are here. There's no way I would be able to afford to stay at Tiverton House or pay for my family to eat here in Los Angeles. I don't have the budget for those things, but the program nurtures us right down to giving us an amazing quilt. Thanks to the skilled surgeons, my wife sees more and more of me each day, and she says she is recognizing features that I once had. I know that the Katz Family Foundation gives money to this cause and that UCLA and the doctors extend themselves to make all this possible, but there are a lot of other people who are making financial contributions as well. I wish I could go around and shake hands and give hugs to everyone who has contributed and who has made all this possible for me and for others. I'm forever grateful to them." In addition to the proceeds of this book going to Operation Mend, you can make direct financial contributions through the following Web site: www .operationmend.ucla.edu.

Operation Mend is a well-planned, well-executed program that builds on UCLA's core medical, service, and leadership competencies. Furthermore, it involves the talent of existing UCLA staff members and physicians and forges partnerships with hospital and community volunteers. Whether it's Patti Taylor, a clinical nurse specialist in UCLA's liver transplant program, and her quilting group creating red-white-and-blue "quilts of valor" for Operation Mend patients, a Buddy Family from the community offering its hospitality and support, or the highly refined technical skills of a surgeon like Dr. Miller, UCLA's leaders have unified the university's vast resources to effectively serve those who serve them.

In every business, we have the opportunity to attack community service with the same fervor that we direct toward our for-profit service offerings. When we take this impassioned approach, we realize the importance of expanding the boundaries of service, and we realize the fullness of the principle "Service Serves Us."

Prescriptive Summary

▶ Consider defining "customer" well beyond its traditional use.

▶ Explore ways to increase the likelihood that your "employees" would choose to be your "customers."

▶ Look for unintended differences in the service experiences of various types of customers or employees.

▶ Evaluate the breadth of your concept of community. Make strategic decisions to maintain or change that breadth.

▶ Identify criteria to guide decisions concerning when service should be offered, even if it won't lead to identifiable profit.

▶ Look to champion causes that connect with your genuine passion, not just those organizations that offer strategic value.

▶ Identify ways to serve those who serve you.

▶ Discuss the idea that "Service Serves Us" and see where those conversations lead.

Your Follow-up Care Plan

A leader is one who knows the way,
goes the way, and shows the way.
—JOHN MAXWELL

UCLA Health System is among the most complicated organizations that you will ever encounter.
In essence, it is at least three businesses in one: a world-class
medical-care provider, an extraordinary medical training center,
and a cutting-edge research facility where the future of medicine is
being created today. Across all these lines of business, UCLA has
the task of developing a culture of safety that integrates technology
and human oversight to prevent harm and death to the customers
it serves. Each business thrives through constant quality improvement, a responsibility for advancing outcomes, and a passion for
streamlining processes to deliver customer-centric care. Despite its
exceptional products, its leaders relentlessly call on staff members
to increase customer satisfaction and maximize the consistency of
service delivery. The leaders champion the message that transactional service is not enough and that human care and compassion
are essential elements of every customer interaction. Finally, the
leaders deliver their products and services in the context of highly
regulated, politically volatile, and often economically challenging
circumstances.

As I approached this summary, I realized that the best way to review key lessons and hopefully inspire you to take action on the concepts presented was to emulate the successful process of UCLA's CEO, Dr. David Feinberg, who talks about patient care at seemingly every opportunity. To that end, please allow me to tell you a patient story—the story of Jay and Katherine Wolf.

Jay and Katherine were living in Malibu, California, where Jay was in his third year of law school at Pepperdine University. The couple had celebrated the birth of their first child, and both Jay and Katherine were in seemingly outstanding health. Katherine was a nonsmoker; she exercised regularly and had no weight-related issues. However, six months after the birth of their son, James, 26-year-old Katherine Wolf experienced a major hemorrhagic stroke secondary to the rupture of a blood supply malformation in her brain. Her neurosurgeon, Dr. Nestor Gonzalez, shares, "Katherine's case is remarkable in many aspects. One of those was the technical challenge of the procedure that we performed. The arteriovenous malformation that she had was one of the worst I had seen in my life. It presented with associated bleeding that was producing a significant increase in the pressure in her head. Her brain was basically herniating into the spinal canal. That is a condition that usually is very, very difficult to reverse, and that in the majority of cases is lethal. The malformation was very close to vital structures of her brainstem. The brainstem, as you may know, controls many of the essential functions for living. My first challenge was to decide whether surgery offered enough hope to save Katherine's life."

Concluding that the risk of inaction was greater than that of action, Dr. Gonzalez engaged in an open discussion with Katherine's husband, Jay, "I think one of the important points of the decision to go forward with the surgery was the communication with the family. I had a very honest conversation with her husband, and I clearly explained to him all of the risks of the surgery, and that they were quite high. But UCLA is one of the few places where we could even try to save a patient like Katherine—that's what we do here. So my team launched into what I knew would be a multiple-hour surgery in which we needed to try to relieve the building pressure and remove the malformation. The surgery proved to be as challenging as I had imagined. I never look at the clock when I work, since my only priority is to be absolutely sure that everything we do for the patient is done perfectly—that no harm comes to the patient as a result of any movement that I make while dissecting. Very, very carefully, we removed every single vessel that was abnormal and removed the hematoma. When I finished, I thought I had been working for 8 hours because I was really tired; in truth, it had been 16 hours." Dr. Gonzalez concludes, "I was very confident that we had done everything we could, but we had to wait on the final result. Would she wake up, walk, or talk again?"

The answer to all three of these questions ultimately was yes, yes, and yes. Katherine responded to a nurse's command to wiggle her toes less than 24 hours after the surgery, but not all aspects of her recovery were swift. She spent four months in acute rehabilitation recovering from damage to seven cranial nerves that resulted in partial facial paralysis, double vision, and decreased coordination of her right hand. She passed swallow tests after 11 months of being unable to eat, and she began to walk with a cane nearly a year after being confined to a wheelchair.

Jay and Katherine praise not only the lifesaving surgery that Katherine received at UCLA, but the compassion and kindness that they received as well. Jay notes, "The staff members at UCLA helped us through an amazingly difficult time. They joined the support community that surrounded Katherine, and they truly cared. Katherine mattered to them, and that mattered to me." Katherine notes, "To me, UCLA means quality, caring, and life. I cannot express how much the staff members encouraged and invested in me and my family."

Jay and Katherine have not kept their praise of UCLA to themselves. Jay shares, "Dr. Feinberg told me that he had seen a lot of friend and family support in medical crises, but that he felt that our situation was a new paradigm because within moments of Katherine's initial brain injury, Facebook groups were started and an actual Web site called katherinewolf.info and the Caring Bridge page were created. People across the country, actually across the world, began supporting us, and there was an amazing outpouring of family and friend visitation. Also, given the severity of Katherine's injury and how long we were at UCLA, we got to be close to people throughout the hospital—from the people at the front desk to the security guards, let alone the doctors, therapists, and nurses. Katherine's story is compelling because of her youth, the outpouring of support from our friends and our community, and the miraculous outcome. I am convinced that Katherine's case was a bright spot for UCLA's staff, and we did all we could to show our appreciation for its professionalism, kindness, and sacrifices for Katherine. We saw that far too often, staff members do not receive the gratitude they deserve from the patients and families whom they so capably served. We will forever be indebted and grateful for UCLA taking the time to be with us and care for us."

All of the lessons of this book are embedded in Katherine's story, and the elements of her experience at UCLA can serve as a template for a follow-up plan for your business. Every aspect of Katherine's safety was built into the processes and procedures of the operating room. All the work of UCLA's leaders to drive a safety culture allowed Dr. Gonzalez to focus on the likely risks of the procedure itself, without undue concern for underlying or neglected safety precautions. Dr. Gonzalez himself owned responsibility for the patient's safety—he weighed the risks of the procedure against its benefits and communicated honestly about the possible outcomes, including death. Everyone who was involved in Katherine's surgery, recovery, and rehabilitation did what was necessary to "leave no room for error" in terms of her safe treatment.

By equipping Dr. Gonzalez and other surgeons with the technology to match their talent and by recruiting and training exceptional staff members at all levels of Katherine's care, UCLA's leaders provided the foundation for a high-quality outcome. By constantly working on process improvements, using detailed quality dashboards to measure outcomes and efficiencies, UCLA had put the essential infrastructure for Katherine's seemingly miraculous survival in place. In essence, Katherine's surgery and postsurgical care realized the leadership's desire to "make the best better."

Dr. Gonzalez believed that Katherine's procedure might not have been attempted at other hospitals. In referring to his willingness to go forward with the delicate operation, he stated, "That's what we do here." Those words encapsulate UCLA's commitment to push the envelope of care in responsible and scientific ways. In the spirit of innovation, Dr. Gonzalez was essentially empowered to ask, "If not here, where else?" His calculated decision to proceed in the context of the watchful eyes of developing surgeons is in keeping with an attitude to "create the future."

The consistent delivery of compassionate care built strong bonds between the Wolfs and staff members at UCLA at all levels of the organization, from security guards to neurosurgeons. Staff members delivered consistent care in accordance with UCLA's CICARE model. They forged an authentic, relationship-based experience with Jay and Katherine. Along the journey, staff members infused hope into, listened to, spent time with, did for, and enabled Jay and Katherine. In essence, the staff members' actions embodied the leadership's message that you must "commit to care."

Finally, Jay and Katherine are brand ambassadors for UCLA. They participate in public presentations, enjoy a strong support community, have a prominent blog presence, are rich with Facebook followers, and honestly advance the message of UCLA's product and service quality. An excerpt from Katherine's message of gratitude can be found in a blog post at the one-year anniversary of her stroke, and it is fairly indicative of her amazingly optimistic perspective on life and her willingness to champion UCLA. Referring to her good fortune concerning how things "happened" amidst the tragedy, Katherine writes, "My husband unexpectedly came home for lunch right before I collapsed. He happened to be home to call an ambulance and be there for my six-month-old baby, who was napping when I collapsed. I was taken to UCLA, which happens to be one of the best hospitals in the country. Dr. Nestor Gonzalez performed my 16-hour brain surgery, and he just happens to be double board certified in vascular neurosurgery and radiology. His skills were specifically useful for my situation. . . . I happened to win $50,000 on a game show (*Are You Smarter than a Fifth Grader?*). The check came in the mail after I was already in the hospital. That money enabled Jay to care for me full time." Katherine's honest, poignant, grateful, and inspirational posts shape the perceptions of UCLA for countless numbers of her blog readers, validating the notion that "Service Serves Us."

So how will you take the leadership excellence of UCLA and fit it into your organization? Will it be an intensive review of your safety processes, with an eye to establishing a "safety culture," as opposed to a top-down set of safety edicts? Perhaps you will look at integrating technologies as safeguards against human shortcomings. Or will your emphasis be on getting back to the basics of product quality improvement? Maybe you need to look at service consistency in your organization, and you will define desired service behaviors, while developing accountability processes such as management rounds and usable performance-tracking systems.

Some of you might reinforce the distinction between "service" and "experience" or lobby your team to invest in customer experience elevation in light of the likely financial and brand-differentiation benefits you will enjoy. You might start every meeting with a customer service story or spend more time offering service to your team members so that they will be inspired by your example. Others of you will begin discussions concerning the five caring processes or define concepts like "customer" or "community" more broadly.

The steps you decide to take are less important than whether you take any steps at all. The English biologist Thomas Huxley said it best when he noted, "The great end of life is not knowledge but action."

So what action steps will you take from the knowledge you acquired while diving into the leadership practices at UCLA? Up to this point, I have offered prescriptive advice at the close of each chapter. This time, I leave you a blank prescription.

Whether it is on a scrap of paper or a post you write on your Facebook wall, please take the time to make a written commitment by completing your "Prescriptive Action" plan. Through steadfast execution of that plan, you will elevate your service one customer at a time, so that, in the words of UCLA CEO Dr. David Feinberg, "Your next customer will be your most important one!"

Prescriptive Action

▶ _____
_____
_____
_____

▶ _____
_____
_____
_____

▶ _____
_____
_____
_____

▶ _____
_____
_____
_____

▶ _____
_____
_____
_____

▶ _____
_____
_____
_____

▶ _____
_____
_____
_____

▶ _____
_____
_____
_____

▶ _____
_____
_____

Appendix A

INSTITUTES AND CENTERS AT UCLA HEALTH SYSTEM

UCLA AIDS Institute

UCLA Brain Research Institute

California NanoSystems Institute

Center for Neurobiology of Stress

Crump Institute for Molecular Imaging

Doris Stein Eye Research Center

Edie and Lew Wasserman Eye Research Center

Inflammatory Bowel Disease (IBD) Center

Institute for Molecular Medicine

Institute of Urologic Oncology at UCLA

Jules Stein Eye Institute

Pfleger Liver Institute

Jane and Terry Semel Institute for Neuroscience and Human
Behavior at UCLA

HEALTH CENTERS

Aging: UCLA Center on Aging

AIDS: CARE Center/Center for Clinical AIDS Research and
Education

Alzheimer's disease: Mary S. Easton Center for Alzheimer's
Disease Research at UCLA

Blood donations: Blood and Platelet Center

Breast cancer: Revlon/UCLA Breast Center

Cancer: Jonsson Comprehensive Cancer Center

Cancer: Simms/Mann UCLA Center for Integrative Oncology

Cerebral palsy: UCLA/Orthopaedic Hospital Center for
Cerebral Palsy

Children's health: Witherbee Foundation Children's Health Center

Children's health: Marion Davies Children's Center

Dermatology: UCLA Dermatology Center

Diabetes: Gonda (Goldschmied) Diabetes Center

Diabetes: Larry L. Hillblom Islet Research Center at UCLA

Digestive Diseases: CURE: Digestive Diseases Research Center

Ear: Victor Goodhill Ear Center

East-West medicine: UCLA Center for East-West Medicine

Esophageal: UCLA Center for Esophageal Disorders

Family health: UCLA Family Health Center,
UCLA Family Medicine

Genetics: Center for Society and Genetics

Genetics: Gonda (Goldschmied) Neuroscience and Genetics
Research Center

Hand: UCLA Hand Center

Heart: Ahmanson/UCLA Adult Congenital Heart
Disease Center

Heart: Ahmanson-UCLA Cardiomyopathy Center

Heart: UCLA Cardiac Arrhythmia Center

Hyperbaric: UCLA Gonda Center for Wound Healing and
Hyperbaric Medicine

Hyperbaric: Gonda (Goldschmied) Wound Treatment and
Clinical Tissue Engineering Center at UCLA

Imaging: Laboratory of Neuro Imaging (LONI)

Medical research: Gordon and Virginia MacDonald Medical Research Laboratories

Muscular dystrophy: UCLA Duchenne Muscular Dystrophy Research Center

Muscular dystrophy: Center for Duchenne Muscular Dystrophy at UCLA

Neurology: Clarence C. Reed Neurological Research Center

Neuroscience: Neuroscience Research Building

Nutrition: UCLA Center for Human Nutrition

Orthopaedics: Orthopaedic Hospital Research Center

Outpatient surgery: Ambulatory Surgery Center at UCLA

Robotics: CASIT/Center for Advanced Surgical and Interventional Technology

Spine: UCLA Comprehensive Spine Center

Student health: Arthur Ashe Student Health and Wellness Center

Stroke: UCLA Stroke Center

Transplant: Dumont-UCLA Transplant Center

Urology: Frank Clark Urology Center

Vascular: Gonda (Goldschmied) Vascular Center

Vascular: UCLA Gonda Venous Center & APU

Voice: UCLA Voice Center for Medicine and the Arts

Women's health: Iris Cantor-UCLA Women's Health Center

RESOURCE CENTERS

Advance directives: Center for Humane and Ethical Medical Care (CHEC √)

Cancer: Simms/Mann UCLA Center for Integrative Oncology

Ethics: UCLA Ethics Center

Library: Louise M. Darling Biomedical Library

Mental health: Nathanson Family Resource Center

Pediatric hematology/oncology: Hope Family Resource Room and Library

Rape treatment: UCLA Rape Treatment Center

Women's health: Iris Cantor-UCLA Women's Health Education & Resource Center (WHERC)

JANE AND TERRY SEMEL INSTITUTE FOR NEUROSCIENCE AND HUMAN BEHAVIOR AT UCLA RESEARCH CENTERS

Ahmanson-Lovelace Brain Mapping Center

Center for Addictive Behaviors

Center for Autism Research and Treatment

Center for Community Health

Centers for Culture and Health Services Research

Center for Neurobehavioral Genetics

Norman Cousins Center for Psychoneuroimmunology

Stefan and Shirley Hatos Center for Neuropharmacology

Stem Cell Research Center

Intellectual and Developmental Disabilities Research Center

INTEGRATED CENTERS

Integrated Substance Abuse Program

Memory and Aging Research Center

Tennenbaum Center for the Biology of Creativity

Appendix B

The following excerpt is from information published and distributed by UCLA Health System:

THE UCLA HEALTH SYSTEM
SELF-STUDY ORIENTATION GUIDE AND
STAFF INFORMATION HANDBOOK
JANUARY 2010

PATIENT CONFIDENTIALITY

Every patient has a right to privacy and it is every employee's responsibility to protect that confidentiality. This means keeping information about patients and their health care private. Both federal law (the Health Insurance Portability and Accountability Act or "HIPAA") and California state law require the protection of all Patient Identifiable Health Information, including all identifiers, images and other information which could be used to determine the identity of a patient. The privacy laws apply to all forms of patient health information, including paper, electronic and verbal information. Unauthorized use of UCLA's information systems, which includes inappropriate view, review, access and/or disclosure of medical and personal information can result in disciplinary action (up to and including termination), notification to the government, fines and reporting to licensing boards, and may constitute grounds for either civil or criminal actions. Do not share your password and LOG OFF when you leave the workstation.

Staff are required to only use or access that amount of patient information that is minimally necessary to complete a task, responsibility or function. Staff are required to only use and access information on patients for whom they are providing care, or which they need the information to complete a task that is part of their responsibilities.

Confidential information includes a wide variety of information about a patient's health care. Examples of confidential information include:

- Patient identifiers such as medical record number, name, date of birth, Social Security Number, address, phone number, contact information, photographic images and any other unique code or characteristic that could be used to identify an individual patient

- Details about illnesses or conditions (particularly AIDS, psychiatric conditions, genetic testing or alcohol/drug abuse)

- Information about treatments

- Health-care provider's notes about a patient

- Patient billing information

- Conversations between a patient and a health-care provider

General patient information in the facility directory such as patient name and condition may be released as provided by California state law and federal privacy regulations without the patient's specific authorization unless the patient requests that they not be listed in the facility directory or census. Your department may have special rules regarding when to release this information. Please consult with your supervisor or manager before releasing information.

Patients have certain rights granted under federal and state law to control their protected health information, including the right to access and receive a copy of their health information, request addendums to or changes to their health information, request restrictions on how and to whom their information is used or disclosed, request alternate methods for communicating with them, and to obtain a list of individuals or organizations to whom UCLA Health System has provided access to their information. These rights apply to both the patient's medical and billing records.

At the time of admission or at the first outpatient direct service encounter, each patient receives a "UCLA Health System Notice of Privacy Practices" which explains how the UCLA Health System uses patient information, and the rights the patients have over their own health information.

PRIVACY AND INFORMATION SECURITY POLICIES AND RESOURCES

UCLA Health System policies and procedures, and University of California policies, relating to the protection of patient privacy can be found on the Office of Compliance and Privacy website, accessible from the UCLA Health System employee website. The website outlines how patients may exercise their privacy rights over their health information, and provides training materials and resources for staff on the legal requirements for protecting and securing patient information.

GUIDELINES FOR PROTECTING PATIENT CONFIDENTIALITY

The federal "HIPAA" regulations require all staff to use physical, technical and other safeguards to keep protected health information secure and private.

- Protect all records. Keep records secured, and ensure that only authorized staff are accessing records for valid treatment, payment and healthcare operations purposes.

- Keep all patient information covered. Do not leave patient information displayed on computer screens. Only authorized personnel may review medical records whether in paper or electronic formats.

- Don't talk about patients in public. Be careful not to discuss confidential information where others, including patients, visitors, or other employees, might overhear.

- Use care with telephones, fax machines, and e-mails. Make sure that all department printers, fax machines and other devices used for transmitting or storing patient information are secure.

- Protect your computer passwords and never share them with anyone else.

- Dispose of trash with confidential patient information on it in secured disposal containers or shred the information.

- Do not look up information not required for your job.

- Use only encrypted flash drives or USB keys to protect the integrity of the clinical information.

- Report suspected information security and privacy violations to your supervisor, through the event reporting system, the Hotline, or to the Office of Compliance and Privacy.

Appendix C

CONFIDENTIALITY AGREEMENT

UCLA Health System

Applies to all UCLA Health System "workforce members" including: employees, medical staff and other health care professionals; volunteers; agency, temporary and registry personnel;
and trainees, house staff, students, and interns (regardless
of whether they are UCLA trainees or rotating through UCLA
Health System facilities from another institution).

It is the responsibility of all UCLA Health System workforce
members, as defined above, including employees, medical staff,
house staff, students and volunteers, to preserve and protect confidential patient, employee and business information.

The federal Health Insurance Portability Accountability Act
(the "Privacy Rule"), the Confidentiality of Medical Information
Act (California Civil Code § 56 et seq.) and the Lanterman-Pe-
tris-Short Act (California Welfare & Institutions Code § 5000 et
seq.) govern the release of patient identifiable information by hospitals and other health care providers. The State Information Practices Act (California Civil Code sections 1798 et seq.) governs the
acquisition and use of data that pertains to individuals. All of these
laws establish protections to preserve the confidentiality of various
medical and personal information and specify that such information may not be disclosed except as authorized by law or the patient
or individual.

Confidential Patient Care Information includes: Any individually identifiable information in possession or derived from a provider of health care regarding a patient's medical history, mental, or physical condition or treatment, as well as the patients and/or their family members records, test results, conversations, research records and financial information. (Note: this information is defined in the Privacy Rule as "protected health information.") Examples include, but are not limited to:

- Physical medical and psychiatric records including paper, photo, video, diagnostic and therapeutic reports, laboratory and pathology samples;

- Patient insurance and billing records;

- Mainframe and department based computerized patient data and alphanumeric radio pager messages;

- Visual observation of patients receiving medical care or accessing services; and

- Verbal information provided by or about a patient.

Confidential Employee and Business Information includes, but is not limited to, the following:

- Employee home telephone number and address;

- Spouse or other relative names;

- Social Security number or income tax withholding records;

- Information related to evaluation of performance;

- Other such information obtained from the University's records which if disclosed, would constitute an unwarranted invasion of privacy; or

- Disclosure of Confidential business information that would cause harm to UCLA Health System.

Peer review and risk management activities and information are protected under California Evidence Code section 1157 and the attorney-client privilege.

I understand and acknowledge that:

1. I shall respect and maintain the confidentiality of all discussions, deliberations, patient care records and any other information generated in connection with individual patient care, risk management and/or peer review activities.

2. It is my legal and ethical responsibility to protect the privacy, confidentiality and security of all medical records, proprietary information and other confidential information relating to UCLA Health System and its affiliates, including business, employment and medical information relating to our patients, members, employees and health care providers.

3. I shall only access or disseminate patient care information in the performance of my assigned duties and where required by or permitted by law, and in a manner which is consistent with officially adopted policies of UCLA Health System, or where no officially adopted policy exists, only with the express approval of my supervisor or designee. I shall make no voluntary disclosure of any discussion, deliberations, patient care records or any other patient care, peer review or risk management information, except to persons authorized to receive it in the conduct of UCLA Health System affairs.

4. UCLA Health System Administration performs audits and reviews patient records in order to identify inappropriate access.

5. My user ID is recorded when I access electronic records and that I am the only one authorized to use my user ID. Use of my user ID is my responsibility whether by me or anyone else.

I will only access the minimum necessary information to satisfy my job role or the need of the request.

6. I agree to discuss confidential information only in the workplace and only for job related purposes and to not discuss such information outside of the workplace or within hearing of other people who do not have a need to know about the information.

7. I understand that any and all references to HIV testing, such as any clinical test or laboratory test used to identify HIV, a component of HIV, or antibodies or antigens to HIV are specifically protected under law and unauthorized release of confidential information may make me subject to legal and/or disciplinary action.

8. I understand that the law specially protects psychiatric and drug abuse records, and that unauthorized release of such information may make me subject to legal and/or disciplinary action.

9. My obligation to safeguard patient confidentiality continues after my termination of employment with the University of California.

I hereby acknowledge that I have read and understand the foregoing information and that my signature below signifies my agreement to comply with the above terms. In the event of a breach or threatened breach of the Confidentiality Agreement, I acknowledge that the University of California may, as applicable and as it deems appropriate, pursue disciplinary action up to and including my termination from the University of California.

Dated: _____ Signature: _____

Print Name: _____

Department: _____

Notes

CHAPTER 1

The history of UCLA Health System and the awards information were obtained from the UCLA Health System Web sites www.uclahealth.org and www.fiftyyears.healthcare.ucla.edu.

"'. . . one of the greatest medical meccas in the world.'" "Great Medical Center Building to Start Soon," *Los Angeles Times* (1886–Current File), November 30, 1950; ProQuest Historical Newspapers, *Los Angeles Times* (1881–1969).

CHAPTER 2

"In fact, a survey of healthcare CFOs published by Healthmedia.com suggests that talent selection and retention (particularly among professional providers) is the single most pressing issue for business success over the foreseeable future (followed by cost management and patient-centric care delivery)." Health Leaders Media, www.healthleadersmedia.com/pdf/survey_project /2010 /CEO_pages_2010.pdf.

CHAPTER 3

"To measure that customer 'love,' Ritz-Carlton utilizes the Gallup Corporation's CE-11 (customer engagement tool), which asks customers to endorse responses like the degree to which the brand is perfect for someone like them, or whether the customer is a proud supporter of the brand. These items drill down much deeper than questions like 'Are you satisfied with our service?' Instead, they measure whether customers are passionate about your company." Joseph A. Michelli, *The New Gold Standard: 5 Leadership Principles for Creating a Legendary Customer Experience Courtesy of the Ritz-Carlton Hotel Company* (New York: McGraw-Hill, 2008)

"For example, the nursing department at UCLA has adopted and modified a model of relationship-based care championed by Creative Health Care Management." Information obtained from the Creative Health Care Management Web site, www.chcm.com.

"That model asserts that relationship-based care is a commitment from bedside to boardroom and builds on evolving theory and research that began in the late 1970s when Jean Watson, a distinguished professor of nursing and founder of the Center for Human Caring, first began to look at 'care' from both the giver's and the receiver's perspective." Information obtained from the Web site www.watsoncaringscience.org.

"The model, the 'five caring processes,' was originally crafted by Dr. Kristen Swanson, affiliate professor of parent and child nursing at the University of Washington." Kristen M. Swanson, Department of Parent and Child Nursing, University of Washington, Seattle, "Empirical Development of a Middle Range Theory of Caring," *Nursing Research* 40, no. 3 (1991).

"'I only wish I could find an institute that teaches people how to listen. Business people need to listen. . . . Too many people fail to realize that real communication goes in both directions.'" Lee Iacocca and Catherine Whitney, *Where Have All the Leaders Gone?* (New York: Scribner's, 2007).

"'To say that a person feels listened to means a lot more than just their ideas get heard. It's a sign of respect. It makes people feel valued.'" Deborah Tannen, Leadership Now, Leading Thoughts, Quotes on Listening, www.leadership now.com/listeningquotes.html.

"Increasingly, UCLA Health System is enjoying highly favorable unedited reviews, such as the following, on customer feedback sites like YELP:" Yelp, "Real People Real Reviews" Web site, www.yelp.com.

CHAPTER 4

"In 1943, Abraham Maslow theorized that human beings are motivated to fulfill an escalating hierarchy of needs, with safety concerns being among the more primitive and basic aspects of human existence." Abraham H. Maslow, "A Theory of Human Motivation," *Psychological Review* 50 (1943), pp. 370–396.

"'If companies believe they will save money by reducing or ignoring safety for their workers, customers, and communities . . . they are mistaken. . . . Not only does [a company's] bottom line benefit positively [from a safety commitment], but their company's reputation stays intact, employees stay safe and healthy; thus, reducing healthcare, workers comp, training, and turnover cost—not to mention keeping customers, the communities they do business in, vendors, and employees happy. Safety is good business.'" President Warren K. Brown, American Society of Safety Engineers, December 2008.

"'A culture of safety is a shared value and belief among employees, managers, and leaders regarding the primary importance of ensuring that the organization's equipment and processes cause no physical harm to employees or customers.'" Sara J. Singer and Anita L. Tucker, "Creating a Culture of Safety in Hospitals," http://iis-db.stanford.edu/evnts/4218/Creating_Safety_Culture-SSingerRIP.pdf, p. 2.

"'The difference between a vision and an hallucination is how many people see it.'" Terry Paulson, Ph.D., CSP, CPAE, *The Optimism Advantage: 50 Simple Truths to Transform Your Attitudes and Actions into Results* (Hoboken, N.J.: Wiley, 2010).

"I've previously written that there is a fine line between 'cult' and 'culture.'" Joseph A. Michelli, *The New Gold Standard: 5 Leadership Principles for Creating a Legendary Customer Experience Courtesy of the Ritz-Carlton Hotel Company* (New York: McGraw-Hill, 2008).

CHAPTER 5

"'principle of social proof'" Robert B. Cialdini, *Influence: The Psychology of Persuasion*, rev. ed. (New York: Harper Paperbacks, 2006), pp. 114–166.

"Business decisions, as many of our colleagues in business and your own experience can attest, are frequently based on hope or fear, what others seem to be doing, what senior leaders have done and believe has worked in the past, and their dearly held ideologies—in short, on lots of things other than the facts. Although evidence-based practice may be coming to the field of medicine and, with more difficulty and delay, the world of education, it has had little impact on management or on how most companies operate. If doctors practiced medicine the way many companies practice management, there would be far more sick and dead patients, and many more doctors would be in jail." Jeffrey Pfeffer and Robert Sutton, *Hard Facts, Dangerous Half-Truths and Total Nonsense* (Boston: Harvard Business School Press, 2006).

Information about the construction of the new Ronald Reagan UCLA Medical Center was obtained from various staff members and also from the UCLA Health System Web sites www.uclahealth.org and www.fiftyyears.healthcare.ucla.edu.

CHAPTER 6

"The federal Agency for Healthcare Research and Quality (AHRQ) simply defines exceptional healthcare as 'doing the right thing, at the right time, for the right person, and having the best quality result.'" "Your Guide to Choosing Quality Health Care," Agency for Healthcare Research and Quality, www.ahrq.gov/consumer/qnt/qntqlook.htm.

"According to the Institute of Medicine, quality occurs when products and services are" The Committee on Quality of Health Care in America, Institute of Medicine, "Crossing the Quality Chasm: A New Health System for the Twenty First Century" (National Academy's Press, 2001).

"U.S. News & World Report has sought to create reliable criteria for comparing U.S. hospitals and each year ranks approximately 5,000 hospitals on the following criteria:" Emily McFarlane, Joe Murphy, Murrey G. Olmsted, Edward M. Drozd, and Craig Hill, "2009 Methodology: 'America's Best Hospitals,'" RTI International, 2009, http://static.usnews.com/documents/health/2009-best-hospitals-methodology.pdf.

"In 2009, for example, UCLA ranked third, behind Johns Hopkins and the Mayo Clinic." "US News Best Hospitals, 2009–2010," *U.S. News & World Report*, Health, http://health.usnews.com/best-hospitals/rankings.

"Dr. Peter Viccellio, clinical professor, vice chair, and clinical director, Department of Emergency Medicine, Stony Brook University Medical Center, Stony Brook, New York, has advocated that patients who are being admitted to a hospital should be routed to their treatment unit as swiftly as possible." Jessica Berthold, "Making Room for More Patients," American College of Physicians (ACP), February 2007.

CHAPTER 7

"'. . . lean thinking'. . ." Yasuhiro Monden, *Toyota Production System: An Integrated Approach to Just-in-Time*, 3rd ed. (Norcross, Ga.: Engineering and Management Press, Institute of Industrial Engineers, 1998).

"Since the timing of physician rounds was established in the 1950s at Johns Hopkins to assist in medical resident training, more than 50 years of tradition limit needed efficiencies." Johns Hopkins Medicine Web site, www.hopkinsmedicine.org/about/history/history3.html.

"'Efficiency is doing better what is already being done.'" Peter F. Drucker, *The Effective Executive: The Definitive Guide to Getting the Right Things Done*, rev. ed. (New York: Harper Paperbacks, 2006).

"Donna's conclusion may be the best definition of equitable care, and it echoes the Agency for Healthcare Research and Quality (AHRQ) definition outlined in Chapter 6—'doing the right thing for the right reason'—without considering extraneous factors." "Your Guide to Choosing Quality Health Care," Agency for Healthcare Research and Quality, www.ahrq.gov/consumer/qnt/qntlook.htm.

"Such was the case at UCLA in 2008, when reports surfaced concerning world-renowned liver transplant surgeon Dr. Ronald Busuttil. Dr. Busuttil was the subject of media criticism for having performed transplants on four Japanese gang figures, including a Japanese gang boss." Associated Press, "Report: UCLA Gave Transplants to Japanese Gang Boss, Other Gang Figures," FoxNews.com, May 30, 2008.

"The issue of 'country of origin' is already factored into the UNOS guidelines, as noncitizens are allowed to receive a small proportion of organs (approximately 5 percent) to ensure that foreign-born residents continue to support organ donations (in southern California, for example, 20 percent of donors are foreign born)." Gerald S. Levey, "'Bad Guy'Transplants," *Los Angeles Times,* June 6, 2008.

CHAPTER 8

"For example, many of the companies profiled in Tom Peters and Robert Waterman's classic book *In Search of Excellence* were no longer viewed as front runners in their industry as early as two years following the book's release, and some had closed their doors." Thomas J. Peters and Robert H. Waterman, *In Search of Excellence: Lessons from America's Best-Run Companies* (New York: Grand Central Publishing, 1988).

"In fact, in a November 1984 issue of *BusinessWeek* magazine titled 'Oops. Who's Excellent Now?' it was observed that of the 43 'excellent' companies surveyed by Peters and Waterman, approximately one-third had experienced financial difficulties." "Oops. Who's Excellent Now?" *BusinessWeek,* November 5, 1984, pp. 76–88.

"It reflects the spirit of innovation presented in one of Stephen Covey's *7 Habits of Highly Effective People,* namely, 'beginning with the end in mind.'" Stephen R. Covey, *The 7 Habits of Highly Effective People* (Running Press, 2000).

"Commercials Are the Culprit in TV-Obesity Link" Tara Parker-Pope, "Commercials Are the Culprit in TV-Obesity Link," *New York Times* (online), February 9, 2010.

"Mediterranean Diet May Help Prevent Dementia, Study Says" Elizabeth Landau, "Mediterranean Diet May Help Prevent Dementia, Study Says," CNN Health (online), February 8, 2010.

"Visual Processing Plays Role in Body Dysmorphic Disorder" Robert Preidt, "Visual Processing Plays Role in Body Dysmorphic Disorder," MSN Health and Fitness (online), February 3, 2010.

"Writing in *The Scientist* in 2005, David Morris notes, 'No pain, no gain' is an American modern mini-narrative. It compresses the story of a protagonist who understands that the road to achievement runs only through hardship." David Morris, "Belief and Narrative," *The Scientist,* March 28, 2005.

"Ultimately, drug company research dollars resumed, and Dr. Slamon created the drug Herceptin to treat the HER-2 positive subtype (representing approximately 25 percent of cases) of breast cancer."Lisa M. Jarvis, "Battling Breast Cancer," *Chemical and Engineering News,* August 7, 2006.

"'You go from the outside to the inside pretty quickly if you're fortunate enough to be involved in a success like Herceptin. So the fact that it worked so well in metastatic disease, and ultimately in early disease, means that a lot more people believe our ideas than when we started in 1986. The problem is, we needed the help back then. The drug could've been and should've been available to patients seven years before it was, and if it weren't for donor money, it would've been another five to seven years beyond that.'" Eli Dansky, "Dennis Slamon: From New Castle to New Science," *Stand Up to Cancer* (online), www.standup2cancer.org/node/194.

"'The Revlon funding made all the difference in the world. Had we had to depend on federal funding, we'd never have been able to get it done. The process by which grants are submitted, reviewed, approved and funded is incredibly long, and it reduces ideas to lowest common denominator approaches. Approaches that are innovative frequently don't get funded.'" Eli Dansky, "Dennis Slamon: From New Castle to New Science," *Stand Up to Cancer* (online), www.standup2cancer.org/node/194.

"'As I watched this movie *Living Proof*, of course I cried, but I also learned new facts about how Herceptin was created, and it was amazing to watch the struggle Dr. Slamon went through to get this drug approved. I have the utmost respect for those brave women who helped with the clinical trials to get Herceptin FDA approved. I also look at the company Revlon in a new way. Just when Dr. Slamon was down and out and almost out of money, Revlon donated over 2 million dollars to help him continue his amazing work. . . . Without Herceptin I don't know where I would be today. If I was diagnosed 20 years earlier, what would my outcome have been? . . . When I was first diagnosed, the doctors asked if I wanted to participate in clinical trials and I was like NO WAY! That would be just too scary for me. But without the brave people that do participate in clinical trials, we would be nowhere. So thank you to all who try to help these amazing doctors.'" Jill Zocco, "Thank You, Dr. Slaman," Sharing my Cancer Crapness blog, http://cancercrapness.blogspot.com/2009/01/thank-you-dr-slamon.html, January 1, 2009.

"'I just finished watching *Living Proof* for the fourth time. The first 3 times were when it originally aired. I watched it 3 nights in a row. I was diagnosed with stage 2 HER-2 positive breast cancer in July 2005 when I was 6 months pregnant with my daughter. Shortly after my surgery, I found out that I was . . . HER-2 positive. I thought I was going to die. My doctor told me that I was lucky. Herceptin was approved only last month for use in treating my type of cancer. I can't tell you how blessed and lucky I feel. I had 52 Herceptin treatments along with chemo and radiation. I have been cancer free for 3 and 1/2 years. This movie was so emotional for me to watch. I sat and cried several times and I feel so thankful for all the time and energy put forth to make this drug a reality for women like me.'" "Dr. Dennis Slamon: The Search for a Cure for Breast Cancer," My Lifetime (online), www.mylifetime.com/movies/dr.-dennis-slamon-search-cure-breast-cancer.

"Herceptin use has now expanded beyond breast cancer into areas such as gastric cancer, where the hormone HER-2 is overexpressed in around 20 percent of all gastric cancer cases."Herceptin.net Web site, HER2-positive gastric cancer.

"For patients like Dominic Blakewell . . ." Mark Wheeler, "The Surgeon Scientist," UCLA Today Faculty and Staff News (online), December 7, 2009.

"Scott Burk, a patient of Dr. Liau . . ." Mark Wheeler, "The Surgeon Scientist," UCLA Today Faculty and Staff News (online), December 7, 2009.

CHAPTER 9

"In their book Launching a Leadership Revolution, Orrin Woodward and Chris Brady suggest that 'leadership influence' is a critical aspect of business success and can be quantified as a function of the effort of the leader multiplied by the scope of those he affects." Orrin Woodward and Chris Brady, Launching a Leadership Revolution (New York: Business Plus, 2005).

"While the organizational structures required by the Magnet Recognition Program are quite extensive, a couple of examples of the ACAA empowerment criteria are" "System Eligibility Requirements," American Nurses Credentialing Center, http://www.nursecredentialing.org/Magnet/ApplicationProcess /EligibilityRequirements/SysEligibilityRequirements.aspx.

"Our ultimate goal is to have new mothers and fathers leave UCLA feeling competent and confident that they can take care of their baby and that they have received consistent information about breastfeeding from all their caregivers." "RRUCLA Delivers Baby-Friendly Practices for Breastfeeding," UCLA Health System Employee News (online), February 2010.

"What compelled me to pursue the research study itself was the attitude conveyed to me and several others before and during the development of the current People-Animal Connection program at UCLA Medical Center. The concept of doing a 'dog visit' was considered 'nice' or 'cute' when in fact it was much more than a thoughtful gesture. I believed that it was important to establish scientific evidence to show specific psychological and physiological effects." Ruth Kleinpell, RN, Ph.D., "Evidence-Based Review and Discussion Points," American Journal of Critical Care 16, no. 6 (2007), pp. 587–588.

"To that end, Kathie and Anna Gawlinski . . ." Ruth Kleinpell, RN, Ph.D., "Evidence-Based Review and Discussion Points," American Journal of Critical Care 16, no. 6 (2007), pp. 587–588.

CHAPTER 10

"Some studies suggest that 80 percent of CEOs think that their business is offering an exceptional experience, although only 8 percent of customers come to the same conclusion." Customer Focus Inc. blog, "Are You Owning the Customer's Experience?" http://www.customerfocusinc.com/index .php?option=com_content&view=category&layout=blog&id=37&Itemid=123.

"Even senior leaders in companies with a customer-centered mystique like Simon Cooper, CEO of the Ritz-Carlton Hotel Company, talk about helping their people continually strive for the 'ultimate customer experience' and set a new gold standard for 'how good *good* can be.'" Joseph A. Michelli, *The New Gold Standard: 5 Leadership Principles for Creating a Legendary Customer Experience Courtesy of the Ritz-Carlton Hotel Company* (New York: McGraw-Hill, 2008).

"As early as 1981, Morris B. Holbrook and Elizabeth C. Hirschman wrote about the importance of emotional experiences in the marketing and sale of products and services." Morris B. Holbrook and Elizabeth C. Hirschman, *Symbolic Consumer Behavior* (Ann Arbor, Mich.: Association for Consumer Research, 1981).

"Even in difficult times, 50 percent of consumers will pay more for a better service experience." Customer Focus Inc. blog.

"Only 14 percent of customers report that they leave a business for product reasons." "Seven Key Findings in Customer Service Research," Customer Focus, Inc., February 12, 2010, http://article.trdunya.com/seven-key-findings-in -customer-service-research.html.

"A full 68 percent will sever a customer relationship because they were treated poorly by a staff member." "Seven Key Findings in Customer Service Research," Customer Focus, Inc., February 12, 2010, http://article.trdunya.com/seven-key -findings-in-customer-service-research.html.

"Companies that are successful in creating both functional and emotional bonding with customers have higher retention rates (84 percent vs. 30 percent) and greater cross-selling ratios (82 percent vs. 16 percent) compared to companies that are not." Shaun Smith, "Winning Customer Loyalty in an Economic Crisis," *Customer Management* (online), http://www.customermanagementiq .com/article.cfm?externalid=676, April 27, 2009.

"The average value of a customer is 10 times his initial purchase." "Seven Key Findings in Customer Service Research," Customer Focus, Inc., February 12, 2010, http://article.trdunya.com/seven-key-findings-in-customer-service-research.html.

"The cost to attract a new customer is 6 times the cost to save one." "Seven Key Findings in Customer Service Research," Customer Focus, Inc., February 12, 2010, http://article.trdunya.com/seven-key-findings-in-customer-service-research.html.

"Low-service-quality companies average 1 percent return on sales and lose 2 percent market share per year." Jim Jackson, "Leading Customer Service with Motivation," Jim Jackson Motivational Blog, September 14, 2009.

"High-service-quality companies average 12 percent return on sales and grow 6 percent per year." "Seven Key Findings in Customer Service Research," Customer Focus, Inc., February 12, 2010, http://article.trdunya.com/seven-key-findings -in-customer-service-research.html.

"Similarly, Steve Downton, Hillbrand Rustema, and Jan Van Veen, authors of the book *Service Economics*, report on three years of research funded by Oracle analyzing the service industry." Steve Downton, Hillbrand Rustema, and Jan Van Veen, *Service Economics*, July 2010.

"'Most industries have readily accepted that improved customer service will lead to increased customer loyalty, increased revenue, and an enhanced bottom line. However, the healthcare industry has lagged in accepting this concept for several reasons:'" John Goodman, BS, MBA, and Dianne Ward, BS, MA, "Satisfied Patients Lower Risk and Improve the Bottom Line," *Patient Safety and Quality Healthcare*, April 2008.

"As is the case with businesses in non-healthcare sectors, more than 40 percent of consumers already research healthcare services online, and 60 per-cent report using the information they gain from that research to make a decision on a healthcare provider." Jessica Kronstadt, Adil Moiduddin, and Will Sellheim, "Consumer Use of Computerized Applications to Address Health and Health Care Needs," prepared for U.S. Department of Health and Human Services, March 2009, ASPE.hhs.gov/sp/reports/2009/consumerhit/report.shtml.

"'The mission/purpose of my company makes me feel my job is important.'" Rodd Wagner, Ph.D., and James K. Harter, *12: The Elements of Great Managing* (New York: Gallup Press, 2006).

CHAPTER 11

"In fact, this was a consideration when Henry Ford began paying his em-ployees $5 a day in 1914, essentially doubling the compensation for auto workers." Lindsay-Jean Hard, "The Rouge: Yesterday, Today, and Tomorrow," *University of Michigan Urban & Regional Planning Economic Development Hand-book*, December 4, 2005.

"'Marwa Naim has her face and life transformed by an American surgeon. It was shrapnel that brought her to Los Angeles. Hot and sharp, it pierced her legs, her stomach and her right hand. It mangled her face around her deep brown eyes, and it tore off her nose. . . . The University of California, Los Angeles (UCLA) Medical Center and its chief of plastic surgery, Dr. Tim Miller, offered to restore her face—for free.'" Kurt Streeter, "Helping One Girl Face the Future with Hope," *Los Angeles Times*, October 15, 2006.

"Ron, whose Katz Family Foundation helps cover costs associated with the program, describes Operation Mend as 'an extraordinary collaboration between the surgeons and staff of Ronald Reagan UCLA Medical Center and Brooke Army Medical Center.'" "About Operation Mend," UCLA Health System, http://operationmend.ucla.edu.

"Whether it's Patti Taylor, a clinical nurse specialist in UCLA's liver transplant program, and her quilting group creating red-white-and-blue 'quilts of valor' for Operation Mend patients, a Buddy Family from the community offering its hospitality and support, or the highly refined technical skills of a surgeon like Dr. Miller, UCLA's leaders have unified the university's vast resources to effectively serve those who serve them." "Nurse Stitches American Quilt to Honor Burned Soldier," *Newswise*, UCLA Healthcare, November 6, 2007.

Sources

Much of the content of this book emerged from interviews with UCLA Health System leaders, staff members, volunteers, and other stakeholders. The following individuals from all levels of the organization made themselves available to provide the information needed to make this book possible:

Barbara Abrams, RN; Dr. Nasim Afsar-manesh; Dr. Juan Alejos; Dan Alivia, RN; Barbara Anderson; Fiona Angus; Steven Arnold; Marti Arvin; Dr. Kathryn Atchison; Dr. James Atkinson; Rabbi Pearl Barlev; Jack Barron, Jr.; Dr. Lori Baudino; Lisa Beck; Hal Bookbinder; Janice Boron, RN; Geri Braddock, RN; Amy Bullock; Jeff Butler; Posie Carpenter, RN; Nicole Casalenuovo, RN; Helen Contraraz; Lea Ann Cook, RN; Heidi Crooks, RN; Pattie Cuen; Dr. Johannes Czernin; Bindu Danee; Lynette DeFrancia, RN; Dr. Jean DeKernion; Delia De Sasia; Kathy Deutsch; Sara Devaney; Jennifer Do, RN; Jeanne Durrant; Joi Edwards; Erik Eggins; Mary Erbeznik, RN; Ana Esquival; Hala Fam; Dr. David Feinberg; Kat Fibiger, JD; Jennifer Fine; Hilary Gan; Tamara Jean Gavilan, RN; Elizabeth George; Dennis Gonzalez, RN; Dr. Nestor Gonzalez; Vernon J. Goodwin; Vanya Green; Alison Grimes; Doug Gunderson; Pam Hoff; Eugene Hsu; Chai-Chih Huang; Clara Huerta; Mercedes Illesces; Kim Irwin; Brenda Izzi; Cindy Jaeger; Peter Ji; Laurie Johnson; Virgil Jones; Dr. Patricia Kapur; Dana Katz; Betsy Korbonski; Janina Krupa; Susan Land; Dr. Gerald Levey; Mary Levin; Dr. Linda Liau; Gene Loveland, RN; Robin Epstein Ludewig; Martha Lusk, RN; Dr. Neil Martin; Lillian Martinez; Maged Matta; Dr. Edward R. B. McCabe; Dr. Lynne McCullough; Suzanne McGuire, RN; Dr. Timothy Miller; Bonnie Millet, RN; Dr. Mark Morocco; Virgie Mosley; Theresa Moussa; Regina Naanos; Shannon O'Kelley; Patti Oliver; Tony Padilla; Dr. Neil Parker; Ellen Pollack, RN; Angie Price; Dr. Angelika Rampal; Sharon Randles; Courtney Real, RN; Carrie Recksieck; Pablo Reyes; Mei Lani Renger, RN; Michael P. Richards; Janet Rimicci; Robin Rosemark, RN; Jennifer Rosenthal; Dr. Tom Rosenthal; Amir Dan Rubin; Ross Scales; Jake Scherzer; Reverend Karen Schnell; Bill Sears; Elaine Rosso Severa, RN; Dr. Bonny Sham, RN; Donna Smith;

Mark Speare; Kit Spikings; Paul Staton; Dr. Michael Steinberg; Deborah Suda, RN; Lynn Sullivan; Grandvell Taylor; Dr. Jan Tillisch; Cullen Torsney, RN; Roxana Vargas; Dr. Jeff Veale; Dr. Cathy Rodgers Ward; Dr. A. Eugene Washington; Paul Watkins, JD; Timothy Wen; David Niles White; Ellen Wilson; Lana Wohlschlegel; Xueqing "Sherry" Xi, RN; Myrtle Yamamoto, RN; and Dr. Michael W. Yeh.

Many patients also were willing to share their experiences at UCLA Health System for inclusion in this book. Any patient-specific information was obtained either directly from the patient, with the patient's permission, or through publicly available information.

Readers of this book are encouraged to share their UCLA patient experiences at www.facebook.uclahealth.org.

Index

About the Author

Dr. Joseph Michelli is an organizational consultant and the Chief Experience Officer of The Michelli Experience. He has dedicated his career to helping leaders create compelling customer experiences and dynamic workplace cultures. In addition to writing *Prescription for Excellence*, Dr. Michelli is the author of such bestselling books as *The Starbucks Experience* and *The New Gold Standard* (based on The Ritz-Carlton Hotel Company). Additionally, he coauthored *When Fish Fly* with John Yokoyama, the owner of the World Famous Pike Place Fish Market in Seattle.

Dr. Michelli transfers his knowledge of exceptional business practices through keynotes and workshops. These informative and entertaining presentations, which are provided by Dr. Michelli and his associates, focus on the skills necessary to

- Create meaningful customer experiences

- Drive employee and customer engagement

- Enhance a commitment to service excellence

- Create quality improvement processes

- Increase employee morale

In addition to dynamic and entertaining international keynote presentations, The Michelli Experience offers

- Consultation on the development of optimal customer and employee experiences

- Service excellence training

- Enhancement of staff empowerment

- Leadership team development services

- Group facilitation and team-building strategies

- Creation of customer and employee engagement measurement processes

- Customized management and frontline training programs

For additional complementary resources concerning *Prescription for Excellence,* please visit www.josephmichelli.com.

Dr. Michelli is eager to help you fill your *Prescription for Excellence* in your business. He can be reached through his Web site, by e-mail at josephm@josephmichelli.com, or by calling either (734) 697-5078 or (888) 711-4900 (toll free within the United States).